DICTIONARY OF CHRISTIAN THEOLOGY

Dictionary of Christian Theology

PETER A. ANGELES

HARPER & ROW, PUBLISHERS, SAN FRANCISCO
Cambridge, Hagerstown, New York, Philadelphia
London, Mexico City, São Paulo, Singapore, Sydney

 For information address Harper & Row, Publishers, Inc., 10 East 53rd Street, New York, NY 10022. Published simultaneously in Canada by Fitzhenry & Whiteside, Limited, Toronto.

FIRST EDITION

Designer: Jim Mennick

Library of Congress Cataloging in Publication Data

Angeles, Peter Adam.

DICTIONARY OF CHRISTIAN THEOLOGY.

1. Theology—Dictionaries. I. Title.

BR95.A54 1985 230'.03'21 84-48235

ISBN 0-06-060237-6

85 86 87 88 89 10 9 8 7 6 5 4 3 2 1

For my mother Kaliope and father Adam Angelos
and my sisters Virginia, Tina and Mariann
for their love

Preface

This dictionary presents readable and informal definitions of important Christian theological terms, for the general reader and students of religion, literature, and philosophy.

The book is intended as an enjoyable, quick at-hand reference and a beginning to advanced work in the field of Christian religion and theology.

Small capitals are used for cross-references.

Throughout the dictionary I have quoted from and referred to the King James Version (1611) of the New Testament. A large number of excellent translations exist. I recommend for easy access and use the paperback, *The Layman's Parallel New Testament,* Zondervan Bible Publishers, Grand Rapids, Michigan, 1970. This edition, in parallel columns along with the King James Version, presents three other excellent translations but done in our century: *The Revised Standard Version* (1952); *The Amplified New Testament* (1958); *The Living New Testament* (1967).

Two other standard sources to which the reader may want to refer: *The English Revised Version* of the Bible (1881–1885), which is a revision of the King James Version of the Bible, and *The American Standard Version* (1901).

For the original Greek text, I have referred to several editions. The two I have cherished and had at my side: Reverend J. A. Spencer's *Four Gospels and Acts of the Apostles in Greek* (Harper and Brothers, Publishers, New York, 1847) and Eberhard Nestle's *Novum Testamentum Graece et Latine* (Privilegierte Württembergishe Bibelanstalt, Stuttgart, Germany, 1951).

Acknowledgments

It would be impossible to acknowledge all who have encouraged and assisted in the preparation of this dictionary. I can mention only a few.

Mrs. Simone Woodcock typed the original draft and saw to the minute corrections throughout the months of writing. Her comments, suggestions, interest, excellent skills, and encouragement at every point in the project gave support and enthusiasm to keep up my spirit. Thanks, Simone.

Dallas Pottinger, my very dear friend, who typed the final copy and gave us the needed impetus at the end. He worked under adverse circumstances during the illness and death of his mother, who in her own way gave her blessing to our work.

Mr. John Loudon, editorial manager, and members of his editorial and production staff, who administratively saw this book through its inception to completion, with patience and faith in its needs and quality.

Processor Adam Sebestyen, my friend, who helped with his library research skills and knowledge of Christian theology, and who loaned me books.

Ms. Ruth Solomon for her encouragement, personal help, and respect for what I was doing.

Mrs. Catharine Lynch, who gave me a few hours each week of needed typing, clerical, filing, and office help, and did library searches and boring chores for me, cheerfully and without complaint, between moments of rushing to classes, her family, and her work at the hospital.

The teacher's aides and support personnel at Santa Barbara City College: Mrs. Kathy Gebhardt, Ms. Mary James, Mrs. Cecilia Tatsch, Mrs. Nadine Schlothauer, each of whom assisted in numerous administrative and clerical ways so that I could devote more time to my teaching and writing.

Dr. Oscar Zaglits, my colleague, learned friend, and advocate, who with kindness gently prompted me along to keep working in spite of difficulties.

Santa Barbara City College faculty, staff, and administrators, who were supportive in so many ways and provided me with the conditions proper for my writing, teaching, and thinking.

My children Beth, Jane, and Adam for their love and acceptance of me; my son-in-law Jon for his energy and interest; my grandson Christopher, who served as an inspiration for this book and hope for the future. And again, to my wife Elizabeth, whose spirit I cannot erase, and who would have enjoyed this book. We would have had endless discussions.

A

abbess (L., *abbatissa,* feminine form of *abbas,* "abbot"). A female superior of a CONVENT or NUNNERY.

abbey (L., *abbatia,* from *abbas,* "abbot"). **1.** A monastery, NUNNERY, habitat, or society of persons, usually secluded from secular affairs, devoted to the religious life and to CELIBACY, and headed by an ABBOT or an ABBESS. **2.** The church of a monastery or CONVENT.

abbot (Gk., *ἀββᾶς [abbas],* from Syraic *abba,* "father"). The superior, leader, or head of an ABBEY or MONASTERY of monks. Traditionally, an elective position by secret ballot by members of the monastery and held for life.

abjuration (L., *abjurare.* "to deny an oath," from *ab,* "from," "away," and *jurare,* "to swear," "to give allegiance"). Renunciation of any deviation from the prescribed faith or behavior. Usually a formal procedure within a church and a prerequisite for continued membership for those in error or for those excommunicated. See also APOSTASY; HERESY; SCHISM.

ablution (L., *ablutio,* from *abluere,* "to wash away," from *ab,* "away," "from," and *luere,* "to wash"). **1.** The ritual performed by a Roman Catholic priest of ceremonial washing of the chalice (and other sacred objects such as the paten, associated with the EUCHARIST) with wine and water. **2.** The ritual of washing the hands before the Eucharist or during a mass. **3.** The ritual by laypersons and priests of rinsing the mouth before and after partaking of the Eucharist.

Ablution is related to the ancient rite of washing in order to rid the washed area of sin or pollution. In Christian theology, ablution is principally related to the sanctification and purification of sacred objects.

absolute, the (L., *absolutus,* pp. of *absolvere,* from *ab,* "away," "from," and *solvere,* "to release." That which is unrestricted, unrestrained, unencumbered). **1.** The underived, uncaused, self-existent, unconditoned, single, complete, all-embracing, and noncontingent Being that **(a)** includes and is the source of all limited and finite things, **(b)** exists necessarily, eternally, and self-sufficiently, and **(c)** is perfect without any of the limitations of finite beings. **2.** The ultimate, underlying Reality, World Ground, or Cosmic Principle that depends upon nothing else for its existence but upon which all things depend for their activity, unity, and variety. **3.** The one, all-inclusive, perfectly interrelated organic and thinking Whole (Reality, Being) that is in the process of actualizing and fulfilling itself through the finite, transient existences of the universe.

absolution (L., *absolvere,* "to set free," "to release," from *ab,* ' "from," "away," and *solvere,* "to loose," "to release"). **1.** In general, the act of forgiving or absolving of sin. **2.** In the Roman Catholic church, **(a)** the remission of sin by the SACRAMENT of PENANCE after CONFESSION; **(b)** the releasing from censures, prohibitions, excommunication; **(c)** the intercession chanted or recited over the body of the dead.

The authority to release a penitent from sin and punishment for sin, thereby reconciling the penitent with God, is given to priests by APOSTOLIC SUCCESSION and exercised formally in the sacrament of penance using phrases such as "I absolve thee of sins in the name of the Father, Son, and Holy Ghost" or "May the Lord God absolve thee of thy sins." (In Roman Catholicism, only God forgives but the church can provide absolution after contrition and confession.)

The three traditional forms of absolution: **(a)** the *indicative,* as above, "I absolve thee of sins"; **(b)** the *precatory* (as for example in the Anglican church), where the priest prays that God will release the sinner from his/her sin; and **(c)** the *declaratory,* which is a declaration or statement as found in a formal prayer (such as the Anglican morning or evening prayer) that God does in actuality forgive the sinner who confesses and is penitent.

Penance, a sincere desire to be forgiven, and a full confession of the sin are necessary for absolution to be successful. At some times, in the long history of absolution, confession was public and/or to the members of the church.

In the Roman Catholic church, it is possible to give absolution without confession of sins when such a confession is not possible (as in the case of war, disaster, injury). At their next confession, though, persons so absolved must declare the sins from which they were absolved. Protestantism has practiced, as in Calvinism (Calvin's *Institutio* iii, 4, 14) a general absolution of the entire congregation after its confession, as well as individual granting of absolution by the minister either in private or in the presence of the congregation. In some Protestant sects absolution may be granted by a layperson. See also PENANCE.

The principal scriptural reference used to support absolution is after Jesus' resurrection at John 20:20–23: "And when he had so said, he shewed unto them *his* hands and his side. Then were the disciples glad, when they saw the Lord. Then said Jesus to them again, 'Peace *be* unto you:. as *my* Father hath sent me, even so send I you.' And when he had said this, he breathed on *them*; and saith unto them, 'Receive ye the Holy Ghost: Whose soever sins ye remit, they are remitted unto them; *and* whose soever *sins* ye retain, they are retained.' "

acolyte (Gk., ἀκόλουθος *[akolouthos]*, "a follower," "an attendant"). One who has been granted the fourth and last of the minor orders (see also ORDERS, MINOR HOLY). An acolyte performs duties such as lighting candles, carrying candles, preparing the wine for the Eucharist, assisting priests at mass, and other church services.

actus purus. Latin, *actus,* "the moving of an object," "impulse," "action," "activity," "the doing or performing of an act," and *purus,* "pure," "unadulterated," "incorrupt," "undefiled." **1.** God exists by his own Pure Act of Being. God's essential action is to Be and to Be as of his nature (and no other nature affecting him). God's essence is acting purely as his nature necessitates and as he must be. See also IPSUM ESSE. **2.** God's Being is Pure Activity. This activity is creating more beings but not any more pure being.

Adam (Heb. *hā-'ādām,* "the man." Means "man," "humanity," "from earth to earth," "the first man"). In the biblical account the first human being (Adam) was a male made of the earth (Gen. 1:26, 27; 2:7). He received the "breath of life" directly from God. He was created in God's image. Adam was put into Eden or a PARADISE. With Eve forming a couple, humankind began.

Adam, the new. Also *the second Adam.* Jesus Christ is a descendant of ADAM (see, for example, Luke 3:21–38). Jesus is regarded by Christians as the second progenitor, the second or new Adam who is far superior to Adam and is what Adam should have been like as a perfect being. Through Adam, earthly, mortal life has been transmitted. Because of Adam's disobedience to God, we are all sinners and receive death as our punishment. Through Jesus, humans are made spiritually whole and just again; humans receive immortality in Jesus' resurrection (1 Cor. 15:22; Rom. 5:14). With Jesus as the new or second Adam, God's will is actualized in the incarnation.

According to Christian tradition, because of the original sin of Adam and Eve, humanity lost God's original gift of eternal life. Jesus Christ, the second person of the Holy Trinity, came down from heaven to provide us with SALVATION and eternal life. Jesus "was incarnate by the Holy spirit of the Virgin Mary and was made human" (Nicene Creed). Jesus Christ thus was the new Adam. By means of his sacrifice on the cross, Jesus washed away the sin of the first Adam and gave back to us all the original gift of eternal life. See also CHRISTOLOGY; INCARNATION, THE.

adiaphora. Greek, ἀδιάφορα "things that do not make a difference." Activities or beliefs that are allowed but that are not necessary, or essential, to one's faith. Protestants such as the Puritans and Mennonites tended to prohibit *adiaphora,* believing that only those activities and beliefs explicitly stated in the Bible were to be allowed and believed.

adiaphorists. Protestants who continued some of the Catholic ways. Some Protestants such as the Anglicans tolerated, allowed, or practiced Catholic ways although they saw no necessity for them in the Bible. See also ADIAPHORA.

adoptianism (L., *adoptare,* "to adopt," from *ad,* "to," and *optare,* "to choose"). The belief that Jesus while a human was adopted by God as his son and thereby brought into Godliness or the Trinity. God thus conferred divinity upon Jesus. This belief was held, for example, by the EBIONITES, by believers in MONARCHIANISM, Paul of Samosata in the third century, Theodore of Mopsuestia, and the Antiochene School; also by Elipandus of Toledo and Felix of Urgel in the eighth century.

adoration (L., *adorare,* "to pray to," "to speak to," "to adore"). **1.** The emotion of VENERATION toward God imbued with personal devotion, HOMAGE, and love. **2.** The act of worshiping God with the deepest reverence possible, thereby honoring him as divine, supremely perfect, and expressing total dependence of all things upon him. Adoration is due only to God and is regarded as the highest form of worship.

adoration of the Cross. See CROSS, ADORATION OF THE.

adoration of the Eucharist. The practice of worshiping, or adoring, the body (bread) and blood (wine) of Christ at the Eucharist.

adoration of the Magi, the. At Matthew 2:1–12 there is reference to the wise men (MAGI) who came from the east to offer gifts to and adore the newly born King of the Jews. The adoration of the Magi is celebrated on January 6, as the Feast of the EPIPHANY, the appearance of Christ to humanity, and is found variously represented throughout the history of Christian art.

adoration of the shepherds, the. A very common representation in Christian art, based on Luke 2:15–20, which depicts shepherds solemnly revering and adoring the Christ child in the presence of "Mary, and Joseph, and the babe lying in a manger."

adorn (L., *adornare,* "to embellish," "to furnish"). **1.** To cover with ornaments; to embellish; to add pleasing, attractive elements to something. **2.** To enhance a religious object, aesthetically, spiritually, and morally. Synonyms: *beautify; grace; emblazon; enrich; dignify; decorate.*

Advent (L., *advenire,* "to reach," "to arrive," from *ad,* "to," and *venire,* "to come"). **1.** The period that includes the four Sundays before Christmas. **2.** The first coming of Jesus Christ. **3.** The expected second coming of Christ.

adventism. The belief that the Second Coming of Christ and the end of the world are imminent. This second ADVENT will be the divine completion of the purpose of human history, and Jesus Christ will physically return as the king, leader, and master, overthrowing the forces of evil at the battle of Armageddon. Jesus' victory will establish a kingdom of righteousness in heaven to last for 1,000 years. All the faithful will be resurrected at that time.

Various Christian adventist groups have existed since the apostles. Montanism in the second century was an organized Christian sect that awaited the end of the world. The Anabaptists during the Reformation also made adventism central to their doctrines. In the United States the adventist movement began basically with William Miller (1782–1849) about 1831. He announced that Christ would return some time between March 21, 1843, and March 21, 1844.

The following are some modern adventist groups that differ about specific doctrines: the Seventh-Day Adventist Church, the Advent Christian Church, Jehovah's Witnesses (who deny the Trinity and the deity of Jesus Christ), the Church of Jesus Christ of Latter-Day Saints, the Pentecostal Church, the Catholic Apostolic Church, the New Apostolic Church, the Church of God, the Primitive Advent Christian Church, and the United Seventh-Day Brethren.

aeon. Sometimes *eon.* (Gk., *αἰών [aiōn],* "lifetime," "an age," "epoch," "for a long period of time"; sometimes *forever* in phrases such as **τὸν δι' αἰῶνος χρόνον** *[ton di'* aiōnos chronon]). **1.** A long period of time—an era or age—present or to come, which has its own inherent quality and which will dissolve into another era or age. **2.** In GNOSTICISM, one of a group of eternal and spiritual beings who, like the angels, serve as intermediaries between the world and God (the Perfect Aeon) and who emanate from and are empowered by God.

affusion (L., *affundere,* "to pour out," "to sprinkle"). Baptism by sprinkling (or pouring) water on the head of the one to be baptized. A method of baptism practiced by early BAPTISTS and other separatists.

agapē Greek, *ἀγάπη*, "love," "brotherly love," "moral love," "spiritual love," "charity"; the plural *ἀγάπαι (agapai)* meant love-feast. *Agapē* is contrasted with two other Greek words for love: *ἔρως (erōs),* "sexual and/or sensual love," and *φιλια (philia),* "friendship," "affinity toward," "affection for," "liking for," "fondness". **1.** The love feast, or feast of sharing, practiced by early Christians. Central to this feast was a common meal and HOLY COMMUNION (EUCHARIST), memorializing Jesus' giving the bread and the cup at the LAST SUPPER. See also CHARITY. **2.** The love of God for humans representing the ideal form that human love should aspire toward. See also Love. **3.** The love of humans for God. **4.** The highest form of human spiritual love. **5.** In early Christianity, a love-feast, or feast of almsgiving, at which the poor were materially helped by the rich, patterned after the Lord's Last Supper. (Because of abuses, such feasts were forbidden by the Council of Carthage in 397).

aggiornamento. Italian, "postponement," "adjournment," or "bringing something up to date." Used specifically to refer to the updating or modernizing of Catholicism.

agnosticism (Gk., *α [a],* "no," "not," the privative letter indicating negation or denial, and **γνωστικός** *[gnōstikos],* "one who knows or has knowledge of"). **1.** The belief that none of the arguments for God's existence demonstrates the existence of that being they purport to prove. Thus no one knows, or can know, whether or not there is a God.

Maybe there is a God; maybe there is no God. **2.** Judgments about God's existence or nonexistence must be suspended because of the limits of our understanding (or, in atheistically inclined agnosticism, because it is highly unlikely that such a being described as God exists in fact). See also GNOSTICISM.

agnosticism, religious. *That* God exists can be known, but *what* God is cannot be known. Religious commitment to God is possible even though we cannot know what that God is like. This commitment is based on foundations such as faith or a feeling of dependence on the presence of some power. In religious agnosticism God is labelled variously as "the Unknown Source (Cause) of the known" (Herbert Spencer) or "Pure Being," "Being-in-Itself," "Being-as-Being" (Paul Tillich). See also THEOLOGY, NEGATIVE.

Agnus Dei. Latin, "Lamb of God." **1.** A name designating Jesus Christ. **2.** An emblem of Jesus Christ using an image of a lamb, usually bearing a cross or banner with a cross. **3.** A disk of wax, imprinted on one side with the image of a lamb, and on the other with the name and arms of the reigning pope. These disks are blessed by the pope during the Easter week of his first year as pope (and every seventh year thereafter). Those who use this disk with faith are safe from evil spirits, fire, storms, catastrophes, injury, emergencies, and sudden death. The blessing, preparation, and distribution of the *agnus dei*s is one of the most intricate ceremonies of the Roman Catholic church. Pieces of the *agnus dei* are put in a small bag, usually heart-shaped and worn as an amulet, or kept somewhere on the body. **4.** The portion of the mass (added by Pope Sergius in the seventh century) at which the priest uncovers the holy chalice, genuflects, bows before the Blessed Sacrament of Jesus' body and blood, strikes his breast three times with his hands joined, and asks the Lamb of God to have mercy on us all. (Or at masses for the dead, the priest requests the Lamb of God to "give them rest," adding after the third repetition "everlasting.") **5.** An anthem sung at communion, or FRACTION in the form of a prayer such as "O Lamb of God, who takest away the sins of the world, have mercy upon us."

Agony at Gethsemane. See GETHSEMANE, THE AGONY AT.

Agony, Christ's Three-Hour. A devotion in the Roman Catholic church offered on Good Friday in memory of the three hours Christ hung upon his CROSS. The devotion usually begins at twelve o'clock, when Christ is believed to have been nailed to his cross. It includes prayers, hymns, chants, meditations upon his suffering, and his seven last words. The devotion ends at three o'clock, the hour Jesus is believed to have died.

agrapha. Greek, *ἄγραφα (agrapha),* "unwritten sayings". **1.** Sayings attributed to Jesus, but not found written, that were current and popular in early Christian times and tradition and are considered by some to be genuine. **2.** Sayings of Jesus, found outside what are regarded as the canonical Gospels. A case in point for those who do not regard Acts as canonical would be Acts 20:35: "Remember the words of the Lord Jesus, how he said, 'It is more blessed to give than to receive.' "

Alexandrian School. Believed in the divinization of humanity by means of the imparting (communication) of divine substance (powers) into it by God—as was done to Jesus. See also COMMUNICATIO IDIOMATUM. SALVATION was the state of being imbued with the divine (divine essence; divine agency or power). This state separated a person from other humans. Stressed the HĒNOSIS of Jesus' two natures, the human and divine. This school of Christian thought developed in Alexandria and was a rival of the school that developed in Antioch. Its principal theologian was Cyril (376–444).

alienation (L., *alienare,* "to alienate," "to estrange," "to withdraw"). The aim of Christianity is to restore humans to a sound relationship with a loving and merciful God. Humans are sinners entirely alienated (estranged) from God. Humans should love, and have a friendship with, God. Humans are alienated from God's mercies. Human sin alone caused and is continuing to cause this alienation, which must be ovecome before a reconciliation with God can be established. See also ATONEMENT; SALVATION. This reconciliation entails forgiveness by God. This forgiveness is entirely undeserved and is freely and unconditionally given by God. Nothing can be done by humans to effect this reconciliation and forgiveness. They are bestowed wholly by the sovereign mercy of the Almighty. God chose three major events to overcome the fact of alienation: the INCARNATION, the CRUCIFIXION, and the RESURRECTION.

allegory (Gk., ἀλληγορία *[allēgoria],* "describing or communicating the meaning of something by representing it through another image or story"). **1.** The use of story (such as the PARABLE of the prodigal son) to convey in a metaphorical (nonfigurative) way a message, usually with moral and spiritual overtones. The message itself is not literally or expressly presented, and the story requires some amount of EXEGESIS. An allegory may be regarded as a prolonged metaphor, e.g., *Pilgrim's Progress.* **2.** A method of scriptural EXEGESIS or interpretation whereby the Bible is seen to have a hidden or subsurface meaning. Since early Christian times, much of the Bible has been regarded as an allegory to be understood not solely for its literal truth but for its philosophical, psychological, doctrinal, and ethical significance. See also TYPOLOGY.

alleluia. See HALLELUIA.

All Saints' Day. A festival held on November 1 commemorating all the martyrs and saints in heaven, known and unknown—including, and especially, those who have no set feast days during the year. See also HALLOW.

All Souls' Day. A commemoration held on November 2 for all those faithful who have died. An intercession with Christ is made for those souls suffering in PURGATORY attempting to enter heaven. Priests may say three masses on All Souls' Day.

almsgiving (Gk., *ἐλεημοσύνη [eleēmosunē],* "mercy," "charity," from *ἐλεεῖν [eleein],* "to pity"). The giving of charity, works of mercy, to those in need in order to alleviate misery and poverty.

Alpha and Omega. The first and last letters of the Greek alphabet: A and Ω. Used by Christians as a symbol of God's omnipotence. These letters are found in connection with the CROSS and with the CHI-RHO symbol of Christ. Based on the Book of Revelation: " 'I am Alpha and Omega, the beginning and the ending,' saith the Lord, 'which is, and which was, and which is to come, the Almighty' " (Rev. 1:8) and, "Saying, 'I am Alpha and Omega, the first and the last: and, What thou seest, write in a book, and send *it* unto the seven churches which are in Asia; . . .' " (Rev. 1:11).

altar (L., *altare,* "an altar," "a high place," from *altus,* "high"). **1.** The communion table. **2.** In general, the raised place or structure on which sacrifices are offered, or at which one worships, or where incense is burned, etc., for religious purposes.

An altar is recognized as a sacred, solemn area with special spiritual significance. (For example, Matt. 5:23, 24.)

amartia. Greek, *ἁμαρτία,* "sin." **1.** Sin, implying missing or coming short of the virtuous mark in life that is being aimed at and that should be hit. **2.** In general, lawlessness. **3.** Specifically, in Christian tradition, conduct not within the boundaries or parameters of God's law.

amen (Gk., *ἀμήν [amēn],* "truly," "certainly," "surely," "verily"). In general, "so be it" or "that is true." It may be used to indicate such things as solemn acceptance of God's plan, a wish that what is asked of God be granted, a termination of a prayer or request, a declaration that one will follow God's will.

Anabaptists (Gk., *ἀνά [ana],* "again," and *βάπτειν [baptein],* "to dip in water"). **1.** Originally used from the fourth century on to refer to those who "rebaptized" persons who had already been baptized (usually by heretics, schismatics, excommunicated priests, evil priests, etc.). **2.** A number of Christian sects that emerged during the REFORMATION in Switzerland, Germany, Holland, and Italy as early as the 1520s. They did not accept the orthodoxy of the NICENE CREED and the prevalent views of the SACRAMENTS. They grounded their theology on direct analysis of the Bible, unencumbered by doctrine, dogma, and historical analysis. They advocated baptism by immersion but rejected PAEDOBAPTISM. They were generally antitrinitarian. They believed in the resurrection of humans after a sleep of their soul at death. They held to a separation of church and state. They declined participation in war and positions in government, often declining to pay war taxes. They opposed usury. They stressed individualism within a community of believers striving for personal righteousness.

Anacephalaiōsis. Greek, *ἀνακεφαλαίωσις,* "a summary." For example, found in St. Paul's epistle to the Ephesians 1:10. The belief that Jesus is the "summary" of humanity; God has finalized all things in Jesus Christ; Jesus is the aim of all creation; Jesus is the highest pinnacle of excellence in the race of humans originating with Adam; Jesus made retribution for our sins, redeemed humankind, and provided immortal life for all who accept him. See also ADAM, THE NEW.

anagōgē. Greek, ἀναγωγή, "a leading up" into higher levels, from ἀνά *[ana],* "up," and ἀγωγή *[agōgē],* "a leading," from ἄγειν *[agein],* "to lead." The mystical, moral, spiritual (and sometimes supernatural) meaning, application, or interpretation of words in the Bible. This form of EXEGESIS is especially associated with theologians such as St. Peter Lombard (1100–1160) and St. Thomas Aquinas (1225–1274).

analogical predication, the theological doctrine of. The attempt (first fully systematized by St. Thomas Aquinas [1225–1274]) to resolve the paradox of how finite minds can have knowledge about the true nature of God. The paradox arises when **1.** God is believed to be so completely different from any of our present and possible concepts that nothing in our understanding can be correctly referred to as a basis for our knowing the nature of God. The characteristics of God cannot be known on the same level of meaning as our human experiences, and thus those characteristics we do ascribe to God cannot be understood univocally (as having one meaning only). Yet **2.** it is also believed that we do have accurate knowledge of God through some means such as revelation, mystical experience, sacred texts, or intuition. These means provide us with characteristics of God believed to be intelligible, consistent, somewhat complete, and unambiguous. These characteristics of God are not to be understood equivocally (as having different meanings).

The word *good* applies to God and also to a person. According to the doctrine of theological predication, *good* is not being used with the same meaning (universally) in each case. God is not "good" in the same identical sense in which a person is "good." But neither is *good* being used equivocally with different meanings. There is a sameness of meaning for the word *good* when applied to both a person and to God. *Good* is neither univocally nor equivocally applied to God. *Good* is applied *analogically.* We say that a dog is a "good" dog. We say that a person is a "good" person. We use the same word to apply to both things, although they differ considerably in their nature and characteristics. We use the word *good* because of the similarity between certain characteristics displayed by a person that are also displayed by a dog, such as obedience, loyalty, trustworthiness, faithfulness, and love. The word *good* is not being used with different meanings, yet it is not being used with identical meanings since there are behavioral and qualitative differences between a person's "goodness" and a dog's "goodness." A person's "goodness" is of a higher order and originates from a different source than a dog's.

The theological doctrine of analogical predication holds that *good* is being used analogically to signify that at the level of the dog's existence, there is a characteristic we call "good" that is analogous to (is similar to, resembles) what we call "good" at the level of a person's existence. So it is with reference to "good" when applied to God and to a person: As the dog's "good" is similar to a person's, so a person's "good" is similar to God's. But the distance between a person's "good" and God's "good" is far greater than that between a dog's "good" and a person's "good" due to God's infinitely greater nature.

The theological doctrine of analogical predication believes that on the basis of this type of analogy, humans can understand how human characteristics, such as "good," "wisdom," "power," "love," and "forgiveness," refer to God's nature even though God is far superior to and different from human nature.

analogy (Gk., *ἀνάλογος [analogos],* "proportionate"). As creatures of God, humans cannot explain God, his Creation, and his works. Humans must rely upon analogy (parables, metaphors, etc.) with human experience to understand God (see also ANALOGICAL PREDICATION, THE THEOLOGICAL DOCTRINE OF). But there are facts, events, and experiences to be explained, such as creation, existence, love, ATONEMENT, FORGIVENESS, the HOLY SPIRIT, the new life in Jesus Christ, RESURRECTION (see also RESURRECTION, HUMAN,) MIRACLES (see MIRACLE), and divine revelation (see REVELATION, DIVINE.) Human imagery and language cannot do an adequate job, but humans must try. Humans thus rely on analogies, metaphors, parables such as being "released," "washing away sin," "being reborn," "cleansing of defilement," "rconciliation in Christ's Spirit," and "the Holy Spirit entering the heart of man."

anamnēsis. Greek, *ἀνάμνησις*, "remembrance," "recollection," "reminiscence," "commemoration," "a memorial," "a recalling to mind." **1.** In general, the ceremonial representation of an important past religious event in order to reproduce the emotions, images, and spiritual significance of that event in the celebrants. **2.** Specifically, used, for example, at Luke 22:19 and 1 Corinthians 11:24 with reference to the Last Supper. Jesus tells his disciples to carry on the tradition of remembering him. See also EUCHARIST, THE.

anaphora. Greek, *ἀναφορά*, "to carry back" from *ἀνά (ana),* "up," "back," and *φέρειν (pherein),* "to carry." The principal prayer and the essential core of the EUCHARIST rite, namely, the Eucharistic prayer of CONSECRATION, climaxing in the COMMUNION. The prayer thanks God for his creation and for his redemption of man by means of the presence of Christ and his Eucharist. After the priest and people offer salutations, the *anaphora* begins by exhorting all to feel joy and lift up their hearts to God. A reply and a prayer of thanks and praise follow, punctuated by the singing of the SANCTUS (the hymn "Holy, Holy, Holy . . ."). This is followed by reference to the redemptive work of God through Jesus

Christ; the Eucharist; an EPICLESIS; INTERCESSION OF THE SAINTS; prayers for communion; and a DOXOLOGY.

Anaphoras vary from church to church within Christianity. For example, in the Eastern Orthodox church two *anaphoras* exist: one by St. Basilios (329–379) and one by John Chrysostomos (347–395). Also *anaphoras* vary in their reference to God, to the Holy Trinity (see TRINITY, THE HOLY,) to the Blessed Virgin Mary, to the HOLY SPIRIT, to Jesus Christ the Son.

anathema. Greek, *ἀνάθεμα*, "that which is devoted to evil," "a curse." St. Paul uses the term to signify "a thing under a curse." The severe and solemn curse (punishment, ban, sentence, suspension) declared by a church against heretics and heretical doctrines. Anathematization is usually followed by EXCOMMUNICATION and is often regarded as a stronger measure than excommunication.

The expression in 1 Corinthians 16:22, *ἀνάθεμα μαρὰν ἀθά (anathema maran atha),* is thought to be an expression of a double curse, or a curse made more powerful with a prayer.

anchor, marine. The cross in the form of a marine anchor is a common and universal symbol for Christianity in the history of Christian art. Early Christians saw a form of the cross in the marine anchor. For example, at Hebrews 6:19, St. Paul says: "Which *hope* we have as an anchor of the soul, both sure and stedfast, and which entereth into that within the veil." See also SHIP FLYING BEFORE THE WIND.

angel (Gk., *ἄγγελος [angelos]*, "messenger of God," "messenger," "angel"). **1.** A supernatural, celestial being, of pure spirit, superior to humans in power, goodness, beauty, intelligence, and abilities, who serves God in many capacities, one being as a messenger, another as an attendant spirit for a human or humans. In this sense, belief in angels is based on ideas such as **(a)** there are intelligences other than ourselves between our intelligence and God's; **(b)** these intelligences are operative and directed by God to assist in the functioning of the universe; **(c)** they may be helpful to humans in making contact with God and in leading them to a more divinelike life.

At Ephesians 3:10, salvation is granted by God even to the angels. At Matthew 4:11 and Acts 5:19 ff., they serve as messengers from God to humans and will surround Jesus, who will be their head, at the Last Judgment. Divine messengers of God are also referred to at Luke 1:13, 26, 28; 2:9; Matthew 1:20. See also REVELATION, DIVINE.

The angels of the Bible have been divded into nine groups or choirs: Seraphim, Cherubim, and Thrones; Dominions (or Dominations); Virtues and Powers; Principalities, ARCHANGELS, and Angels. **2.** The EXOUSIAI (powers of darkness) from which Christ delivers us (Col. 1:13; 2:15; Rom. 8:38, 39; Eph. 1:21; 6:12). St. Paul did not believe in the existence of good angels in the sense of **1.**

angelic doctor. Refers to St. Thomas Aquinas. See also FATHERS, THE FOUR LATIN; THOMISM.

Angelus, the. A popular DEVOTION or prayer recited in the Roman Catholic church that presents the INCARNATION of Jesus and venerates his mother Mary. It consists of verses, responses, and prayers. Indulgences are gained when the *Angelus* is recited.

Anglican Communion, the. Composed of eighteen separate churches throughout the world, united by a common tradition since the founding of the Church of England (see also ANGLICANISM), a common liturgy, faith, church organization, and attitudes.

Anglicanism. The form of Christian faith that stems from the church founded in 1534 by King Henry VIII, who declared himself "the headship" of the Church of England in a SCHISM from the Roman Catholic church.

Anglo-Catholicism. Refers to those within the Church of England who have accepted Roman Catholicism, but without a pope or allegiance to a pope. They favor the traditions of the Eastern Orthodox church and the Roman Catholic church in contrast to Protestant churches. Their theological and historical inspiration does not come from the reformers of the Reformation.

anhomoeans (Gk., ἀνόμοιος *[anomoios]*, "unlike"). Those early Christians who believed that Christ was unlike God, not of the same substance or identical essence. See also TRINITY, THE HOLY.

anhypostasia. Greek, ἀνυποστασά, "not a personality (person, subject) on its own," from α *(a)*, "not," and ὑπόστασις *(hypostasis)*, "subsistence," "substance," "personality." An early Christian belief that the human nature of Jesus had no HYPOSTASIA, no personal locus of its own, but achieved a personage only by means of the function of the LOGOS upon Jesus (see also ENHYPOSTASIA).

animism (L., *anima*, "soul," "air," "breath of life" from Gr., ἄνεμος "that which breathes"). Belief that inanimate objects are also alive and imbued with spirits, demons, life-forces. These objects may be NUMINOUS or ominous in form and activity and are to be treated accordingly as sacred, with respect, or as offensive, with dread.

annihilationism (L., *annihilare*, "to reduce to nothing," from *ad*, "to," and *nihil*, "nothing"). The belief of some Christians that sinners shall cease to exist after this life. The wicked shall not enter eternal HELL; both the body and soul are completely annihilated forever.

Annunciation of the Blessed Virgin Mary. The announcement, as stated in Luke 1:26–38, by the angel Gabriel to Mary at Nazareth that she had been chosen by God to be the virgin mother of his son. Celebrated by churches on March 25 as Annunciation Day. (Also known as the Feast of the Annunciation; the Feast of the Incarnation; LADY DAY.)

At Luke 1:28: "the angel came *in* unto her" and Gabriel said, 'Hail thou that art highly favored, the Lord is with thee: blessed art thou among women.' " Depictions of this in the history of Christian art show Mary in a state of *pensiveness* ("Mary was troubled at his saying, and cast in her mind what manner of salutation this should be," Luke 1:29); *humility*, with Mary's hands crossed on her breast; and *purity*, symbolized by her clothing, centrality, demeanor, and uniqueness. See also INCARNATION, THE.

This annunciation, or announcement, to the Blessed Virgin Mary is different from the annunciation to the Shepherds (Luke 2:8–14) at which an angel appeared to shepherds tending their flock and announced to them ("the glory of the Lord shone round about them: and they were sore afraid," Luke 2:9) the *birth* of Jesus Christ the Savior.

anointing (L., *inungere,* "to anoint"). The pouring (spreading, rubbing, smearing) of holy oil upon a person or thing in order to make it sacred (see also CONSECRATION). This rite is used in, for example, BAPTISM, ordination, UNCTION, (see also UNCTION, EXTREME and UNCTION, HOLY) and dedication of churches, objects, or altars. Anointing has traditionally been regarded as a sacramental rite that conferred the sevenfold gift of the Holy Spirit. Anointing of the sick has scriptural basis, for example, at James 5:14 ("Is any sick among you? Let him call for the elders at the church; and let them pray over him, anointing him with oil in the name of the Lord"), and has been practiced since early Christian times in this general manner: a leader of the Christian community prays over the sick person, then anoints the person with holy oil, which symbolizes—or has the power to produce—among other things, healing, forgiveness, salvation, at the invocation of the name of Jesus Christ.

Anointing exists as part of the coronation of kings. For example, the coronation of an English monarch follows the ritual established at the coronation of King Edgar in 973: the monarch's declaration; the people's acclaim and acceptance; the anointment; the investiture of the king's regalia; the crowning; the enthronement.

anthem (Gk., *ἀντίφωνον [antiphōnon],* "antiphon," "anthem," "sounding in response to," from *ἀντί [anti],* "over," "against," and *φωνή [phōnē],* "voice," "sound"). **1.** A hymn sung in response. **2.** Prose or poetry set to sacred music. **3.** A selection from the Psalms set to sacred music. **4.** A song praising God or expressing joy or gladness to him. See also ANTIPHON.

anthropomorphism (Gk., *ἄνθρωπος [anthrōpos],* "man," "mankind," and *μορφή [morphē],* "form," "shape," "figure"). **1.** The representation of God as having human form and attributes. **2.** The belief that God has characteristics similar to humans such as intelligence, awareness, intention, will, emotions, feelings, sensations, desires, drives, but to a more perfect and powerful degree. (The Greek philosopher Xenophanes [fl. 530 B.C.] was one of the first to point out that humans make

God in their own image in the passage: "If oxen and lions had hands, and could paint with their hands, and fashion images, as men do, they would make pictures and images of their gods in their own likeness; horses would make them like horses, oxen like oxen. Aethiopians make their gods black and snub-nosed; Thracians give theirs blue eyes and red hair.")

Christian theology does not accept the derogatory implications of anthropomorphism. Christian theology is based on the presupposition that most of God's characteristics can be known by extrapolation from those structures that constitute the essence of human nature. God is personal. God is a person. God has a personality. Persons can know other persons only by means of knowing their own personage. Some such form of anthropomorphism is inevitable and a necessary condition for knowing this personal God. Christian theology thus sees anthropomorphism not as a false projection of human attributes upon God but as a description and an awareness in one's life of those attributes given to and present in God. Christian theology also stresses the converse of anthropomorphism: God created humans in his/her image. See also ANALOGICAL PREDICATION, THE THEOLOGICAL DOCTRINE OF.

antichrist (Gk., ἀντι *[anti]*, "against," and Χριστός *[Christos]*, "Christ"). **1.** Any person, ideology, or institution opposed to, or denying, Christ and Christianity. **2.** The enemy of Christ who will appear before the Last Judgment and persuade humans to work against Christ, but who will be defeated by Christ.

The word *antichrist* appears in the Epistles of St. John. For example, at 1 John 2:18: "Little children, it is the last time: and as ye have heard that antichrist shall come, even now are there many antichrists; whereby we know that it is the last time"; 2 John 7: "For many deceivers are entered into the world, who confess not that Jesus Christ is come in the flesh. This is a deceiver and an antichrist"; and at 1 John 4:3: "And every spirit that confesseth not that Jesus Christ is come in the flesh is not of God: and this is that *spirit* of antichrist, whereof ye have heard that it should come; and even now already is it in the world."

antinomian (Gk., ἀντί *[anti]*, "against," and νόμος *[nomos]*, "law"; being against the law). **1.** In general, one who desires to be free from the regulations and laws of a society. One who wants to live either **(a)** *outside* society in a state of nature (like the ESSENES) and/or in a social structure of his/her own choosing (like the monk or nun), or **(b)** *within* society but adhering to as few social norms as possible. **2.** Specifically, in Christian theology **(a)** one who believes that faith alone, not conformity to the civil and moral law, is necessary for SALVATION, or **(b)** those who despise, and hold themselves above, all laws and social restrictions because of some special faith, grace, or knowledge that makes for salvation.

Christian antinomians refer to passages from the Gospels such as Galatians 2:16 ("Knowing that a man is not justified by the works of the law, but by the faith of Jesus Christ, even we have believed in Jesus Christ, that we might be justified by the faith of Christ, and not by the works of the law: for by the works of the law shall no flesh be justified"); Galatians 3:10 ("For as many as are the works of the law are under the curse: for it is written, Cursed *is* every one that continueth not in all things which are written in the book of the law to do them"); Romans 10:3, 4 ("For they being ignorant of God's righteousness, and going about to establish their own righteousness, have not submitted themselves unto the righteousness of God. For Christ *is* the end of the law for righteousness to every one that believeth") to support their position that salvation does not come from following the *nomos* (law, the conventional, custom), that following the *nomos* may indeed hinder one's salvation, and that following the *nomos* is unnecessary if one follows the spirit, way, and faith of the Gospels.

The following are some theological highlights of the antinomian position in addition to the scriptural ones above. **1.** Those in legal power are the principal opponents of Christ's spirit. **2.** As Christians, Christians must assert and proclaim their being and spirit by faith in, and love of, Jesus, and not by following the *nomos*. (Christians "show" their Christianity not by following the *nomos,* but by exhibiting in everyday life the spirit and ways of Jesus Christ.) **3.** The spirit of Jesus Christ is the supplanter of the *nomos*. All laws end up ideally as the way of Jesus Christ. **4.** Those who follow the *nomos* are alienated from the true spirit of Christ, are devoid of grace, and carry a spiritual burden. **5.** Rely upon the *nomos* for spiritual salvation and goodness and they will never come.

Antiochenes. Dedicated to an exegesis of the Bible (as opposed to philosophical and theological analysis). They recognized and accepted both the human and divine natures of Jesus but stressed SYNAPHEIA in contrast to HĒNOSIS. Jesus was a human in whom God dwelled as one would in a temple (compare with Matt. 3:16, 17). A school of Christian thought that developed in Antioch and was a rival of the school that developed in Alexandria.

Their principal theologian was Nestorius (381–451), patriarch of Constantinople (see also NESTORIANISM). Nestorius was attacked by Cyril (376–444) of the ALEXANDRIAN SCHOOL and with the help of Caelestin, a bishop of Rome, had him excommunicated at the Council of Ephesus in 431. Other important representatives of this school: Malchion (third century) Lucian of Antioch (fourth century), and St. John Chrysotomos (347–395).

antiphon (Gk., ἀντίφωνον *[antiphōnon],* "antiphon," "anthem," "sounding in response to," from ἀντί *[anti],* "over," "against," and φωνή *[phōnē],* "voice," "sound"). **1.** A musical response, as in a CHANT or HYMN. **2.** Devotional prose or poetry set to sacred music and sung as a part of the liturgy. **3.** That which is sung before and after the Psalms. See also ANTHEM.

antipope. A POPE elected, or selected, by other than the traditional methods of the Roman Catholic church. There have been 37 antipopes. The last was in 1449.

apocalyptic (Gk., *ἀποκαλύπτειν [apokalyptein],* "to uncover," "to reveal," from *ἀπό [apo],* "from," and *καλύπτειν [kalyptein],* "to cover"). **1.** In general, pertaining to those writings that prophesy the divine, predestined course for (or end of) history. For example, the last book of the New Testament (the Revelation of St. John the Divine) is called the Apocalypse because for Christians it prophesies the coming of God's kingdom. **2.** Anything viewed as a prophetic revelation.

apocatastasis. Greek, *ἀποκατάστασις,* "a restoring." Acts 3:21 refers to the "restoration" by Jesus the Messiah of the blessings had in paradise. The belief that in the end all God's creatures (creation, beings) will be saved. Angels, humans, devils, Satan will all share in the grace of God's salvation. (Sometimes referred to as Universalism; some forms of Universalistic faith contain this belief. Sects such as ANABAPTISTS, Christadelphians and Moravians hold to this view.)

apocrypha. Greek, *ἀπόκρυφος [apokruphos],* "hidden," "spurious" from *ἀπό [apo],* "from," and *κρύπτειν [kryptein],* "to hide".) Writings (documents, statements) that claim a sacred origin but whose authorship and/or authority is in doubt. Implies they are false, fictitious, and not canonical, although some have been considered by some as appendages to the Bible. There are numerous writings regarded as New Testament *apocrypha.* Some: the APOCRYPHAL GOSPELS; Acts of the Apostles; Epistles; Apocalypsis.

apocryphal Gospels. See GOSPELS, APOCRYPHAL.

Apollinarianism. The belief following Apollinarius, Bishop of Laodicaea (ca. 310 to ca. 390) who opposed ARIANISM, that Jesus was sinless—a perfect human, without any capacity to sin—and that Jesus was not wholly God and not wholly man, but a mixture of the two. Apollinarianism was condemned as a doctrine of the Trinity at Rome in 374–380 and by the Council of Constantinople in 381, which affirmed the perfect divinity and perfect humanity of Christ.

apologetics (Gk., *ἀπολογητικός [apologētikos],* "to speak in defense of"). **1.** In general, the endeavor to rationally justify the divine origin of a faith. **2.** Specifically, a branch of Christian theology that systematically defends Christian revelation, beliefs, and way of life, and in particular, the divine origin, authority, and faith in Jesus Christ as Savior and Master.

apologia. Greek, *ἀπολογία,* "to speak in defense of." **1.** A defense or justification of a doctrinal position that to others appears incorrect. **2.** In a negative sense, projecting interpretations upon Scripture; reading things into material to be understood.

apologists, Christian. **1.** In general, Christian theologians who defend their faith against the critics (heretics, schismatics, pagans) of their times. **2.** Sometimes used specifically to refer to the early church theologians of the first four centuries (such as Aristides, Justin Martyr, Athenagoras) who, by means of treatises, not only defended Christianity against attack but attempted to educate people about the Christian faith, to correct its many misinterpretations, and to distinguish it from other faiths and philosophies.

apophatic way, the (Gk., ἀπόφασις *[apophasis],* "denial," from ἀποφάναι *[apophanai],* "to speak out," "to deny"). Apophatic is the method of denying something in order to create an awareness or support a point. In Christian theology the apophatic way denies all the characteristics of God in order to assert his utter transcendance and superiority. The major points: **1.** God is ineffable (indescribable, undefinable). **2.** Human language is unable in any way to reveal or approximate God's real being. **3.** All human attempts to know God fail, and the language used (in relationship to his true reality) is inappropriate, blasphemous, and sacrilegious. **4.** Human language is created to deal with the finite experiences of God's creatures—and not with the nature of God. **5.** Nevertheless, our inadequate attempts suggest or evoke the majesty and glory of God. See also THEOLOGY, NEGATIVE; VIA NEGATIVA.

apostasy (Gk., ἀποστασία *[apostasia],* "defection," from ἀπό *[apo],* "from," and στῆναι *[stenai],* "to stand"). **1.** In general, the renunciation or abandonment of the religious vows taken, usually by one ordained. **2.** Specifically, intentional abandonment or disavowal of the Christian faith. (Apostasy implies a voluntary acceptance at one time of Christian faith.) An apostate is one who has *apostatized.* **3.** Occasionally, the fall of Adam and Eve is referred to as the first apostasy, the first alienation from God's will and command. Apostasy is usually punished by excommunication.

apostle (Gk., ἀπόστολος *[apostolos],* "one sent forth," "envoy," from ἀπό *[apo],* "from," and στλλειν *[stellein],* "to send"). **1.** In general, one who is given power and sent to use this power on behalf of the one who has sent him/her. **2.** Specifically, one of the twelve followers or disciples of Christ sent out to preach the way of Jesus. Used synonymously with DISCIPLE. **3.** Can also apply more generally to others besides the original twelve apostles—such as Barsabas, also known as Barssabas or Barnabas, who went out after Jesus' death, and St. Matthias, who was chosen by lot by the apostles to replace Judas Iscariot, the betrayer of Jesus (Acts 1:23–26: "And they appointed two, Joseph called Barsabas, who was surnamed Justus, and Matthias. And they prayed, and said, 'Thou, Lord, which knowest the hearts of all *men,* shew whether of these two thou hast chosen. That ye may take part of this ministry and apostleship, from which Judas by transgression fell, that he might go to his own place.' And they gave forth their lots: and the lot fell upon Matthias; and he was numbered with the eleven apostles."). See also APOSTLES, THE TWELVE; DISCIPLES, JESUS' TWELVE. **4.** More specifically, Jesus himself who at Hebrews 3:1 is called "the Apostle and High Priest of our profession."

Apostles' Creed. A creed ascribed to the Twelve Apostles (and which may have been a baptismal confession): "I believe in God the Father Almighty, Maker of heaven and earth; and in Jesus Christ his only begotten Son our Lord, who was conceived by the Holy Ghost, born of the Virgin Mary; suffered under Pontius Pilate, was crucified, dead, and buried. He descended into Hades; the third day He rose from the dead; He ascended into heaven; and sitteth on the right hand of God the Father, Almighty; from thence He shall come to judge the quick and the dead. I believe in the Holy Ghost; the holy Catholic church, the communion of saints; the forgiveness of sins; the resurrection of the body; and the life everlasting. Amen."

The creed is spoken, chanted, or sung as an act of praise in the worship service to God and proclaims God's salvation for us. It is the ecumenical creed of the Western church. (The NICENE CREED is the ecumenical creed of the Eastern church.)

Apostles, the Twelve. The twelve disciples (see also DISCIPLES, JESUS' TWELVE) of Jesus. But more than the tweve disciples came to be called "apostles." For example, St. Paul was authorized as an apostle directly by God (Gal. 1:1) and St. Barnabas by the Holy Ghost through a local ecclesia (Acts 13:2). Luke and Mark are regarded as apostles. Used synonymously with *the Twelve Disciples.*

The origins of the Christian churches are for the most part apostolic (based on the apostles; see also APOSTOLICITY). Their basis is in apostolic writings, apostolic faith, and APOSTOLIC SUCCESSION. (Refer, for example, to Matt. 10:5ff.; Luke 9:2ff.; Mark 3:14.)

apostolate. The office (mission, status) of an APOSTLE.

Apostolic College. The Roman Catholic church regards the Apostles as constituting the first Apostolic College with Peter at its head. It is believed that scriptural authority for this is found at places such as Matthew 10:1ff.; 16:18–20; Luke 22:29; and John 21:15ff. Peter's successors are the popes (the bishops) of Rome. Jesus' authority is transmitted through Peter and the popes, through the Apostolic College that consists of the successors of the Apostles. See also APOSTOLICITY; KEYS, THE POWER OF THE.

Apostolic Fathers. The Christian authors and APOLOGISTS immediately following the New Testament writings, regarded as the pupils of the original APOSTLES (or of those who had been taught by the original apostles), such as Clement of Rome, Ignatius of Antioch, Hermas, Polycarp, Papias, the authors of the Epistle of Barnabas, the Epistle to Diognetus, and the Didache. See also PATRISTICS: PATROLOGY.

apostolicity. **1.** In Ephesians 2:19ff. it is stated that the church was built on the foundation of the APOSTLES and sustains and maintains their beliefs, doctrines, and practices. A Christian church in possessing the writings of the Apostles has in them the true doctrines of Christianity and can trace (should be able to trace) its existence back to the Apostles and to the churches they founded. **2.** The belief that there is one primary church founded by the Apostles from which all true Christian churches should originate. Apostolicity is one of the four signs of the Christian church as found in the NICENE CREED. **3.** The belief that the true faith taught by Jesus to his Apostles is transmitted through them and their successors in an unbroken chain on down to the present EPISCOPACY of a church. Apostolicity implies that the doctrines of Jesus have been preserved and contained intact as a whole. **4.** Specifically in Roman Catholicism, the one church of the Apostles is that of St. Peter maintained by means of the continuity of dogma and APOSTOLIC SUCCESSION, through the Pope of Rome (where St. Peter founded his church) as heir of St. Peter, who was considered the Prime of the Apostles. Roman Catholicism (the Church of Rome) holds that only those who are under the jurisdiction of the pope, only those who have doctrinal loyalty to the pope are to be regarded as within the true Apostolic church.

apostolic see. **1.** In general, a SEE founded and governed by an APOSTLE. **2.** Specifically, the Roman Catholic church—the see founded on the belief that the pope is the spiritual and apostolic successor of St. Peter, who is regarded as the only apostle who has apostolic successors. See also APOSTOLIC SUCCESSION.

apostolic succession. The belief that EPISCOPACY is spiritually obtained from the APOSTLES by means of a continuous succession of events and people. See also APOSTOLICITY. For example, the Roman Catholic church regards itself as apostolic because it was founded by Christ through the Apostles; its doctrines, beliefs, and sacraments are those of the Apostles; the pope and bishops are links in an unbroken chain leading back to the Apostles; it regards itself as the true and only successor of Jesus. Scriptural references such as Matthew 16:18ff. are used to support the notion that Jesus appointed Peter as the head of the Twelve Apostles, as the "rock" or foundation upon which he would build his universal church in the interim between his death and his PAROUSIA. See also KEYS, THE POWER OF THE. Another example: the Church of England (of Canterbury) claims to trace its succession back from the present archbishop, to other archbishops, to St. Augustine, to Gregory, back to Peter and Paul. In this case, the succeeding persons are officeholders in the sense of succeeding the Apostles (but not, according to the Church of Rome, "successors" of the Apostles). The Greek Orthodox church also maintains apostolic succession.

apotheōsis Greek, ἀποθέωσις. Deification of someone during that person's life or after. In such areas as Greek patristic and in mystical theology, deification *(apotheōsis)* was possible by means of union, a oneness with God effected by Christ. Once this oneness in Christ took place, then humans participated in the divine nature of God. (Refer, for example, to 2 Pet. 1:4.)

appropriation (L., *appropriare,* "to appropriate," "to set apart for a particular use or person"). Attributing a property belonging to the Godhead as a whole, to one Person (one member of the Trinity) because of a common and greater resemblance to the particular properties of that Person. Examples: appropriating (as St. Augustine [350–430] did) *unity* to the Father; *equality* to the Son; and relatedness in *love* to the HOLY SPIRIT. St. Thomas Aquinas (1225–1274) appropriated *power* to the Father; *wisdom* to the Son; and *goodness* to the Holy Spirit. St. Bonaventura (1217–1274) appropriated *oneness* to the Father; *truth* to the Son; and *love* to the Holy Spirit. Calvin (1509–1564) appropriated *origin to the Father; wisdom to the Son; and virtue* to the Holy Spirit.

Appropriation applies to the sources of *activity* of the three Persons of the Trinity: *ex quo* (from whom) relates to the Father; *per quem* (through whom) relates to the Son; and *in quo* (in whom) relates to the Holy Spirit. Appropriation is also applied to the *functions* of the Trinity: the Father as Creator; the Son as REDEEMER; the Holy Spirit as the Sanctifier.

Aquinas, Thomas. See THOMISM.

archangel (Gk., ἀρχάγγελος *[archangelos]*). An angel at the uppermost level in the hierarchy of angels (see also ANGEL). Some prominent archangels: SAINT MICHAEL, SAINT GABRIEL, SAINT RAPHAEL (who are honored as archangels by a feast day in the Roman Catholic church on September 29), Saint Uriel.

archbishop (Gk., ἀρχιεπίσκοπος *[archiepiskopos],* "a principal bishop," from ἀρχί *[archi],* "chief," "first," "prime," and ἐπίσκοπος *[episkopos],* "bishop," "overseer"). A chief bishop. A bishop who is a head or leader of an ecclesiastical area usually containing other bishops.

archdiocese. The DIOCESE of an ARCHBISHOP—that district of a church over which an archbishop has authority.

Arianism. Based on the beliefs and writings of Arius (ca.250–ca.356), a priest of Alexandria. He preached that Jesus (the LOGOS), as Jesus, is not eternal like the Father (God). Jesus was created (begotten) by the Father and is not of the same substance as God. Jesus as the *Logos* mediates between God and humanity. Jesus is God's representative in this world.

Jesus had free will (could choose between right and wrong) and he used it to become divine. Arianism was condemned as heretical in 325 by the First Council of Nicaea. See also ATHANASIANISM.

Armageddon (Gk., Ἀρμαγεδδών). The final battle to be fought at the Final Judgment Day ("the great day of God") between the forces of God and those of evil (refer to Rev. 16:16).

Ascension Day. The Thursday, forty days after EASTER, that commemorates Jesus' ascension into heaven from the Mount of Olives. Tradition has it that the ascension occurred in the presence of his Mother Mary, the apostles, and the disciples. Jesus' ascension is the last of his appearances on earth after his Resurrection.

The PATRISTIC writers considered Ascension Day as the crown of all Christian feasts. For example, St. Augustine (354–430): "This is that festival which confirms the grace of all the festivals together, without which the profitableness of every festival would have perished. For unless the Saviour had ascended into heaven, his Nativity would have come to nothing . . . and his Passion would have borne no fruit for us, and his most holy Resurrection would have been useless."

Ascension of Jesus, the. The ascendance into heaven of Jesus' resurrected body is found in Acts 1:9–11: "while they beheld, he was taken up; and a cloud received him out of their sight. And while they looked stedfastly toward heaven as he went up, behold, two men stood by them in white apparel; which also said, 'Ye men of Galilee, why stand ye gazing up into heaven? This same Jesus, which is taken up from you into heaven, shall so come in like manner as ye have seen him go into heaven.' " (See also Acts 1:1–14; Luke 24:50–53; Eph. 4:10; John 20:17; Mark 16:19.)

In Christian faith, the Ascension of Jesus differs from the concept of Jesus' Resurrection. Jesus was resurrected and that resurrected body, forty days later, ascended into heaven. For Christians, Jesus' ascension is the principal foundation of the SACRAMENTS, and Christian HOPE and FAITH. The Ascension is believed to be the pinnacle point for humanity—the topmost mature spiritual state (an indissoluble union with God) that endows one with liberation from bondage and previous limits. The Ascension is considered as God's ultimate purpose for humanity—the summit point of SALVATION. The Ascension of Jesus is often thought of as man (Jesus) being put in God's place in the act of reconciliation, whereas at the INCARNATION, God has put himself in man's place. Often Jesus' ascension is referred to as his *exaltation.* See also RESURRECTION, THE.

asceticism (Gk., ἀσκητικός *[asketikos],* "one who exercises"). **1.** In general, the view that humans should deny their desires. **(a)** The strong version: humans should deny all desires without exception. **(b)** The weak version: humans should deny base desires of the body (lust, lasciviousness, sensuousness) and the world (material possessions, fame, achievement). The desires of the flesh must be repressed. Only in this way can humans free the soul to attain virtue and salvation. Ascetism has been associated with celibacy, austerity, obedience, submissiveness, martyrdom, poverty, fasting, abstinence, flagellation, discipline, penance, mutilation of the body, self-mortification, solitariness, contemplation, meditation. See also RENUNCIATION. **2.** Austerity and the renouncing of activities or things that may be correct and desirable for the sake of other values such as simplicity, order, control, altruism, respect, future benefits.

asceticism, Christian. The rigorous discipline and tasks required to abnegate all reference to a self or ego and thereby allow the total embodiment of the HOLY SPIRIT and the presence of God's GRACE. Generally a typical form: **1.** Katharsis (purgation), the process of renouncing personal wants, needs, and attachments; **2** enlightenment (illumination), by practicing the Christian VIRTUES and conforming as closely as possible to the ideal of Jesus Christ the SAVIOR; **3.** oneness (union) with God in which all things become one in the presence of God or are absorbed into a total unity with God. See also entries on MYSTICISM. In this sense asceticism is a preparation for or a prelude to higher levels of the contemplative life.

Christianity considers some degree of asceticism to be necessary for the development of the spiritual life and for the fulfillment of a Christian life in imitation of Jesus Christ. See also CHRIST, IMITATION OF.

a se. Latin, "existing of itself, self-sufficiently, of its own power underived from any other source." Applied only to God as the only self-sustaining being. God's essence is existence (to exist); God's eternal existence is God's essence.

aseity (L., *aseitas,* "being by, for and of itself"). The state **1.** in which a thing is utterly, completely, absolutely independent of all other things, **2.** upon which all other things depend for their total existence, and **3.** which manifests its nature (essence) in a perfectly pure way without manifesting nonessential characteristics. In Christian theology, the word *aseity* applies only to God. See also GOD, THE ATTRIBUTES OF.

Ash Wednesday. The first day of LENT, forty days before EASTER. Ashes, symbolizing REPENTANCE and CONTRITION, are put on the forehead in the form of a cross by the priest with this thumb, as he says: "Remember . . . that thou art dust and unto dust thou shalt return." The palms used the previous Palm Sunday are burned and the ashes are used in the ritual.

In early Christianity, Christians who were guilty of sins underwent public confession and penance. For forty days sinners wore sackclothes that were blessed by a bishop, and they had the ashes put on their foreheads. The congregation sang and expelled the penitents from the church, in a symbolic gesture of Adam and Eve being expelled from the Garden of Eden.

assensus. Latin, "assent." In medieval theology and philosophy, an essential item in FAITH, together with FIDUCIA (trust) and NOTITIA (understanding).

Assumption Day. See ASSUMPTION OF THE BLESSED VIRGIN MARY.

Assumption of the Blessed Virgin Mary. The belief, similar to Christ's Ascension (see also ASCENSION OF JESUS, THE), that Mary, the Mother of God, was also taken up body and soul into heaven. This belief dates back to earlier than the sixth century. The assumption of Mary is known to have been celebrated in Palestine in the fifth century. Assumption Day, or the *Feast of the Assumption,* is celebrated on August 15, and in the Eastern Orthodox tradition is referred to as the *κοίμησις (koimēsis)* or the "Feast of the Falling-asleep," one of the most important and celebrated feast days. Controversy still exists as to whether the Virgin Mary was taken up into heaven at death, or before death. According to Christian tradition, Mary the Mother of God died at Mount Sion and was buried in the Garden of Gethsemane. Christian legend has it that she died in the presence of the Apostles (except St. Thomas, who did not arrive in time). The Apostles found her sepulchre full of flowering lilies when it was opened on the third day after her burial. The lily they had placed was gone.

On November 1, 1950, Pope Pius XII codified the belief in the Assumption of the Blessed Virgin Mary in the papal BULL *Munificientissimus Deus.*

Athanasian Creed. One of the formulations of Christian faith, composed in Latin in the fifth century, stressing the doctrine of the Trinity and the Incarnation. St. Athanasios (293–373), a Greek Church Father, was probably not the author. See also APOSTLES' CREED; NICENE CREED.

Athanasianism. Based on the writings of St. Athanasios (293–373) who supported the view of Christ's divinity (against, for example, the Arians), which held that Jesus as the Son of God was of the same identical essence and substance with his Father. Arius (ca.250–ca.356), who believed that Jesus was created by God but was different in essence and substance from the Father, was voted down at the Council of Nicaea (318–325) by Athanasios and his supporters.

athanatism (Gk., *α [a],* "not," and *θάνατος [thanatos],* "death"). **1.** The belief in the survival of the soul (the consciousness, the mind, the self, the ego, the personality) in some form or other, and in some place or other, after death. **2.** The belief in immortality. Opposite of thanatism.

atheism (Gk., *ἀ [a],* "no," "not," and *θεός [theos],* "God"). **1.** Used to refer to the attitudes of those who refused to revere the god(s) of the city (state, political bodies, the emperor) and thus were implicated in deviating from the policies (and politics) of the city's rulers. In this sense, Christians were accused of being atheistic since they did not venerate the god(s) of the state at that time. **2.** Those who were "without God in the world," that is, the Christian God (Eph. 2:12 where the Greek plural *ἄθεοι ἐν τῷ κόσμῳ [atheoi en tō kosmō]* is used, which can be translated literally as "atheists in the world": "That at that time ye were without Christ, being aliens from the commonwealth of Israel, and strangers from the convenants of promise, having no hope, and *without God in the world."*). **3.** The belief that God does not exist (or the denial that God exists). Atheism in this sense appears systematically in the rationalism of the enlightenment and finds it culmination in philosophies such as secular Humanism, Materialism, Marxism, Existentialism.

atonement (From "at" and "one," "to make as one," "to unite"). **1.** To make into one ("at-one-ment"). **2.** To bring together in reconciliation. **3.** To make amends, or to mend. **4.** To remove obstacles preventing a union, or acceptance. **5.** A state of concord, peace, agreement. **6.** The act of making reparation of expiation. **7.** The act whereby a wrong act one has done is intentionally rectified or undone in order to produce reconciliation and harmony, overcome estrangement, and enrich the relationship that has been broken. **8.** The spiritual activity of removing the hindrances that prevent a loving relationship among humans. **9.** The spiritual activity deliberately undertaken to correct the repercussions of evil and to restore a relationship of love. **10.** Specifically in Christianity, atonement is related to the life and work of Jesus Christ ending at Calvary, the redeeming effect upon humans of Christ's obedience (and discipline), his suffering (sacrifice) and crucifixion (death).

The Christian concept of atonement is scripturally based upon passages such as Mark 10:45 ("For even the Son of man came not to be ministered unto, but to minister, and give his life a ransom for many"): 1 Timothy 2:6; Titus 2:14; Colossians 1:20; 2 Corinthians 5:19; etc. (The first three especially have been used to support the "ransom" or "substitutionary" concept of Christ's atonement. See also CHRISTOLOGY.)

attrition (L., *atterere,* "to rub," "to wear down by friction"). The grief (guilt, remorse, sorrow) for having sinned only because of the fear of punishment by God. Sometimes referred to as imperfect CONTRITION. Attrition alone is not enough to receive forgiveness for one's sin. Attrition has been regarded as a precursor of contrition and sufficient in preparing a human for the Sacrament of Penance, which requires contrition. Attrition has also been regarded as a manifestation of God's gratuitous grace *(gratia gratis data)* whereby the beginning stages of overcoming evil are manifested; whereas contrition has been regarded as a consequence of God's sanctifying GRACE, or grace of charity *(gratia gratum faciens)* by which evil is truly destroyed and perfect contrition elicited. Attrition prepares a human for the grace of charity that produces contrition.

Augsburg Confession. The principal confession of faith for Lutherans. Philip Melanchthon compiled it. Its preface and epilogue were written by Gregor Brück, chancellor of Saxony. It was presented to the Imperial

Diet of Augsburg on June 30, 1530 and approved by King Charles V with Luther's approval. The original text given to the king (emperor) is not extant. The declaration included theological positions held by Luther and those adopted by Lutherans at previous conferences (such as at Marburg, Schwabach, Torgau). The document contains twenty-one articles on doctrine, followed by seven more that describe the evils and abuses of the Roman Catholic church that have been, or can be, or will be, corrected by events such as those that were taking place by reformers. See also REFORMATION, THE.

The Augsburg Confession presents the basic and essential tenets of Lutheranism in the context of hope for Christian brotherhood and unity.

Augustinianism. Based on the writings of St. Augustine of Hippo (354–430). He was born in North Africa and was baptized from paganism on Easter Eve, 387. One of the cornerstones of the Roman Catholic church. Some of the tenets: **1.** God is Pure Being, immaterial, eternal, pure intelligence, immutable, and a unity. (Augustine was influenced by Plato and the Neo-Platonic philosophy of Plotinus.) **2.** The soul rules the body (as in Platonism) and its spiritual condition causes good and evil. **3.** Humans have free will, and evil exists because they choose it rather than choosing good. (St. Augustine also held to the view that evil was the absence or privation of good, not of any subsistent existence and hence not produced by an omnipotent and omnibenevolent God.) **4.** The soul can participate in (imitate, partake of) the divine Ideas of God and his Will. **5.** God can illuminate (enhance, reveal to) the soul and grace it. **6.** Humans are corrupted by sin and cannot of themselves reach God, salvation, or divine truth. **7.** Humans must rely upon God's grace, must allow the Holy Spirit to work on them through Jesus Christ, must learn through faith (and its understanding), and must live according to faith (and its practice). **8.** Faith is a gift of God—of God's grace. **9.** Faith and repentance (SALVATION in general) are the temporal expressions of God's eternal predestined selection. **10.** Merits, good works, do not precede nor serve as preconditions for faith and repentance. **11.** God's grace presents his Son with those whom he has selected (chosen, elected). **12.** The gospel of Christ must nevertheless be preached so that humans can come into faith. **13.** The Father, Son, and the Holy Spirit are one and the same without distinction. Opposed to PELAGIANISM.

auricular confession. See CONFESSION.

autopistic faith. See FAITH, AUTOPISTIC.

autotheism (Gk., *αὐτός [autos]*, "self," and *θεός [theos]*, "God"). The doctrine in contrast with the Trinity that Jesus Christ was God himself—not the Son of God; not the Holy Sprit associated with Jesus or God but *a se ipso, non a Pater*—existed in and by himself and not by means of a Father. See also TRINITY, THE HOLY.

autotheos. Greek, *αὐτόθεος*, from *αὐτός*, *(autos)*, "self-same," and *θεός* *(theos)*, "God." Refers to Jesus as containing his own *status* as a God-figure, in distinction to God the Father and the Holy Spirit.

autousia. Greek, *αὐτουσία*, from *αὐτός (autos)*, "self-same," and *οὐσία (ousia)*, "essence." Refers to Jesus as containing his own *essence* as a God figure distinct from God as Father and the Holy Spirit. See also AUTOTHEOS.

awe. **1.** The emotion of REVERENCE mixed with emotions of greatness, fear, dread, the terrifying, the sublime, the sacred. **2.** The emotion of great reverential terror or fear felt in the presence of God. **3.** Solemn and profound wonder at the majesty of God's creation.

B

baptism (Gk., *βαπτίζειν [baptizein]*, "to dip in water"). The ceremony of applying water to a person by immersion and/or sprinkling and thereby (according to some Christian sects) purifying, sanctifying, initiating, and naming the recipient as a Christian. Baptism is administered by pouring (or sprinkling, or immersion in) water, at the same time declaring "I baptize thee . . . in the name of the Father and of the Son and of the Holy Ghost." The ceremony can be very ritualistic as in the Roman Catholic church and Eastern Orthodox church where elements such as exorcism, salt, spittle, oil, water, linen cloth, a font, candle light, chanting, etc. are used, or it can be a simple declaration of acceptance into the Christian faith. Infant baptism (see also PAEDOBAPTISM) is practiced by most Christians. Many Protestants practice a "believer's baptism"—baptism at an age where one understands the tenets and direction one is accepting. Baptism in most Christian sects requires a sponsor (a godparent or godparents) who publicly vow and promise to rear the person in the faith.

A variety of attitudes about baptism exist in the Christian faith, not all accepted by Christian groups. Some: **1.** Baptism is a SACRAMENT—the sacrament of rebirth—that produces a supernatural regeneration to a new life in Jesus Christ. In counterdistinction to the Roman Catholic church, which holds that there are seven sacred sacraments, most Protestant groups regard baptism and the Last Supper (Holy Communion) as the only two sacred sacraments ordained by Christ. (See Matt. 28:19.) Some Protestant groups affirm that only those two are necessary in order to be saved. Among Protestants there is division as to whether or not these sacraments are of supernatural import or merely symbolic gestures. **2.** Through baptism persons are admitted into the visible Church of

Christ—the Body of Christ. A person gains membership into the Christian community by means of baptism. **3.** An unalterable CHARACTER is received at baptism. **4.** Grace is received at baptism. **5.** Only a baptized person can be graced by God. **6.** The Holy Spirit enters into the baptized person. At the INFUSION of the Holy Spirit, the recipient is reborn, allowing the participation in a divine life as a child of God. **7.** Baptism creates a new person, and in early Christianity a new name was taken to signify this. **8.** Baptism remits all sin and permits the reception of God's grace. (See John 3:5; Mark 16:16.) Original sin is cancelled. The soul is returned to a state of pure, original innocence. The self is changed in spirit, heart, nature, and purpose. **9.** A baptism is the only means by which humans can deliver themselves from original sin—the sin and guilt inherited from our first parents, Adam and Eve. (A form of baptism and CIRCUMCISION were practiced by the Jews at the time of Christ to admit proselytes into the Jewish faith and to signify repentance for the remission of sins.) **10.** Repentance of faith are necessary for the realization of the full benefits of baptism. **11.** Unbaptized infants cannot ever be admitted into the Kingdom of Heaven (see also LIMBO). (The Latin Fathers speak about unbaptized infants as suffering a pain of *sense*. The Greek Fathers preach that they suffer a pain of *loss*.) A stronger form: No one who has not been baptized can be saved or admitted into the KINGDOM OF GOD. At John 3:5, Christ says: "I say unto thee, Except a man be born of water and of the Spirit, he cannot enter the kingdom of God." (Baptism *in utero* has been conducted in order to baptize a fetus as in the case of a stillborn child.) **12.** Lay baptism, as opposed to being baptized by one ordained, may be practiced in situations of emergency. **13.** In cases where it is unknown whether or not the person has been baptized, "conditional baptism" has been practiced, where the form is in some fashion such as "If thou hast not already been baptized, I baptize thee in the name of . . . ." **14.** One cannot—and should not—be baptized a second time.

baptism, Jesus'. The Holy Family returned to Nazareth after Herod's death and it was there that Jesus developed into manhood. Jesus' ministry begins with his baptism by SAINT JOHN THE BAPTIST in the River Jordan (see Matt. 3:13–17; Mark 1:9–11; Luke 3:21, 22). In the history of Christian art, Jesus is traditionally depicted as standing in the river as St. John pours the river water over Jesus' head, the DOVE of the HOLY SPIRIT descends from God the Father in heaven, and two angels stand on the bank of the river prepared to clothe the naked Jesus as soon as he steps from the river.

baptism of desire. The desire for the sacrament of baptism accompanied by CONTRITION, which produces the effects of baptism. In general, baptism and membership in a church are necessary for salvation, but there has been a tradition in Christian faith that merely the desire to belong to the true Church of Jesus Christ satisfies baptismal requirements for membership in Jesus' Church. Evidence of this desire is found in one's faith, charity, conscience, everyday actions.

baptism of blood, the. **1.** Achieved by those who died for the faith before they could be baptized. **2.** Baptism accomplished by means of martyrdom. See also MARTYR.

Baptists. There are several historical origins for the Baptists in the early seventeenth century (although Baptists have traced their origins back to the first century). The two most prominent ones: John Smyth (1554–1612), an Anglican minister, was removed in 1602 by his ecclesiastical superiors for heretical beliefs. He formed a small group of separatists that moved to Holland in 1606 to form a Baptist church. (AFFUSION was the method practiced until 1641 when IMMERSION became the prescribed method.) Thomas Helwys (1550–1616) left Amsterdam in 1611 and went to England to form the first Baptist group there. The offshoots of this group were called "General Baptists" because they believed that salvation was possible for everyone. In 1638 another group formed called "Particular Baptists" who were influenced by Calvinism and its notions of predestination and the elect. In the United States, credit is given to Roger Williams (1604–1684), an expelled Puritan minister in the Massachusetts Bay Colony, for founding the First Baptist church in America in Providence, Rhode Island, in 1639. (Roger Williams did not remain a Baptist long.) John Clarke (1609–1676), an English physician, secured a final charter from Charles II, establishing Rhode Island as a colony in 1663, and became the minister of the Baptist church at Newport, Rhode Island.

Some of their tenets: **1.** The Bible is the supreme source of inspiration and direction, as opposed to an institution or ecclesiastical authority. **2.** Humans must be free to worship without interference or compulsion from the state. (In general, Baptists take a positive attitude toward the state and political involvement.) **3.** Stress upon the primacy and right of individual conscience to interpret the infallible teachings of the Bible. **4.** Immersion is the true form of Baptism. Christ was so immersed by SAINT JOHN THE BAPTIST. **5.** No supernatural significance is attached to the sacraments. Any sacraments practiced have symbolic, personal value in the act of rededication to the life of righteousness in Jesus Christ and of service to all humans. (Baptists celebrate the Lord's Supper, or a communion serivce, on the first Sunday of each month, as a memorial following Jesus' command to observe that event in his memory.) **6.** Clergy or the church cannot save a person, but only the belief in Christ as one's personal savior (which results in personal redemption shown by faith, good works, and a devoted Christian way of life). **7.** The confession of sin is a private, personal, and solemn matter between each individual and God, having nothing to do with clergy or the church. **8.** Congregationalism, or the complete autonomy of each Baptist denomination, or church. (It is customary for the local churches to ordain.)

basileia. Greek, *βασιλεία*, "kingdom," "reign of God," "sovereignty." **1.** The eschatological reign of God at which he judges all nations at the end of the present world and at which God initiates a new AEON. **2.** The earthly kingdom of God to be established here on earth at the Second Coming of Jesus, in which Jesus Christ's teachings will prevail in thought and deed, all evil and devils will be subjugated (Mark 1:15), the salvation of humankind will be achieved, and all will live in bliss and joy.

Christians pray for the *basileia*. The *basileia* will be inherited, or bestowed upon us by God (Luke 12:32; 22:29). The *basileia* is not, and cannot be, humanmade. It is a utopia that can be created only by the supernatural God. Only God knows (Mark 13:32) when the *basileia* will come and who will be allowed in it. But according to Christian faith, the prerequisites for entering the *basileia* are qualities such as: faith, penance, love, baptism, participation in the sacraments, etc. The keys of the *basileia* were given to Peter (Matt. 16:19). See also KEYS, THE POWER OF THE; KINGDOM OF GOD, THE; PAROUSIA.

The EUCHARIST is often regarded as the spiritual anticipation of the banquet, or feast, of the final *basileia* of God. St. Paul makes a distinction between the *basileia* of Christ, which refers to Jesus' Church (Col. 1:13) and the *basileia* of God, which refers to the moral and spiritual teachings (preachings) of Jesus Christ.

beasts. See CREATURES, THE FOUR LIVING.

beatification (L., *beatificare,* "to make happy," and *facere,* "to make"). **1.** The act by means of which a pope initiates veneration of a deceased person in the church whose life and actions merit it. **2.** The public declaration by the Roman Catholic church that a deceased person has entered the realm of "the blessed." Beatification is often the stage prior to canonization or sainthood.

beatific vision (L., *beatificare,* "to make happy," from *beatus,* "happy," and *facere,* "to make," and *visio,* from *videre,* "to see"). **1.** The direct blissful perception of God had by angels and saints. **2.** The vision of God as God is in himself, not as known by inference, teachings, or authority. This vision is a joy that exists only in heaven and awaits those who have been redeemed. (Some exceptions have been made for those who received the beatific vision from God while still mortal men, such as Moses, St. Paul, St. Thomas Aquinas.) The essence of the blessed life in heaven. The *summum bonum* of all life and existence. Regarded as the highest pleasure and glory attainable by humans and that toward which all humans aspire. Humans were created for the purpose of meeting God face-to-face. It is held out to humans as their ultimate and final reward for a perfect life. **3.** The perfect awareness or perception of God, imparted by God, stressing our nearness and importance to God, our absorption into his glory based on our being possessed by the Holy Spirit and obedience to Jesus Christ. This perception of God is the essence of the beatific vision, or of a human's beatitude that God has promised and that will be received at death, or before a human's resurrection, or possibly during life, or at the Final Judgment. Concepts of the beatific vision have been based on New Testament references such as: Revelation 21:4; 1 Corinthians 13:12; 1 John 3:2; I Timothy 6:16.

beatitude (L., *beatitudo,* "blessing," "blessedness," "felicity"). **1.** Jesus' promise of coming blessings for those who believe in him. **2.** Those blessings that are described as the qualities necessary for Christian perfection (see also BEATITUDES, THE). **3.** The complete and ultimate perfection of the human being who has been blessed by God's supernatural grace. **4.** One who has received the BEATIFIC VISION. **5.** The state of blessedness received at one's resurrection and/or entrance into God's BASILEIA.

Beatitudes, the. The statements made by Jesus in the SERMON ON THE MOUNT (Matt. 5:3–12) that refer to the eight spiritual blessings: "Blessed are the poor in spirit: for theirs is the kingdom of heaven. Blessed are they that mourn: for they shall be comforted. Blessed are the meek: for they shall inherit the earth. Blessed are they which do hunger and thirst after righteousness: for they shall be filled. Blessed are the merciful: for they shall obtain mercy. Blessed are the pure in heart: for they shall see God. Blessed *are* the peacemakers: for they shall be called the children of God. Blessed *are* they which are persecuted for righteousness' sake: for theirs is the kingdom of heaven. Blessed are ye, when *men* shall revile you, and persecute *you,* and shall say all manner of evil against you falsely, for my sake."

In the history of Christian art, these blessings are depicted as maidens.

benediction (L., *benedicere,* "to bless," from *bene,* "good," and *dicere,* "to say"). **1.** In general, a blessing. **2.** The formal, ritualistic act of blessing someone such as an ABBOT or PRIOR on their installation to a sacred office. **3.** That part of a liturgy at which a blessing is bestowed or requested, such as the blessing bestowed upon a penitent before CONFESSION. **4.** The blessing of the bread and wine in OBLATION and CONSECRATION. **5.** The rite or ceremony presenting the Blessed Sacrament to the congregation for ADORATION. The priest makes the sign of the cross over the people with the Blessed Sacrament and blesses them. **6.** The blessing pronounced by popes, patriarchs, bishops, or priests over persons, or things, such as oil, water, salt, ashes, palms, rosaries, vestments, etc.

The benediction blessing is done by means of the hand making the form of the cross.

benefice (L., *beneficus,* "beneficent"). The benefits accruing to a cleric such as living arrangements (see also RECTORY), curacy, rights, powers, titles in the performance of religious and spiritual duties. Originally referred to a grant of land *(beneficium)* given for life as a reward for services rendered. In canon law, refers to the compensations given for the performance of spiritual duties in an ecclesiastical capacity. The holder of a benefice is often called an "incumbent," such as a VICAR, RECTOR, PRIEST.

bestiary (L., *bestia,* "beast"). A book written about the supernatural qualities attributed to animals (including birds, fishes, and reptiles), real or fabled. Bestiaries were popular from early Christian times and especially popular during the Middle Ages. Some of the symbolic creatures in these bestiaries: adder, amphisbaena, basilisk, dragon, griffin, LION, mermaid, PELICAN, phoenix, unicorn.

Bible, the Holy (Gk., *βιβλία [biblia],* "the books"). Also referred to as the BIBLE; HOLY WRIT; SCRIPTURE; WORD OF GOD. In the New Testament the Holy Bible is called "The Scripture" (Acts 8:32; Gal. 3:22; 2 Tim. 3:16; James 4:5), "The Scriptures" (Matt. 21:42; Luke 24:27), "The Holy Scriptures" (2 Tim. 3:15). The book containing the sacred works accepted by Christians as the unique and only revealed word of God, revealing his supreme power and authority, his commands and divine will, his actions in the universe, and what our relationship should be to him. The Bible, comprising the Old and New Testaments, is a collection of over sixty-six books composed by different writers over a period of approximately 1,800 years. The OLD TESTAMENT was written in Hebrew and the New Testament in Greek. The word "Bible" is not found earlier than the fifth century. The priests who were in charge of the manuscripts referred to them as *"the* Books". The Greek word for *Book* is *βίβλος* (biblos) and it became the title of the entire collection of the books, or sections, which we now call *the* Book, or Bible.

During the first 400 years of Christianity, over ten Catalogues of Canonical Books appeared, each differing slightly. The Old and New Testaments as we have them today, including six Apocryphal books of the Old Testament, were ratified as canonical by the third Council of Carthage in 397 A.D. (Since then, there have been controversies as to the proper cataloguing of the canonical books of the Bible.) The Latin Vulgate (see also BIBLE, THE VULGATE) translated by St. Jerome (384–406) is the classic and standard work used in the Roman Catholic church. The English King James Authorized Version (see also BIBLE, THE KING JAMES) translated from the Hebrew and Greek in 1611 stands as the biblical basis for English Protestantism. Luther's German Bible, translated by Luther in 1522–1534, from the original Hebrew and Greek, is the biblical standard for Lutheranism and German Protestantism. (Luther's translation was the first Western European Bible not based on the Latin Vulgate

Bible of the Roman Catholic church and was translated into the German of the time, in a language so rich and poetic that it inspired German literature for centuries.)

The first complete English translation of the Bible was the Wycliffe Bible (1380), which was a translation of the Roman Catholic Latin Vulgate. (Bede in the eighth century had begun a translation of the Latin Vulgate into the English of his time.) Some of the subsequent translations: the Tyndale Bible (1525), which was a translation of the New Testament from the original Greek (Tyndale [1491–1536] translated parts of the Old Testament before his violent death in Brussels) and was the first English printing of the Bible. Some of the many translations of the Bible: The Coverdale Bible (1535); the Matthews' Bible (1537); the Great Bible (1539); the Geneva Bible (1560); the Bishop's Bible (1568); the Authorized Version (1611) (see also BIBLE, THE KING JAMES); the English Revised Version (1881–1885); the American Revised (1885–1900); the American Standard (1901); the Revised Standard Version (1951); the new Jerusalem Bible (1968); the New English Bible (1961 and 1970); the New Ecumenical Bible (1973).

In the Roman Catholic faith, the Douay-Rheims Bible (1582 and 1609) is an English translation from the Vulgate that has had wide appeal. Its 1746 revision is a standard Catholic English version of the Bible. The New American Bible (1970) is a Catholic work translated directly into English from the original languages used in the Bible.

Some of the ancient manuscripts from which translations of the Bible have been made: the Vatican Greek Manuscript (probably the oldest manuscript, it is from the fourth century and has been in the Vatican Library since 1450; it is an Uncial manuscript); the Sinaitic Greek Manuscript (found in 1859 by the German scholar Tischendort in the convent of St. Catherine at Mount Sinai; this manuscript is in the St. Petersburg, now Leningrad, Library, and is venerated as one of the greatest treasures of the Eastern Orthodox churches); the Alexandrian Greek Manuscript (from the first half of the fifth century; given to Charles I in 1628 by Cyril Lucar, the patriarch of Constantinople, and now in the Library of the British Museum); the Greek Codex of Ephraem (written in the early part of the fifth century and now housed in the Royal Library of Paris).

Bible, the King James. Often simply referred to as the *Authorized Version.* In 1604, King James I appointed fifty-four scholars to translate a new version of the Bible in order to help settle biblical disputes among scholars. The book was published in 1611 and has since been the most popular of all translations in the English language. Several revisions have been published in order to incorporate new manuscripts and modern philological scholarship, such as the English Revised Version, (1881–1885); the American Standard Version (1901); the Revised Standard Version (1951). See also BIBLE, THE HOLY.

Bible, the Vulgate (L., *vulgatus,* "usual," "typical," "common"). Latin translation of the Bible by St. Jerome (342–430) from the Hebrew, Greek, and Chaldean originals, initiated and supported by Pope St. Damasus. Also referred to as the "common" version—because of its common use in the Latin Church and its translation into the common Latin of the time. St. Jerome worked on this translation in Bethlehem for nearly twenty-five years, from 384–406. The Gutenberg Bible of 1456 was a printing of the Vulgate. The Vulgate has been used as the standard and official translation of the Bible by the Roman Catholic church. See also BIBLE, THE HOLY.

biblical theology. See THEOLOGY, BIBLICAL.

bibliolatry (Gk., *βιβλίον [biblion],* "book," and *λατρεία [latreia],* "worship," "servitude to"). Book worship, especially of the Bible. Used as a pejorative term to refer to such things as **1.** accepting the Bible as the literal word of God, **2.** worshipping it as the only source of wisdom, **3.** demanding the suppression of rational inquiry about its inerrancy.

bibliomancy (Gk., *βίβλος [biblos],* "book," or *βιβλίον [biblion],* "the Bible," and *μαντεία [manteia],* "divination"). A form of divination. The Bible is opened at random, a passage is fingered, and from this prophesies of the future and one's fate are ascertained.

binitarianism. The tendency to present the Holy Trinity, in a twofold rather than a threefold relationship. In pre-Nicenian times this was especially common. Some such schools: Monarchianists (see also MONARCHIANISM); some Arians (see also ARIANISM); Macedonians; Pneumtomachi).

bishop (Gk., *ἐπίσκοπος [episkopos],* from *ἐπί [epi],* "over," and *σκοπός [skopos],* "inspector," "one who has oversight of others," "one who supervises others"). Regarded by many in Christendom as the highest order of minister in Jesus' Church—the spiritual overseer of the followers of Christ and charged with the spiritual well-being of his congregation. In the first century *ἐπίσκοπος [episkopos]* ("bishop") and *πρεσβύτερος [presbyteros]* (presbyter) were used as synonymous. In the second century, St. Ignatius (died 107 A.D.) makes a distinction among bishops, priests, and deacons.

The following are some general descriptions that have been given to a bishop but that must be accepted with modification, depending on the Christian sect and its use of the term. (Many Protestant groups have no bishops.) **1.** Bishops are elected and consecrated and given their charge. (In the Roman Catholic church, Bishops are selected by the pope.) **2.** A candidate for bishop must be thirty years of age, be of legitimate offspring, a priest for several years, of good character, and of sound faith. **3.** Bishops receive a power (see also LAYING ON OF HANDS; APOSTOLIC SUCCESSION) that enables (empowers) them to do such things as confer HOLY ORDERS on others. This power is never lost even if the bishop is excommunicated. **4.** Bishops can consecrate churches, places, things, etc. **5.** As head liturgical ministers, bishops can preside at the EUCHARIST, at all the sacraments, at ABSOLUTION; grant marriage licenses; license curates; allow minor dispensations; settle disputes. **6.** Bishops teach and enforce doctrine. **7.** Bishops do charitable works, direct and take care of the souls of their parishioners. **8.** Bishops exercise administrative, financial, judiciary, and supervisory powers over their diocese. (In early Christian Church structures, bishops were autonomous and in ultimate authority over their diocese. Early Christian tradition held that submission to the bishop's decrees was one of the criteria for acceptance into the church. Opposition to a bishop showed a SCHISM, HERESY, or APOSTACY.)

In the Roman Catholic church, a bishop is one who holds the office established by Jesus Christ himself when he established his Church through Peter. A bishop has received divine rights and thereby is able to govern a local diocese, which represents a part of the universal Church of Christ. A bishop is a member of the episcopal college of the church and is administratively and spiritually in communion with the pope, who rules the episcopal SEE of St. Peter. Some of the New Testament references upon which the concept of bishop is founded: Acts 20:17–36; Philippians 1:1; 1 Thessalonians 5:12; 1 Timothy 3:2ff.; Titus 1:5ff.

The pope cannot abolish the episcopate of bishops. The pope, though, has the primacy of power and jurisdiction. Bishops are not mere representatives of officials of the pope. They delcare their own proper rights, authority, and privileges from Jesus Christ himself. They supervise their congregation in Christ's name (not the pope's) and regard themselves as the true successors of the Apostles.

The insignia of the office of a bishop are items such as the CROSIER or PASTORAL STAFF; MITRE; ring PECTORAL CROSS; gloves; sandals; etc. See also ORDERS, MAJOR HOLY.

blasphemy (Gk., *βλασφημία [blasphēmia],* "a curse," "vilifying"). **1.** Impious, mocking, undignified speech about or attitudes toward God, sacred or religious things. **2.** Claiming the powers, privileges, and authority of God—or attributing them to someone who is not God. Regarded as a sin.

bless. **1.** To make sacred by a religious rite or word: God blessed the seventh day. Blessings were given by Jesus Christ and by the Apostles. Blessing may take a liturgical form as in the sacraments. Blessings are given when authority, an office, a task is bestowed upon one. Blessings are given upon objects as in consecration. **2.** To pray or beg for the favor of God, as in "Bless them who persecute you." **3.** To make the sign of the CROSS upon something, for example, against evil spirits.

Blessed Virgin. See MARY.

blessing. **1.** The act of one who blesses. A BENEDICTION. **2.** A beneficent gift bestowed by God. **3.** Used in hymns, devotional literature, and doxologies in the context of exclamation, praise, love, and gratitude for the goods granted to humans by God upon whom all things depend for their existence without exception. In primitive times, God's blessing was the cause of fertility in animals. In the Hebrew and Christian faiths, God blesses humans and nature to make them multiply. Christians believe that God's unending blessings are bestowed upon man and the universe, that God's blessings shine through those graced by him, and that the ultimate blessing from God is in the very fact of there being a universe controlled by him. Christians hold that this is a final stage of history during which God blesses through the Spirit and Person of Christ, that to be blessed is to be fully subservient to Jesus Christ, and that the ultimate blessing of God is to be received, through Christ, into an eternal life of bliss (Rev. 22:14). See also BEATITUDE.

bliss. **1.** Exalted, heavenly joy. (See also ECSTASY.) **2.** Blessedness (see also BLESSING.) **3.** BEATITUDE.

blood of Christ. **1.** In general, in early times, *blood* suggested the power to effect change. In the Old and New Testaments, it connoted **2.** death, often violent death, and **3.** the source of life and spirit (as in Genesis 9:4ff., where blood is regarded as the foundation of life and therefore had God as its source).

In Christianity, the phrase *blood of Christ* has been interpreted in many interrelated contexts: Christ gives his blood for our salvation. The old covenant (see also COVENANT, THE OLD) is fulfilled and thereby ceases; the new covenant (see also COVENANT, THE NEW) is established. Jesus Christ's blood is necessary for everlasting ATONEMENT. Jesus' blood has sealed the New Covenant relationship between God and his people in Christ. Jesus Christ's blood has the power to give SALVATION; it cleanses us from SIN (1 John 1:7; Heb. 9:14; Rev. 1:5; 7:14); it sanctifies (see also SANCTIFY) as in Hebrews 10:29; it forgives (Eph. 1:7); it reunites, revitalizes, reestablishes God's people (Eph. 2:13); it provides REDEMPTION (Rev. 5:9); it is found to respiritualize us in the Holy Communion (1 Cor. 10:16; 11:25); it is the source of REPENTANCE (Rom. 3:25; 5:9; Col. 1:20–23); it assists in our confession of sin (1 John 1:7–10); it helps us turn to God in FAITH (Heb. 10:19).

According to Christian tradition, Christ of his own accord shed his blood (his life) for humanity in order to sacrifice himself and thereby forgive the sins of humanity (Matt. 26:28). In this way God's New Covenant was initiated; a new, innocent, pure, redeemed people came into existence. This people is the Church of Jesus (the BODY OF CHRIST). The blood of Jesus Christ is, or represents, the source of the Church's existence and continuation. The blood sacrifice of Jesus is presented at the LAST SUPPER, the sacrifice on the CROSS, and in the offering of the MASS.

blood, precious. **1.** Jesus' blood shed during the PASSION OF CHRIST. The tradition holds that Jesus' lost blood was united with his body at his resurrection, except for that which now remains as part of holy relics such as the spear that pierced him. This blood is worshiped, for example, at the Feasts of the Most Precious Blood on Friday after Lent or the First Sunday in July. **2.** The sacrificial and saving blood Jesus had to shed as the price for the redemption and salvation of humans. (At 1 Pet. 1:19 humans are redeemed "with the precious blood of Christ." At John 19:34 and 1 John 5:6–8 blood and water flow from Jesus' side signifying in Christian tradition the Spirit of God [water] and the redemptive sacrifice of Jesus Christ [blood]. Also refer to: Eph. 1:7; Rom. 3:25; 5:9; Acts 20:28.) **3.** The very wine of the EUCHARIST, which is Jesus' very (precious) blood. (Refer to scriptural texts such as Mark 14:24; 1 Cor. 10:16; 1 John 1:7; John 6:54–58.)

body of Christ. **1.** Jesus' natural body of flesh, bones, and all that pertaining to human nature that suffered and was crucified, which body Jesus took with him at his INCARNATION. **2.** Jesus' glorified body: those aspects of Jesus' natural body exhibited after his RESURRECTION. **3.** Jesus' symbolic body: The BREAD symbolizing Jesus' body and which is eaten and digested by us. **4.** Jesus' crucified body: the body that is symbolized by the bread in the EUCHARIST; the body offered on the CROSS. **5.** Jesus' spiritual body controlled by the spirit or *πνεῦμα (pneuma)*. **6.** The Christian church of which Jesus is the mystical, spiritual leader. (Also referred to as the Mystical Body of Christ.) The Church of Jesus Christ has been called the "body" of Christ. This "body" possesses actual historical existence, a unity, a direction, a structure, members, functions, offices (for example, a pope, bishops, holy orders, laypersons, etc.) and is a living, continuing expression of the HOLY SPIRIT, whose Lord is Jesus Christ. St. Paul: "Now ye are the Body of Christ, and severally members thereof. . . ." That the Church is the body of Christ was a common belief among the early Church Fathers such as Athanasius (293–373), the Cappadocian Fathers, Cyril of Alexandria (376–444), etc. St. Augustine (354–430) taught that the Church is in its totality the Body of Christ—the Church is Christ whole, alive, and active in affairs of the world. Some principal scriptural references: 1 Corinthians 6:12–20; 10:14–22; 12:4–17; Romans 12:4–8; Ephesians 1:23ff., 2:11–18; 4:4, 12, 15ff.; 5:23, 30; Colossians 1:18, 24; 2:19; 3:15. See CONCOMITANCE.

bondage, freedom from. See FREEDOM FROM BONDAGE.

bonum diffusivum sui. Latin, referring to God's "diffusing his Goodness" throughout all things in the universe. St. Thomas Aquinas (1225–1274) held that there was one and only one *summum bonum* (highest good), only one intrinsic good (a good in and for itself)—all other goods, such as pleasure, are subordinate to this one good granted by God himself: existence. All other goods are dependent upon this BLESSING from God.

bread. **1.** A symbol of the common food for all humanity. **2.** One of the elements used in the EUCHARIST and the Lord's Supper. **3.** A symbol of Jesus' Body offered in sacrifice upon the CROSS: "I am the living bread which came down from heaven: if any man eat of this bread, he shall live for ever: and the bread that I will give is my flesh, which I will give for the life of the world" (John 6:51). See also LAST SUPPER, THE.

brethren. Plural of brother. Used by religious groups to refer to their members or adherents. It has a solemn and sacred connotation. See also DISCIPLES.

brethren of Jesus. In passages of the New Testament (such as in Mark 6:3) James, Joses, Juda, and Simon are called brethren, or brothers (*ἀδελφοί adelphoi*) of Jesus. (The Greek Orthodox tradition interprets them a stepbrothers of Jesus.) Controversy exists as to whether they were sons of Mary, older or younger than Jesus, or merely Jesus' relatives. See also entries under JESUS.

breviary (L., *breviarium,* "abridgment," "a summary"). The liturgical book containing the daily public or canonical prayers, hymns, psalms, lessons, etc. Used especially in the Roman Catholic and Eastern Orthodox churches. Breviaries date back to the second century, where they collected together what was available only in scattered or separate manuscripts. Pope Gregroy VII in about 1085 had a first abridgment made of the ancient Church offices. About 150 breviaries were compiled and in use before the Reformation. Pope Urban VIII wrote a breviary in 1631 whose use is popular even today. In 1911 a Roman Catholic breviary was revised based on the one officially proclaimed at the Council of Trent: the *Breviarium Romanum* of 1568. In the Roman Catholic church, all clergy and nuns must recite the breviary daily.

A breviary is usually divided into four parts, each part dedicated to a season of the year. Each of the four parts is subdivided into daily sections consisting of selections from the Bible, the Church Fathers, the Saints, prayers, antiphons, responses, etc. Each day has eight sections corresponding to the canonical hours, which must be repeated by the clergy without omission.

Breviaries—Eastern, Roman, and Protestant—contain commonly told stories about saints, angels, the Virgin Mary. St. Denis, for example, honored on Oct. 9, walked two miles carrying his head in his hand. Resurrection of the dead by saints is a common event in breviaries.

bull (L., *bulla,* "a seal"). A solemn declaration (mandate, formal brief) from the pope in the form of a document that has attached to it a seal (the *bulla*) of gold, or lead, on which is engraved the effigies of SAINT PETER and SAINT PAUL, the name of the issuing pope, and the year of his pontificate.

A "consistorial" bull requires the signatures of cardinals as well as of the pope.

C

Calvary (L., *calvaria,* "a bare skull," from *calvus,* "bold"). **1.** The place where Christ was crucified, outside Jerusalem (see Luke 23:33). **2.** In the Roman Catholic church, any representation of the crucifixion of Christ or of various scenes of Christ's Passion.

Calvinism. The adherence to the doctrines of John Calvin (1509–1564) as found primarily in his *Institutes of the Christian Religion* (1536–1559), which was a systematic presentation of reformed thought and serves as the basis for many non-Lutheran churches in the tradition of the Reformation. A few of the principal doctrines: **1.** divine predestination; **2.** redemption of humans by the death of Jesus Christ; **3.** conversion as a method of bringing humans to God; **4.** the perserverance of the Saints; **5.** the election by God's Grace of the saved (these are regarded as "the Five Points of Calvinism," stated at the Synod of Dort held on November 13, 1618 to May 9, 1619 in the Netherlands); **6.** total depravity of humankind; **7.** the transmission of sin from Adam; **8.** justification by faith; **9.** limited atonement; **10.** the irresistibility of grace; **11.** effectual calling; **12.** the sovereignty of God in the bestowal of salvation and grace; **13.** the complete dominance by God of all occurrences in the universe; **14.** the divinity of Christ and Christ as the only Savior; **15.** the Bible is the foundation for God's plan and God's revealed word; **16.** Christ is the sole mediator between humans and God; **17.** participation in the sacraments is essential as a visible sign of professing God and Christ.

Candlemas (Anglo-Saxon, *candelmaesse,* "mass for the candles). Also *Candlemas Day*. Celebrated on February 2. The Feast of the Presentation of Jesus in the Temple (see PRESENTATION OF JESUS IN THE TEMPLE, THE FEAST OF THE). Candles are blessed for religious, sacred use and purchased for uses such as last rites, to ward off impending peril, at times of storms, to burn at mass or benedictions. The procession of the congregation carrying lighted candles during Candlemas is a symbol of the entry of Christ, as the Light of the World, into the Temple of Jersualem. Christ's light is placed in human hands (see also LIGHT). In essence, Candlemas is the last feast connected with CHRISTMAS.

canon (Gk., *κανών [kanōn],* a "rule," such as used by carpenters or masons to straighten or measure by; a "rod" [shuttle] such as is used in weaving to pass the threads of the woof between those of the warp, implying measurement, setting a standard or norm). **1.** An ecclesiastical rule, law, decree (see also CANON LAW). Specifically, in Roman Catholicism, one enacted by a council of the church and confirmed by the pope. **2.** A rule specifically binding on the clergy. **3.** A resident member of a cathedral usually appointed by the bishop. (A canon must have at least six years in the priesthood.) **4.** One who lives according to the beliefs, principles, rules of his church or religious institution. **5.** The collection of biblical books regarded as genuine, authoritative, and inspired (see also CANON OF THE BIBLE). **6.** That part of the mass consisting of prayers that begins after the Preface and the SANCTUS, with the prayer *"Te igitur."* **7.** In the Roman Catholic church, also used to refer to a catalogue of saints.

canonical hours. Also *canonical services.* **1.** The times of, and prayers to be spoken at, the daily services as presented in the BREVIARY. **2.** The times and services ordered by ecclesiastical or monastic authorities during which devotion is given, by reading, chanting, etc., to the canonical or accepted writings of the Bible (or other authorized sources).

canonization. The process of adding a person, according to a decree from the pope, to the list (or canon), of saints for veneration. Canonization brings with it several secular honors: **1.** the saint's name is listed in the calendar of saints; **2.** the saint's name may be invoked in church prayers; **3.** churches and other areas may be dedicated (consecrated) in the saint's memory; **4.** public mass may be said in honor of the saint; **5.** a festival is proclaimed in honor of the saint; **6.** the saint may be shown in paintings or ikons with a halo and surrounded by a heavenly glory; **7.** the relics of a saint may be venerated.

canon law. **1.** The laws (legislation, regulations, rules) of church body or authority that regulate or govern its proceedings and activities. Such regulations have scriptural bases in places such as Matthew 26:19; 28:18; John 20:23; Acts 15:28, 29. **2.** The body of formal rules by which a church is governed, such as the Roman Catholic church's *Corpus Juris Canonici* (1918). Regarded as divine law (as opposed to civil or secular law) insofar as it originates in divine revelation and/or is part of natural, moral law. See also JUS DIVINUM and JUS NATURAE.

canon of the Bible. Also *canon of Scripture.* A phrase that designates the collection of divinely revealed books comprising the Bible and that serves as the basis of the Christian faith. (See also BIBLE, THE HOLY)

Dispute exists, and has existed since the origins of Christianity, as to which books were to be regarded as canonical. For example, the Book of Revelation has been doubted. So have Hebrews, James, 2 Peter, 2 John, 3 John, and Jude. (Those whose canonicity is in dispute are called "deutero-canonical"—from the Greek δεύτερος *[deuteros]*, "second"—or "of secondary order.") In the Roman Catholic church, the COUNCIL OF TRENT unequivocally decreed all forty-five books of the Old Testament and all twenty-seven books of the New Testament to be revered as authored by God.

The canonical books of the Bible are contrasted with the APOCRYPHAL (uncanonical) books of the Bible, which are considered not to be divinely revealed, not to possess divine authority, and thereby not to be a part of the Bible and the rule of faith. See also CODEX.

Cappadocian Fathers. A group of early church fathers, all from Cappadocia, such as Basil of Caesarea (ca. 330–79), Gregory of Nazianzus and Constantinople (329–389), Gregory of Nyssa (ca. 330–395). They were right-wing, conservative Origenists. The Cappadocian perspective was accepted by the Council of Constantinople (381).

cardinal (L., *cardinalis,* from *cardo,* "hinge," "that on which anything turns or depends). Originally, any priest attached permanently to a church (and thus in a *cardo,* "hinge" position). It has also referred to a parish priest of Rome, a bishop of the seven dioceses of Rome, and to a district deacon. These gradually formed into the "Sacred College," or the "College of Cardinals," ranking directly under the pope, which counselled him, was in control during any vacancy of the position, and elected a new pope in a secret meeting. Cardinals are considered ecclesiastical princes ("princes of the Church") appointed by the pope, who constitute his own council, and are next to the pope in the Roman Catholic church hierarchy, taking precedence over all other dignitaries. In 1506, the number of cardinals was fixed at seventy: six bishops, fifty priests, fourteen deacons. In 1958, Pope John XXIII selected over seventy-five cardinals from all over the world.

The three ranks of cardinal: **1.** cardinal bishop (usually bishops of sees around Rome); **2.** cardinal priest (who may be, and usually is, a bishop); **3.** cardinal deacon (who may be a priest).

The dress of a cardinal is scarlet in color and differs only slightly from that of a bishop. A red hat is the distinctive sign of a cardinal. (The hat is low crowned, broad brimmed, and is not worn but carried behind the cardinal at ceremonies. After the cardinal's death, this hat is hung from the ceiling in the vault of the church at which he is buried.) The insignia of a cardinal's rank: biretta and cap, a soutane, zucchetto, mozzetta, a pectoral cross (see CROSS, PECTORAL), a ring with a sapphire.

cardinal virtues. See VIRTUES, CARDINAL.

carnal (L., *carnalis,* from *caro, carnis,* "flesh"). **1.** Animalistic. **2.** That which has to do with the body as the source of cravings, appetites, desires, sensuality, lust, indulgence. **3.** Material, worldly; hence temporal, transitory, and valueless. See also CARNAL KNOWLEDGE. Opposed to SPIRITUAL. Cognates: carnage, carnality, carnally.

carnal knowledge. **1.** In general, sensual knowledge, knowledge of the flesh (see also CARNAL). **2.** Specifically, the knowledge gained in the act of sexual intercourse and/or the act of sexual intercourse itself. Usually used in the context of a sinful act and evil knowledge.

casuistry. Applying moral rules to specific contexts, situations, or individual cases in order to cover or excuse particular deviant moral behavior.

Casuistry assumes that broad, universal ethical principles cannot apply to all cases without exception; some are irrelevant or inapplicable in individual circumstances. Also the finiteness of human existence implies some partiality to absolutes.

catechesis. The technical word for the instruction (learning) given to those about to be baptized or confirmed into a church. See also CATECHISM.

catechism (Gk., κατηχίζειν *[katēchizein],* "to impress or instruct, by word of mouth," from κατά *[kata],* "according," and ἠχεῖν *[ēchein],* "to sound"). **1.** In general, the method of impressing (imparting, teaching, instructing) religious belief by means of asking questions and receiving prescribed answers. **2.** The set of formal questions presented to candidates or initiates of a religion, who respond with a recitation or answers, before they are accepted into the faith. **3.** Specifically, the book that contains a summary of a faith—its beliefs, practices, doctrines—which is usually in the form of questions and answers. This summary is usually to be learned before CONFIRMATION into a church.

The teacher is the *catechist.* The student is the CATECHUMEN. The content is often referred to as the CATECHESIS. The method of, or guide to, instruction is the catechism.

catechumen (Gk., κατηχούμενος *[katēchoumenos],* "one who has been instructed"). **1.** One who receives basic instruction in religious faith or doctrine. **2.** A candidate for a SACRAMENT who is receiving instruction (CATECHISM) in the sacrament. **3.** Often refers to a neophyte in a religious tradition or faith. **4.** One who is under instruction for baptism.

cathedra (Gk., καθέδρα *[kathedra],* "a seat"). The official chair, or throne, of a high ecclesiastical official such as the pope, a bishop, etc. When such persons speak *"ex cathedra,"* this implies that they are speaking from the authority of their position and all that it entails, such as correctness, finality, tradition, precedent, objectivity, and divine sanction.

catholic (Gk., καθολικός *[katholikos],* from καθ' ὅλου *[kath' holou],* a contraction for κατά *[kata],* "regarding," "concerning," and ὅλος *[holos],* "the whole"). **1.** In general, universal, common to all, pertaining to all humanity. **2.** The early Christian Universal Church that was to be comprised of baptized believers from all ranks, nations, and races. (Matt. 28:18, 19: "And Jesus came and spake unto them, saying 'All power is given unto me in heaven and in earth. Go ye, therefore, and teach all nations, baptizing them in the name of the Father, and of the Son, and of the Holy Ghost.' " Mark 16:15–18: "He that believeth and is baptized shall be saved; but he that believeth not shall be damned. And these signs shall follow them that believe; In my name shall they cast out devils; they shall speak with new tongues; They shall take up serpents; and if they drink any deadly thing, it shall not hurt them; they shall lay hands on the sick, and they shall recover.") **3.** The Western church after its separation from the Eastern church, which took the title of Orthodox. Thus, the Roman Catholic church, or a Roman Catholic.

Catholics, Old. Distinct from Roman Catholics of the Roman Catholic church, whose head is the pope. Refers to Catholic groups who have separated from the Church of Rome. The very first separation was the Church of Utrecht, Holland, with three bishops, which separated in 1724. But Old Catholics were formally organized at a Congress at Munich, September 22–24, 1871, in opposition to the 1870 Vatican Council's definition of papal infallibility. There are Old Catholics in Germany, Holland, Austria, Switzerland, Poland, Italy, Greece, the United States. They are in communication with the Eastern Orthodox churches and the Church of England.

Old Catholics reject the pope as the head of the church, believing Jesus Christ is the sole head of the Church. Clergy are allowed to marry. The worship services are presented in the vernacular. Confession is voluntary. The doctrine of the IMMACULATE CONCEPTION is denied.

cause, first. See FIRST CAUSE.

celibacy (L., *caelebo,* "unmarried"). The state of being unmarried and bound to that state by means of vows not to marry or engage in acts of sexual intercourse and sensuality.

Marriage, sexuality, and temptations of the flesh were considered undesirable results of the FALL, which when avoided helped in gaining a perfection in life. See also CHRIST, IMITATION OF. Celibacy is an accepted way of life for the clergy in the Roman Catholic and Greek Orthodox churches. In the Greek Orthodox and Coptic traditions, a seminarian may marry and be ordained, but his advance in the church hierarchy above a parish priest is then forbidden. The rule of celibacy in the Roman Catholic church is not necessarily regarded as having divine sanction. It does have an ecclesiastical foundation. The stress upon celibacy for the clergy reached a high point in the seventh century. Pope Gregory VII, in 1074, formalized it for the priesthood. Protestants interpret the New Testament as permitting marriage to the clergy. Christ called Peter, who was a married man. There is the opinion that Paul was married. Matthew 19:12 has been used as a scriptural defense of celibacy; here Jesus recognizes and recommends celibacy for the sake of the BASILEIA. Also refer to 1 Corinthians 7:25, 26.

Celibacy and *chastity* are often used as synonyms. They both imply the deliberate denial of one's sexual activities and power of procreation.

Celibacy (virginity), poverty, obedience, and martyrdom have traditionally been considered as the counsels by Christ to Christians (see also COUNSELS OF PERFECTION).

Chalice, the Eucharistic (L., *calix,* "cup"). The ancient name for the cup or goblet, used for the Eucharist, or Holy Communion. It represents the cup used by Jesus Christ at his Last Supper and holds the consecrated wine. It is made of silver or gold. In the past, chalices were made of glass, wood, pewter, or other metal. The chalice has a bowl, stem, and base. The stem usually has a knap in the middle for better handling. The bowl has no turned-over lip. The base is usually wide. A design of the crucifix, or other sacred symbol, is found on one side of the base, which side is kept turned toward the celebrant. In Christian art, the chalice is used to represent one of the instruments of the Passion. See also CUP OF WINE; PASSION, INSTRUMENTS OF THE.

chant (L., *cantare,* "to sing"). To sing or recite in worship in the manner of intoning in a monotone modulation of the voice.

chaos (Gk., *χάος [chaos],* "gap," "chasm," from *χαίνειν [chainein],* "to gape"). **1.** In general, that disorganized, confused, formless, and undifferentiated state of primal matter before the presence of order in the universe. That condition of the universe in which random change is the principal ruler. An uncontrolled state of affairs. **2.** In Christian theology (distinct from the theory of God's CREATIO EX NIHILO), the universe as it was before the embodiment of God's rational plan—before God manifested himself throughout the universe, bringing about the world order as it is now. That disorganized matter that God took and fashioned into an ordered universe. See also CREATIONISM; CREATION, THE DOCTRINE OF GOD'S; LOGOS. **3.** Sometimes regarded as itself a principle that prevents order or demolishes order.

character (Gk., *χαρακτήρ [charaktēr],* from *χαράσσειν [charassein]* "to make sharp," "to engrave"). **1.** As in St. Augustine, Jon Scotus, and the Scholastics, the special supernatural quality (power, spiritual effect) imprinted by the SACRAMENTS. (This spiritual quality imprinted by the sacraments is analogous to GRACE given by God.) This charismatic imprint (mark, quality, sign) cannot be erased by sin or any other activity. It is indelible and permanent. Neither SIN nor APOSTASY can affect its presence. (But they may affect its efficacy or fruition.) **2.** At the COUNCIL OF TRENT (1545–1563), specifically applied to a property (predicate, attribute) of BAPTISM, CONFIRMATION, and HOLY ORDERS: "If any one shall say that in three sacraments, namely, baptism, confirmation and holy orders, there is not a character impressed upon the soul, that is a certain spiritual and ineffaceable mark *(signum),* whence these sacraments cannot be repeated, let him be anathema" (see also EPISCOPI VAGANTES). It is a generally held belief that because the sacraments receive this indelible character, they do not have to be repeated. (See also BAPTISM and HOLY ORDER for the exceptions.)

charis. Greek, *χάρις,* "grace," "charity." Some of the meanings of *charis* that flow into the Christian concepts of GRACE and CHARITY: **1.** That which causes pleasure, joy, loveliness, acceptableness. **2.** Goodwill, favor, being in one's correct view. **3.** Goodness, kindness, beneficence. **4.** A gracious act, a favor granted to someone. **5.** The spiritual or emotional result of a gift received, such as thankfulness, joy. See also CHARISMA.

charisma Greek, χάρισμα "a gift," "something given or bequeathed." **1.** A unique, special divine gift of spiritual significance to be used for the benefit of the faith. **2.** A grace of unmerited talent, poise, powers from God signifying a divine use and purpose. A gratuitous gift from God that cannot be asked for, cannot be wrung from God by humans, and cannot be received by the normal functions of the sacraments. **3.** Unmerited salvation from God. **4.** The SPIRITUAL GIFTS that the Holy Spirit gives those who are baptized (as in St. Paul: 1 Cor. 12:1–31; Gal. 5:22ff.). See also SPIRIT, THE FRUIT OF THE.

The principal spiritual gifts that have been recognized as *charisma:* wisdom, prophecy, faith, hope, love, glossolalia, healing, miracle working, leadership.

charismatic. Also *charismic* (Gk., χάρισμα *[charisma]*, "a gift"). One who shows divine powers and abilities such as healing, spiritual leadership and respect, divination, miracle working, divine enthusiasm (see also CHARISMA; PENTECOSTAL).

Some of the major qualities by means of which a charismatic presence is recognized: adulation, respect (and in the case of Jesus, worship) of the leader; total belief in and commitment to the ideas, ways, and purposes of the leader; personal involvement by believers with the wishes, authority, and commands of the leader; the pervading sense of righteousness, piety, devotion, and spirituality shown by the leader in pronouncing the good news of Jesus Christ—in proclaiming the spirit of Jesus Christ and Jesus as Lord and Master of all.

charity (L., *caritas,* "dearness," "love," from *carus,* "dear," "loved," from Gk., χαρίζειν *[charizein]*, "to share") **1.** Benevolence; love (see also AGAPĒ; in the New Testament ἀγάπη *[agapē]* is translated not only as love but as charity). "Though I speak with the tongues of men and of angels, and have not charity, I am become *as* sounding brass, or a tinkling cymbal. And though I have *the gift* of prophecy, and understand all mysteries, and all knowledge; and though I bestow all my goods to feed *the poor,* and though I give my body to be burned, and have not charity, it profiteth me nothing. Charity suffereth long, *and* is kind; charity envieth not; charity vaunteth not itself, is not puffed up. Doth not behave itself unseemly, seeketh not her own, is not easily provoked thinketh no evil;" (1 Cor. 13:1–5). Refer also to 1 Corinthians 8:1; 13:8, 13; 14:1; 16:14; Colossians 3:14; Romans 5:5; 14:15; 1 Thessalonians 3:6; 1 Timothy 2:15; 4:12; 2 Timothy 2:22; 3:10; Titus 2:2; Revelation 2:19. See also CHARIS. **2.** Goodwill; good naturedness. **3.** Affection and generosity toward those poor and/or suffering. **4.** Help for the poor, and/or suffering. **5.** Almsgiving to the needy.

child of God. A human becomes a child of God at BAPTISM, which may signify this by kinship or by adoption (Protestantism stresses the former). When thus accepted by God, the human receives a supernatural ability or dispensation for infused (see also INFUSION) virtues such as hope, charity, faith.

chiliasm (Gk., χίλιοι *[chilioi]*, "a thousand"). The same as MILLENARIANISM. Christ will govern the earth for a thousand years preceding the final moment for all things. (Compare with Rev. 20:1–7.)

Chi-Rho. Sacred monogram XP, which are the first two letters of the Greek word ΧΡΙΣΤΟΣ *(Christos)*, meaning "Christ the anointed one."

The Chi-Rho monogram has been replaced by monograms such as IC, XC, IHC, IHS. In each, the monogram is composed of letters found in the Greek word for Jesus Christ: ΙΗΣΟΥΣ ΧΡΙΣΤΟΣ *(Iesous Christos)*.

chrism (Gk., χρῖσμα *[chrisma]*, from χρίειν *[chriein]*, "to anoint"). In the Roman Catholic church, the holy oil, consecrated by a bishop, used for BAPTISM, CONFIRMATION, and ordination (at which the holy oil imprints CHARACTER), or at other ceremonies such as anointing of a king, consecration of altars and other sacred objects. (See also ORDAIN.) (Chrism is not used for extreme unction. An unperfumed oil without balsam is used.)

The bishop breathes over a vase (jar) of oil three times in the form of a cross. He exorcises (see also EXORCISM) the evil spirits from the oil. He then mixes balsam with the oil and says: "Be this mixture of liquors atonement to all that shall be anointed of the same, and the safeguard of salvation for ever and ever." The chrism is saluted with the words *ave, sanctum chrisme,* ("hail, holy chrism").

chrismatory. The vessel in which the CHRISM is kept.

chrisom. The white cloth (or robe, or mantle, or blanket) signifying purity, thrown over a child when baptized.

Christ, blood of. See BLOOD OF CHRIST.

Christ, body of. See BODY OF CHRIST.

Christendom. **1.** The Christian world. **2.** Specifically, the Christian world up to the rise of nationalism and the REFORMATION. The period was basically characterized by a unity of church and state: one church, one state inextricably combined. Dissent against the state was dissent against the church; heresy against the church was an offense against the state. During this period, the SACRAMENTS and general church policy were enforced by the civil arm of the state. **3.** The hoped-for and desirable future state of Christianity, working as an important and vital force in human hearts and institutions. The future harmony and efficacy of Christian thought and behavior throughout the world.

christening. **1.** Synonym for BAPTISM. **2.** The giving of a Christian name.

Christian (Gk., Χριστός *[Christos]*, "the anointed one, Christ," and ιαν *[ian]*, "like," "similar to"). Literally, one who lives a life like Christ. See also CHRIST, IMITATION OF. One who believes in Jesus Christ as his/her only Lord (God) and Master through which spiritual, personal, and physical SALVATION is achieved. A believer in CHRISTIANITY or the Christian faith.

Christianity. The religion of Christians. Christian faith. An outline of its major tenets: **1.** A belief in the Holy Trinity—God the Father, Jesus the Son, and the HOLY SPIRIT. **2.** Jesus Christ restores humans to a new humanity lost at the Fall of Adam (see also ADAM, THE NEW). **3.** Humans must accept the Lordship of Christ and his method of SALVATION. Believers in Jesus Christ create a new relationship with God that overcomes the estrangement with God's purpose and unites humans with God through faith and participation in a community of the faithful. **4.** God is just, pure, holy, good; he is love; he is the creator. **5.** God chooses humans through which he expresses his way and will. **6.** God has provided us with the MESSIAH, the Christ, and the NEW COVENANT. **7.** Jesus died for our sins, and this is the highest form of sacrifice. **8.** Miracles performed by God occur. **9.** The Bible is the sacred, inspired, and revealed Word of God. **10.** The prophecies of the Bible have been, and will be, fulfilled. **11.** The books of the Bible have a consistency and harmony far surpassing that of the human mind. **12.** The spiritual power of Jesus Christ and the Holy Spirit upon the moral life and character of a person is divine, supernatural, and a state blessed enough to serve as a sign of the superiority and uniqueness of a Christian and of the Christian faith. **13.** Christian truth is unalterable, undeniable, and absolute, transmitted primarily through the New Testament. **14.** Christian truth is final and cannot be replaced. All other religions are inherently false, a result of social forces alone and manifestations purely of historical circumstances and accidents. **15.** Christianity is not merely a historical manifestation of a religious movement, one of many, but the only legitimate, true religion—the only correct relationship between humans and God. God himself established Christianity as the only revealed way to him and his wishes. Christianity possesses the true Revelation inaccessible to any other religion. Through Jesus Christ, God became Perfect Man at a unique moment in history. (See also CHRISTOLOGY.)

Christian Science. The system of faith for healing illnesses of the body and mind based on the belief that all cause-effect relationships are mental (existence is mental), and that suffering, pain, sin, and death can be overcome by one's mental processes in conjunction with an acceptance and understanding of the divine powers of Jesus Christ inherent in his philosophy of healing and teaching as found in the Scriptures. Christian Science was founded by the Reverend Mary Baker Glover Eddy, of Concord, New Hampshire, in 1866.

Christ, imitation of. The true Christian must live in the imitation of Christ, which means a new life, a reborn life, in Christ's spirit. Evidences according to St. Paul of this better life, and the mysterious working of Christ in each human, can be seen in the lives and actions of Christians (for example 1 Cor. 13). According to Christians, the signs of following Jesus Christ as Lord and Master are many: obedience, poverty, love, charity, self-abnegation, self-giving, avoidance of sin and temptation, acceptance of faith. According to St. Paul, the life of Jesus Christ must act in an analogous fashion in the lives of Christians upon whom the HOLY SPIRIT works. That one successfully imitates the Christ is due solely to the operation of the Holy Spirit.

During several historical periods of Christian faith, the highest form of the imitation of Christ was martyrdom—an ultimate form of self-abnegation. (See also MARTYR.) Other periods stressed the imitation of Christ as he was in his own history—to emulate or mimic Jesus Christ as a historical figure. Bernard of Clairvaux (1090–1153), St. Francis of Assisi (1181–1226), and Thomas á Kempis (1380–1471) are examples of this interpretation of *imitatio Christi*. In the imitation of Christ, Christians have tended to view his unmarried state as an ideal state to be sought after. Primarily because of the FALL, this ideal state is thought not to be attainable by most humans. See also CELIBACY.

Christmas. (from *Christ* and *Mass*). Also referred to as the Feast of the Nativity, or simply the NATIVITY. The annual festival held on December 25 commemorating the birth of Christ. The date of December 25 as celebrating Christ's birth was fixed in Rome about 380. That date is not a precise date for Jesus' birth.

Christology. (Gk., Χριστός *[Christos]*, "Christ" and λόγος *[logos]*, "the rational study of"). **1.** The inquiry into the life, person, works, faith, significance, and divinity of Christ. **2.** The attempt to support the contention that Jesus is divine, is the Christ (e.g., Acts 2:36; 5:42; 9:22; 18:5, 28; etc.) and humankind's only Lord and Master (1 Cor. 12:3; Phil. 2:11; Acts 16:31). **3.** The attempt to answer the very question Jesus asked of himself (Mark 8:27): "Who do men say that I am?" The answers varied: "John the Baptist," Elias (Elijah) "one of the prophets." Jesus turned to his disciples and asked, "But whom say ye that I am?" The answer received from Peter was "Thou art the Christ." (Mark 8:29. Mark is the principal Gospel addressing itself to the question about the personage of Jesus. Mark 1:27: "What thing is this? what new doctrine *is* this? for with authority commandeth he even the unclean spirits, and they do obey him." Mark 2:7: "Who is this that forgives sins?"; Mark 4:41: "And they feared exceedingly, and said one to another, What manner of man is this, that even the winds and sea obey him?" Also: Matt. 16:17, 18; John 6:66–69; Mark 14:61, 62.) **4.** The attempt to show that God is present and active in Jesus Christ who is the mediator between us and

God. According to Christianity, humans know God, and only know God, in the act of knowing how God is present in Jesus as the Christ. God-in-himself can never be known; God-in-himself can only be known through God-with-us (Jesus Christ). Jesus Christ was the incarnate and risen God, the Lord of Creation. **5.** The attempt to show not only the nature (essence, personage, uniqueness) of Jesus as Christ but to show the advantages (benefits, practical results) in accepting the spirit of Christ and allowing it to work its wonders upon one's soul, mind, and body. **6.** The attempt to show that Jesus, the divine being, beseeches all humans to encounter Christ, to witness Christ to accept the faith that brings salvation. (Mark 8:27–29; John 20:24–29; Acts 1:8.) See also ATONEMENT; SOTERIOLOGY.

Christology approaches the subject of Christ from a theological admission or confession of belief and openly admits a subjectivity and attachment to the unique importance and divinity of Jesus. The aim of Christology is to evoke a personal relationship with the divine reality of Jesus as the Christ. Christology is bound *not* to see Jesus: only as a moral and perfect human or teacher; only as a model archetype or paradigm; only as a sensitive and compassionate creature. Christology is committed to viewing Jesus through the faith that he indeed is God come to earth as flesh. John, the Fourth Evangelist, expresses the starting point for Christology: "these are written that you may believe that Jesus is the Christ, the Son of God, and that believing you may have life in his name" (John 20:29–31).

Some of the major theories about Christ in the field of Christology: *Christ as the Culminator.* All the events of the Old Testament progress in a connected sequence to a culmination in Christ. All the promises of the Old Testament are climaxed in Jesus Christ (2 Cor. 1:20). The history of God is worked out in the Old Testament by means of such forms as the law, the sacrificial structure, the temple, the synagogue, the customs and traditions, and achieves its ultimate culmination in God as man, Jesus Christ, and in Christianity as the unique and final state of mankind's fulfillment. God's purpose has been expressed in Christ and in the Christian spirit. Now it must be embodied in the world.

Christ as the New Adam. Christ is the new Adam of a revitalized race, a newly empowered race (of Christians). This race is a new people spiritually begotten by Christ out of sinners into a new life and consciousness. Christ imparts love, righteousness, and a rebirth in joy. See also ADAM, THE NEW.

Christ as Servant. Christ describes himself as the servant and minister of God. All Christ's life was dedicated in total obedience to God's will. Christ was totally subservient to God. This was dramatically epitomized at the LAST SUPPER, Christ's final great task, where he washed his disciples' feet to make them aware that he was a servant of God, not of man.

At John 6:38 (compare with John 4:34; 10:15–18), Christ identifies himself with the prophecies of the suffering servant in Isaiah 52:13–53:12; 42:1, 19. St. Paul at Philippians 2:7–8 also refers to Christ as the servant of God.

Christ as the High Priest. Christ is seen as the eternal heavenly high priest (Heb. 5:10). But a unique priest: He freely offered himself as a sacrifice (Heb. 7:27; 8:3; 9:11, 25; 10:5–9) and thereby purged our sins and sinful natures, preparing us for a new life. Christ was the one and only high priest who could do this (I Pet. 2:24).

Christ as the Reconciliator. Christ is seen as the reconciliator or conciliator bringing us back to God, the source of our spiritual being. Christ overcomes our ALIENATION or estrangement (as in Rom. 5:10). God reconciles us to himself (as in 1 Cor. 5:18ff.; Eph. 2:16; Col. 1:20–22). For Paul (Rom. 5:8–11 and in 2 Cor. 5:18–21), Christ died for us at the time we were sinners, alienated from God; God was in Christ reconciling through Christ the world unto himself.

In Romans 5:11, Paul speaks of our now having "received the atonement (reconciliation)." This suggests the creation of a new life, a new relationship and bond created by God in and through Christ—a relationship that is no longer alienated. This relationship is a gift bestowed that establishes a new status and personality. God then continues to sustain this new reconciliation, or relationship (2 Cor. 5:19).

Christ as Sufferer and Forgiver. Christ's life was a life of suffering but also of forgiveness, and a life of complete love and trust in God. Christ revealed God's forgiveness (in the very act of Christ himself forgiving). Forgiveness as the core of atonement is a revelation of the love of God. This awareness must stimulate a loving, forgiving response in man. Christ endured the utmost in suffering for us and on our behalf—a suffering no mortal human could take willingly upon himself. Realizing this, we are moved to thankfulness, penitence, love, and a new life in grace and atonement.

Christ as the Perfect, Single, Ideal REDEEMER. See also REDEMPTION. Christ delivers us from bondage (see also FREEDOM FROM BONDAGE). Hebrews 10:14: 'for by one offering He hath perfected forever them that are SANCTIFIED." Christ is offered but once to bear the sins of many (Heb. 9:28). Christ is the finality, an unrepeatable happening, come into being as the Redeemer once for all time. Christ purges our sins and he sits fulfilled on the right hand of the majesty on high (Heb. 1:13). Christ reconciles us to God and guarantees the final blessed, eternal end of our SALVATION (Rom. 5:9ff.; 8:32, 38, 39). The REDEMPTION he obtained for us is eternal and was achieved at the cost of his life (Acts 20:28). Christ accomplished full righteousness (Matt. 3:15) and brought to fruition eternal salvation for all (Heb. 5:9; John 6:38–58).

Christ as the Sacrifice. Man's sin had to be expiated. A sacrifice for sin was necessary. The sacrifice had to be as perfect a creature—as sinless a creature—as possible. Man's defilement could be removed only by means of such a sacrifice. The removal of man's defilement would enable man to communicate with God. Christ was created sinless by God to provide that sacrifice; Christ lived a life in which he conquered sin and temptations. Christ voluntarily offered himself in perfect acceptance and obedience to God. Christ's death was the completely perfect sacrifice to ensure atonement. We are now able to communicate with God and live in God's presence.

Christ is seen as a sacrifice in 1 Corinthians 5:7; Ephesians 5:2; Hebrews 7:27; 8:3; 9:6–15, 23, 25, 26, 28; 10:10, 12, 14, 26; Hebrews 13:10–13. See also SACRIFICE; PROPITIATION.

Christ as the Satisfier. God was outraged by the sinfulness of the only creature created in his image. Christ, as a man, accepted the penalty for all human sin and in atonement offered himself as satisfaction in man's place. This God allowed and accepted, indicating his forgiveness and love in the culminating act of the RESURRECTION.

Christ as Ransom. Christ's death was the ransom paid to the Devil who demanded that price—God's only begotten son—in order to release humans whom he had in control.

At Matthew 20:28 and Mark 10:45 Christ uses the term λύτρον *[lutron]* of himself. *Lutron* means ransom, or the price one has to pay to buy a slave from his bondage. At these passages, this ransom or price is related to the "cost" of the cross and to the blood that must be shed. Refer also to Ephesians 1:7; Colossians 1:14; 1 Peter 1:18ff.; Hebrews 9:12–15; Revelation 5:9.

Christ as Conqueror of Satan. Associated with PATRISTIC thought and that of Luther (1483–1546). Christ waged war with the DEVIL (SATAN). The Devil was defeated completely and will not gain ascendancy again in the presence of Christ. Christ secured a victory for humans over death and spiritual misery. Christians can now look forward with hope to a life with Christ here, hereafter, and forever. Christians must share their light and message in love and faith.

Christ allowed his suffering and death to assist man in atonement with God and in severing the bonds to Satan. Christ reconciles the world to God.

Christ, the (Gk., Χριστός *[Christos],* "the anointed one," "the Messiah"). The MESSIAH, or the one anointed by God, whose coming was prophesied and awaited by the Jews. For Christians, JESUS fulfilled this prophecy and expectation. (For Jews, the Christ is yet to come.) Jesus as the Christ is prophet (see JESUS AS PROPHET), priest (see PRIEST, CHRIST AS), and KING. According to Christianity, Jesus Christ must be seen as human and as God; Jesus Christ must be seen as a historical, and as a living, acting divine presence, a divinity who has risen. See also entries under JESUS.

Christ as human is pointed out throughout the New Testament. For example: "But when the fullness of the time was come, God sent forth his Son, made of a woman, made under the law" (Gal. 4:4); "Hereby know ye the Spirit of God: Every spirit that confesseth that Jesus Christ is come in the flesh of God:; And every spirit that confesseth not that Jesus Christ is come in the flesh is not of God: and this is that *spirit* of ANTICHRIST, whereof ye have heard that it should come; and even now already is it in the world." (1 John 4:2, 3). See also FLESH, JESUS AS. Also refer to Corinthians 5:16, Hebrews 2:17; 4:15 (where Jesus "was in all points tempted like as *we are, yet* without sin"). Jesus' humanness is portrayed by his hunger, thirst, weariness, creatureliness, temptations of the flesh, and death.

Christ as divine is pointed out throughout the New Testament. For example, at Mark 8:38, Jesus talks about his coming in glory, an allusion to his messiahshp: "Whatsoever therefore shall be ashamed of me and of my words in this adulterous and sinful generation; of him also shall the Son of man be ashamed, when he cometh in the glory of his Father with the holy angels." Refer also to Mark 13:26; Matthew 24:27; John 1:14. See also CHRISTOLOGY; KĒRYGMA.

church authority. Obedience obtained by the church as the guardian of Christ's teachings and commands, through an institution, empowered officials, councils, popes, CANON LAW, church fathers or founders, etc.

Four dangers felt by Christian authority in modern times: **1.** The historical pronouncements of a church may tend to be regarded as purely historical events and relative to the cultural and philosophic opinions of that historical period. **2.** The pronouncements of a church may tend to be evaluated and in some cases disregarded in accordance with present-day systems of thought and societal wishes. **3.** The pronouncements of a church may be set aside as custom, ritual, as "good for the spirit" but not as reasonable or rational sources of religious conviction, belief, or truth. **4.** The pronouncements of a church may be replaced by the individual's own conscience.

churches of Asia. See SEVEN CHURCHES OF ASIA, THE

church fathers. See FATHERS, THE FOUR GREEK; FATHERS, THE FOUR LATIN; PATROLOGY; PATRISTICS.

Church of England, the. See ANGLICANISM.

Church, the (Gk., **κυριακόν** *[kyriakon]*, "the Lord's house," from **κῦριος** *[kyrios]*, "lord," or **κῦρος** *[kyros]*, "power"). **1.** The BODY OF CHRIST (as in the Pauline description of "The Body of Christ"); as the incarnation of Jesus Christ into society and the will of the people. **2.** The KINGDOM OF GOD on earth, or at least as a tool (means, instrument) to attain the Kingdom of God on earth. **3.** The Temple of Christ's presence. (A variety of metaphors [images, symbols] have been applied to the Church: the Body of Christ; the Bride of Christ; the Temple of God; the House of God; the Assembly of God; the Repository of Divine

Truth [Wisdom]; the Tabernacle of God; the Kingdom of Christ [God]. **4.** For Luther, the Church was identical with the Word of God and the Sacraments (as opposed to the papacy, the hierarchy of the Roman Catholic church, the organized, social, administrative and ritualistic structure of the Church). Basically, for Luther the Word of God meant a community of fellowship of believers in the Gospels. This is the true Body of Christ. For Calvin, too, the essence of the Church—the Body of Christ—was the Gospels and the Sacraments functioning among a community of believers according to the power of the HOLY SPIRIT.

The foundation of Christian churches rests upon: **(a)** authority (as in APOSTOLIC SUCCESSION;) **(b)** preaching; **(c)** teaching; **(d)** service; **(e)** mission work. A Christian church believes itself to be the institutional tool chosen by God in the name of Christ to reveal his Word by means of the BIBLE, to preach it and to assist humankind in living its message and receiving its inspiration, light, and blessings.

Church, the invisible. The ideal, perfect Church of Jesus Christ, that community in which all those who have been saved here on earth will dwell in bliss, peace, harmony, and love. The followers of the Apostle John held the notion that only God knows the true members of the church or community. If one is to estrange oneself, the estrangement occurs with God, not a church with a membership. The Alexandrians recognized an invisible church: the Church of Christ as composed of all humanity in a mystical bond. St. Augustine (354–430) refers to an invisible aspect of the Church in that only God knows who of those in the visible church were truly devout and sound. See also CHURCH, THE VISIBLE.

church, the visible. The structured, organized, and administering Church of Jesus Christ working as a community and within a social order not of its own. Contrasted with CHURCH, THE INVISIBLE. St. Paul affirms a visible church of God (which he identifies, for example, at Corinth). Such a church has a community, a membership, and one can estrange oneself from it. St. Augustine (354–430) held that there was a true, visible church—the historical Catholic church—consisting of those who accepted the faith. See also CHURCH, THE INVISIBLE; CIVITAS DEI.

circumcision (L., *circumcisus,* from *circum,* "around," and *caedere,* "to cut"). The act of cutting off the prepuce or foreskin of the penis as a religious rite practiced by Jews and Moslems as a general symbol of spiritual purity.

In Genesis 17:10 circumcision was a mark of the seal of the covenant between Abraham and God—a mark of descent from Abraham. The Jewish rite of circumcision initiated male children on their eighth day of life. It was used as a sign to show that the male Israelite belonged and was entitled to worship as an Israelite. Jesus was circumcised and this is commemorated on the first of January in the Feast of the Circumcision.

At Acts 15:24, Gentile converts were exempted from the rite of circumcision. St. Paul accepted circumcision of the heart (Romans 2:25–29) and baptism as the "circumcision of Christ" (Col. 211ff.; Phil. 3:3; Gal. 5:6).

Civitas Dei. The heavenly city (society, civilization) as opposed to CIVITAS TERRENA, the earthly city. Associated with St. Augustine of Hippo (354–430) who interpreted history as a series of events happening to two levels of being, roughly the secular and the sacred—the kingdoms on earth and God's judgments on them such as Babylon, Jerusalem, Greece, Rome; and the kingdom in heaven into which the reborn go who have accepted the FAITH. Both kingdoms are created and controlled by God. God disposes of the earthly kingdoms and uses earthly kingdoms to select the saved and bestow eternal blessings upon them. God deserves order, justice, brotherhood, and the Christian virtues (see VIRTUES, THEOLOGICAL), and the extent to which an earthly city fails to express these, to that extent it will fail and be destroyed.

Civitas Terrena. The earthly city (society, civilization) as opposed to CIVITAS DEI, the heavenly city.

clergy (Gk., **κλῆρος** *[klēros],* "one's portion," "one's inheritance," "one's lot"). **1.** In general, those persons in a church who share the power, authority, and offices of that church. (In early Christianity this meant all the members of a Christian community. The entire church is God's **κλήρος** *[klēros].* The plural **κλέροι** *[kleroi]* referred to the specific pastoral areas designated to individual disciples that were a part of the more general pastoral community called **κλερονομία** [KLERONOMIA]). **2.** Specifically, those formally ordained by a church to serve the will of God (and the church) and thus distinguished from the LAITY.

clericalism (Gk., **κληρικός** *[klērikos],* "pertaining to a priest," into L. as *clericus,* "priest"). Used in a derogatory sense of excessive devotion to the interests of the clergy, or excessive influence by the clergy or ecclesiastical authorities. *Cleric* is used synonymously with *clergyman* or *clergywoman. Clerical* pertains to the CLERGY.

cloister (L., *claustrum,* "bolt," "bar," "bounds," from *claudere,* "to close"). **1.** A monastic building or establishment. **2.** Often used interchangeably with MONASTERY.

Cloister, monastery, ABBEY, CONVENT, nunnery, PRIORY suggest seclusion from the ordinary, everyday affairs of the world.

codex (L., *codex,* "a book," "a writing"). A book of Scripture bringing together what is regarded as its authentic, authoritative, and inspired works. See also CANON OF THE BIBLE.

coinherence (L., *co,* "with," and *haerere,* "to stick," "to hang"). In general, the inherence or existence together of two or more qualities (attributes, properties) in one substance, which acts as a unity. In Christian theology, a doctrine regarding the Holy Trinity of mutual interconnection (interpenetration, indwelling) of the three members of the Trinity in which any one member (the Father, Son, or Holy Spirit) is inextricably to be found in the other two; any two members are invariably present in any one. The principal scriptural base is John 10:28–38.

A belief propounded primarily by Novatians. It was accepted by Church Fathers such as St. Athanasius (293–373), Cyril of Alexandria (376–444), Iranaeus (ca. 115–202), the Cappadocians, St. Augustine (354–430).

collegialism (L., *col* or *collum,* "neck," and *legare,* "to send," "to choose as a deputy"). The view that the CHURCH is a *collegium* (literally "college")—a society of self-governing, voluntary members independent of the authority of the state (but to which it involuntarily subjects itself) and whose own authority is vested in the entire body of members, not a governing board as such. See also CONGREGATIONAL; EPISCOPALISM.

collegiality. A concept whereby the administration of the Roman Catholic church is to be shared and the primacy of the pope (see also POPE, THE PRIMACY OF THE) altered. The pope serves as the Vicar of Jesus and the bishops serve as successors to the Apostles.

communicatio essentiae. Latin, "communication of essence." A doctrine relating to the Holy Trinity that Jesus the Son receives his essence (*οὐσία*: or *[ousia]*) from God the Father. The HOLY SPIRIT receives its essence from both God the Father and Jesus the Son. This exchange or transference is self-contained and takes place within the unique and undifferentiated single essence of God (of the Godhead).

communicatio idiomatum. Latin, "communication of similarities." **1.** The communication, or transference, of divine qualities to humans. See also ALEXANDRIAN SCHOOL. **2.** The impartation of the glorified body and blood of Jesus at the Lord's Supper or EUCHARIST. **3.** The communication (transference, imparting) of qualities (attributes, properties) in Jesus from his human aspect to his divine aspect, and vice versa. Both the divine and human natures of Jesus Christ must be predicated of, and are interchangeable in, his being.

communion (L., *communis,* "common"). **1.** An act of sharing. **2.** Christians regarded as a united body of common faith, ritual, and discipline. **3.** The ANTIPHON or PSALM sung or recited at Holy Communion (see also COMMUNION, HOLY). **4.** The sharing and commonness experienced at the celebration of the EUCHARIST or the LAST SUPPER.

Communion, Holy. Sometimes simply *communion.* **1.** The celebration of the EUCHARIST or the LAST SUPPER. The receiving or partaking of the wine and bread, the spirit and body of Christ. The history of communion, its frequency, the prior requirements for it such as fasting or confession, its method, etc. is long and varied. The Roman Catholic church establishes a minimum of one communion a year (Fourth Lateran Council [1215]). Recent tendencies are to allow communion as frequently as wished. The Church of England prescribes three minimum communions a year. The Eastern Orthodox churches prescribe fasting before partaking of communion. **2.** The Anglican churches often refer to church services as "the Holy Communion." See also COMMUNION.

The practice of kneeling to receive Holy Communion was strongly objected to by the Reformers during the Reformation. They believed it was truer to historical events that the Sacrament was one that included sitting at a meal (and many believed at a table, as Jesus is depicted sitting at a table—the Lord's Table—with his disciples). Where kneeling is used in the reformed churches, there is a desire to disassociate kneeling from indications that the consecrated bread and wine are being adored or idolized.

Communion of Saints, the. See COMMUNIO SANCTORUM.

Communio Sanctorum. Latin, "communion of saints." The conception is found in Colossians 1:12, John 1:3ff.; 1 Corinthians 15:29; 2 Corinthians 13:13. **1.** The communion of saints with God the Father through Jesus the Son. **2.** The communion of deceased Christians with those still living. The implication is that those dead can be influenced by those alive. The converse of this is a further implication. At Revelation 6:10, the martyrs worship God and beseech him to cast judgment upon those who have murdered them. Also, an early Christian practice was to invoke the saints to pray to God for them in order to receive SALVATION. See also INVOCATION; INVOCATION OF THE BLESSED VIRGIN MARY.

Conception, the Immaculate. See IMMACULATE CONCEPTION OF THE BLESSED VIRGIN MARY, THE MOTHER OF GOD.

concomitance (L., *concomitans,* from *con,* "with," and *comitari,* "to accompany"). In general, the state of accompanying something or of being conjoined with it. In Roman Catholicism the bread in the EUCHARIST becomes Christ's body in actuality and the wine becomes Christ's blood in actuality, commanded by Christ's words "This is my body" and "This is my blood." But in essence, there is no real separation in the risen Christ between his body and blood (nor between his humanhood and his divinity; nor between his soul and body). They are concomitant in the sense that Christ is fully, completely present in the bread and/or in the wine. The whole of Jesus Christ, both his body *and* blood is contained in either (and in both). If one were to receive only the bread, then Christ would have been fully received. If one were to receive only the wine, then Christ would also have been fully received. Contrast with CONSUBSTANTIATION. See also TRANSUBSTANTIATION.

Concord, Formula of. The last of a series of Lutheran confessions that constitute the Book of Concord. The Formula of Concord was put together in 1577 by Jakob Andreae of Tübingen and others, extensively using the Book of Torgau of 1576. In 1580 the German Lutheran states approved the Formula. The confession is in two major parts: the short *Epitome* and the extensive *Sana, plana ac perspicua repetitio et declaratio,* which has an introduction and twelve articles of faith for Lutherans.

Some of the items of faith: The Bible is to be appealed to as final authority by the clergy and the laity. Human nature is irredeemably corrupted by original sin. The human will is utterly opposed to God's will and by itself is not capable of goodness but needs the presence and activity of the HOLY SPIRIT. JUSTIFICATION and SALVATION are only possible by true faith alone (SOLA FIDE)—they are not possible by means of good works or meriting action. Predestination of all things by God is affirmed. Beliefs about the EUCHARIST, the LORD'S SUPPER, Jesus' position in the Holy Trinity, his descent into Hell, etc., are established and defined. An appendix presents the doctrine of COMMUNICATIO IDIOMATUM.

concupiscence (L., *con,* "with," and *cupere,* "to desire"). **1.** In general, lust. **2.** Specifically, sexual lust. The drive for sensual, or sexual, pleasure in contrast to the spiritual or divine drive (see also ENTHUSIASM that leads humans to the love of God and righteousness. Concupiscence is an aspect of the necessarily sinful nature of finite humans and their tendencies toward a life of VICE as opposed to VIRTUE.

confessio. Latin. **1.** The tomb (grave, burial place) of a confessor, martyr, or saint as in "the confessio of St. Peter." See also CONFESSION. **2.** The memorial (shrine, structure) built over the tomb of a martyr or saint. **3.** The crypt in a church (basilica or cathedral) under the high altar in which the relics of a saint or confessing martyr are buried. **4.** The affirmation of the Christian faith in the face of punishment, persecution, and/or death.

confession (L., *confessus,* pp. of *confiteri,* from *con,* "with," and *fatire,* "to confess"). **1.** To acknowledge or make known one's sin in order to obtain ABSOLUTION. Confession may be public or private (as to a priest—it is then referred to as an "auricular" confession). **2.** The parts of a liturgy during which the church members as a whole express acknowledgement of their sins, for example, in the Morning and Evening Prayer in the Book of Common Prayer, or the EUCHARIST. **3.** A statement proclaiming the Christian CREED, CANON, belief, or FAITH. (Institutional examples of this: Augsburg Confession [1530]; Westminster Confession [1643]. **4.** In early church history the declaration of the Christian faith by one persecuted or by a martyr. The word CONFESSIO is often used to refer to the burial place of martyrs or saints, usually the spot where they uttered their confession of faith.

References to public confession may be found in James 5:16: "Confess your faults one to another, and pray one for another, that ye may be healed." (Also, for example: Matthew 3:6; Acts 19:18.) In early Christian theology, confession was public but voluntary (the first indication of compulsory confession is in 763).

Confession is most commonly understood as the private conveyance of sin to a priest—into the *auris* (ear) of a priest, hence the term *auricular.*

This form of confession is also often called "sacramental confession" since it is regarded as essential to the sacrament of PENANCE. The Lateran Council (1215) stated that persons must confess their sins to their priest at least once a year. The COUNCIL OF TRENT (1545–1547) proclaimed that confession was demanded by God and was necessary for SALVATION.

Protestantism has practiced, as in Calvinism (Calvin's *Institutes* iii, 4, 14), **1.** a common confession of the entire congregation, **2.** individual confession in the presence of the whole congregation, and **3.** private confession to the minister. In some Protestant sects, confession may be heard and ABSOLUTION granted by a layperson.

Other scriptural bases for confession are Matthew 10:32ff. and Romans 10:9ff.

Objections to confessing to others—either publicly or privately to a priest—have existed since the early Church Fathers. St. Chrysostomos (347–394) and St. Augustine (354–430) are two early examples of theologians who saw confession as a private matter between a penitent and God. Other humans could not heal one's anxiety, conflict, distress, and spiritual agony—only direct contact with God could do this; other humans could hear a confession but could never know the inner spirit of the confessor and whether or not deceit entered into the confession—only God has access to this inner spiritual reality; other humans know the words of the confessor but not his/her inner spirit, heart, and mind; humans were curious about the transgressions of others, curious about the lives of others, but indolent at correcting their own—only God can direct a human into the course of righteousness.

Some objections specifically directed to sacramental or auricular confession: **(a)** only God can absolve and forgive our sins. This is a right only God can—and must—possess. (In sacramental confession, absolution, not ultimate FORGIVENESS, is given.) **(b)** Priests do not have power derived from Christ (see also APOSTOLIC SUCCESSION) to serve as judges who grant or withhold absolution. The Council of Trent held that priests held the *vim et numen* (energy and divinity [divine light]) of the eternal God. Priests cannot act in God's stead or in the person of Christ. **(c)** The power of the Church (the priestly class) is increased both institutionally and psychologically. **(d)** Confession is heard under the seal of silence but can be, and has been, misused. **(e)** Both the priest and the penitent are subject to temptation, immorality, and indecencies of thought. (In a full confession, it is regarded as a mortal sin [see SIN, MORTAL] not to reveal truthfully and candidly all the details of a sin.) Priests themselves may fall into immorality and lose their innocence and spirituality.

confirmation (L., *confirmare,* "to make firm"). **1.** In general, any INITIATION or rite that inducts a person into a church. **2.** The act or rite of corroborating (validating, verifying) one's baptism into a church by means of vows and promises made at, or for one at, baptism. **3.** The rite supplemental to BAPTISM that admits one to the full rights and privileges of a church.

In the Roman Catholic church, confirmation is regarded as one of the seven SACRAMENTS and as a necessary precursor to the sacrament of Holy Communion (see COMMUNION, HOLY). The person often takes the name of a patron saint and has a sponsor. Confirmation impresses an indelible CHARACTER (as do also baptism and priestly ordination). A special gift is sealed or anointed different from such events as CONVERSION and baptism (see Acts 8:12–17; 19:1–7). Confirmation allows the person to share in the charismatic, missionary, and prophetic abilities of the Roman Catholic church, powers that it received at Pentecost.

In general, the Roman Catholic rite of confirmation consists of **1.** the laying on of hands, **2.** anointing with CHRISM (sacred olive oil with balsam), and **3.** the words "I sign thee with the sign of the cross and strengthen (confirm) thee with the chrism of salvation, in the name of the Father and of the Son and of the Holy Ghost." Usually bishops conduct confirmation.

confirmation in grace. A scholastic doctrine taught, for example, by St. Thomas Aquinas (1225–1274) and St. Bonaventure (1217–1274): an unmerited special gift has been bestowed upon a person's will by God such that one's will is free but incapable of sin (though the power to sin is there). Examples of confirmation in grace: the Blessed Mother, Virgin Mary, St. Joseph, St. John the Baptist, the Apostles.

congregational (L., *congregare,* "to congregate," from *con,* "with," and *gregare,* "to collect into a flock or group"). A form of church organization that grants the church's powers to the brethren (brotherhood, members, disciples) of each local church body; each local church is an independent, ecclesiastical unit but is united with others in fellowship, belief, and common action. See also COLLEGIALISM.

consecration (L., *consecratus,* pp. of *consecrare,* "to consecrate," from *con,* "with," and *sacrare,* "to consecrate," from *sacer,* "sacred"). **1.** The act (ceremony, ritual) of making something sacred (or of declaring it to be sacred). To sanctify; to hallow. **2.** The act of spiritually setting something apart from PROFANE use and dedicating or devoting it to the sacred service and/or worship of God. **3.** The ritual that dedicates bishops to God's will and confers on them the formality of the office. The ordination of a bishop is called his consecration. **4.** The ritual whereby objects such as a building, church, land, altar, chalices, vessels, garments, rugs, chairs, water, ashes, bells, time, etc.. are sanctified for the purpose of use in a divine service or for a divine purpose. (Once consecrated, an object cannot be secularized. Objects that are only dedicated [see also DEDICATION.] can be unconsecrated.) Usually only bishops and popes have the right and power to consecrate. **5.** The most significant act in the EUCHARIST that spiritually affects the bread and wine. See also CONSECRATION OF THE EUCHARIST.

Two major points of view exist in Christian theology about consecration: **(a)** the act of consecrating gives to the consecrated object special divine and spiritual powers and favors (rights, privileges) that it did not possess before. Proper relationships with these objects enable one to also receive some of these powers and favors. **(b)** Consecration is only symbolic and prescribes only a proper and prescribed attitude toward the consecrated objects.

Consecration of the Eucharist. The ritual by which the bread and wine in the celebration of the EUCHARIST are made divine or holy. Eastern Orthodox and Catholic theology see this consecration as an actual conversion of the wine into Christ's blood and the bread into Christ's body. In the Roman Catholic church, this conversion or transformation occurs at the utterance by the priest of the words: *Hoc est enim corpus meum,* Latin for "This is my body," followed by *Hic est enim calix sanguinis mei, novi et aeterni testamenti* . . . ("For this is the chalice of my blood of the new and eternal testament . . ."). "The HOLY SPIRIT is invoked for this physical and spiritual transformation of the bread and wine. See also EPICLESIS.

Protestants hold one of two positions: **1.** The denial of this transformation and of any real divine presence in the bread and wine, although the bread and wine receive a sacred quality at their consecration (and cannot be used for any PROFANE purpose). The bread and wine remain the very same natural, chemical substances. **2.** No such "consecration" occurs at all. The bread and wine are to be regarded as symbols or reminders (reminiscences) of the life, love, and suffering of Jesus Christ for us. See also ANAMNESIS; CONSUBSTANTIATION.

consubstantiation (L., *consubstantialis,* "with or of the same nature and kind [essence and substance]," from *con,* "with," and *substantia,* "substance," from *substare,* "to be under," "foundation," "stand firm"). Associated with Martin Luther who, opposing the doctrine of TRANSUBSTANTIATION, believed that the actual substance of the bread and wine in the EUCHARIST remained the same but that the substance of Jesus Christ's body and blood were intimately related with them. (The *Augsburg Confession* of August 1530 and *The Articles of Smalkald* prepared by Martin Luther in 1539 are the principal sources for this concept). Some of the principal points of consubstantiation: **1.** There is a real, actual presence of the body and blood of Jesus Christ in, with, and under the bread and wine. The body and blood of Christ become present but *coexist* with the substance of the bread and substance of the wine, which substances remain after their consecration, as still bread and wine in an empirical, absolute sense. They are not in substance transformed. **2.** This divine presence is not connected to the bread and wine by any consecration by priests. (No human activity causes this divine presence of the body and blood of Jesus Christ; Christ himself causes this by means of his omnipotence.) **3.** This divine presence is not present in the bread and wine as it stands on the altar (or anywhere in space). **4.** This divine presence enters the bread and wine through Jesus Christ at the moment the bread and wine are consumed. **5.** No unusual or special veneration or adoration need be given to the bread and wine before or after any eucharistic consecration. **6.** In general, the denial of the sacrificial dimension of the EUCHARIST and LORD'S SUPPER is implied. See also IMPANATION.

The Council of Trent (1543–1547) expressly anathematized those who were propagating the concept of consubstantiation. The Roman Catholic church accepts TRANSUBSTANTIATION, a theological doctrine that was explicitly formulated to counter the Reformation's, and in particular Luther's, acceptance of consubstantiation.

contemplation (L., *contemplari,* "to contemplate," "to meditate upon," to gaze at attentively," from *con,* "with," and *templum,* "temple"). **1.** In general, meditation or the act of contemplating or putting attention upon. **2.** A level of prayer, usually regarded as higher than meditation. In popular usage, meditation as in Transcendental Meditation is a form of mental activity (focus, reflection, or even nonfocus), whereas contemplation is regarded as a "spiritual" activity such as of devotional prayer and/or reflection that attempts to enrich religious understanding, improve commitment, and inspire dedication. **3.** The act of attempting to behold some spiritual object or to gain spiritual insight. **4.** The experience of **(a)** complete or **(b)** partial absorption into the Oneness of all things or into God (see also entries on MYSTICISM).

continence (L., *continere,* "to hold together" or "to repress"). **1.** In general, self-restraint, self-command, self-mastery, self-governance; especially with reference to strong passions. See also ASCETICISM. **2.** Specifically, the exercise of sexual self-restraint (total or partial). Specifically in Christian theology, the spiritual and moral state of a human in which bodily desires, evil thoughts or intentions are controlled by one's spirit (in the presence of, or controlled by, the HOLY SPIRIT, or Jesus, or God).

contrition (L., *contrere,* "to grind," "to bruise," "to rub together and pulverize," from *con,* "with," and *terere,* "to rub"). **1.** In general, the repentance of sin perfected by the love of God, which love itself makes a person avoid sin. **2.** Specifically, the deep sorrow felt for having displeased God by acting sinfully. This sorrow must involve a sincere hatred of sin and a resolve not to sin again.

Contrition is necessary in order to be forgiven or pardoned by God. Contrition has been referred to as perfect repentance, in contrast to ATTRITION, which is imperfect repentance because it is not motivated by the pure love and total acceptance of God but rather by not wanting to be rejected or forsaken by God. See also METANOIA.

convent (L., *conventus,* "a meeting," from *convenire,* "to come together"). **1.** In general, a community of monastics (see also MONASTICISM) such as monks, friars, or NUNS, who live a religious life under a superior. **2.** Presently used to refer to a NUNNERY, or a community of female monastics. Usually this female community must consist of a minimum of twelve nuns.

conversion (L., *convertere,* "to convert," from *con,* "with," and *vertere,* "to turn"). **1.** In general, the state or act of being converted. **2.** The spiritual and moral change that occurs in a human—a change of commitment and with conviction from what is not true or worldly to what is true and divine or godlike. **3.** To accept a monastic or religious life or faith not previously believed in. **4.** The turning (or returning) to a faith in God. **5.** The change of substance in the EUCHARIST, from bread and wine to the body and blood of Christ.

Conversion implies a spiritual revitalization, re-orientation, and change of personality and of beliefs—a breaking with the past. Conversion is attributed to the HOLY SPIRIT or the direct action by God upon the psyche. Conversion often implies, in popular thought, a suddenness and swiftness in the "turnabout" of the psyche. Occasionally, as used in Christian tradition, conversion is not sudden but a day-to-day, accumulating spiritual progress or renewal. (For example, Calvin in his *Praelection on Jeremiah:* "We are converted to God . . . gradually and by sure degrees." Although for Calvin all conversions are produced not by any power in humans but by the power of God's grace.)

Conversion is often used interchangeably with NEW BIRTH or REBORN. See METANOIA.

convocation (L., *convocare,* "to call together," from *con,* "with," and *vocare," "to call").* **1.** Specifically, an assembly of clergy who are called together to consult on church policy and affairs. **2.** In general, a church convention, assembly, meeting, council, or synod that also includes laypersons.

co-redemptrix. Applied to the Virgin Mary as the redeemer of the world together with *("co")* her son Jesus Christ. See also REDEMPTRIX.

corporeal acts, the seven. Also known as the Seven Corporeal Works of Mercy. Based on Matthew 25:35–36: "For I was hungered, and ye gave me meat: I was thirsty, and ye gave me drink: I was a stranger, and ye took me in: Naked, and ye clothed me: I was sick, and ye visited me: I was in prison, and ye came unto me." **1.** Feeding the hungry; **2.** giving drink to the thirsty; **3.** giving shelter to strangers; **4.** clothing those naked; **5.** visiting the sick; **6.** helping (relieving) prisoners; **7.** burying the dead.

Corpus Christi (L., "the body of Christ"). A feast celebrated by the Roman Catholic church on the Thursday after TRINITY SUNDAY that honors the EUCHARIST. A procession through the city with the Blessed Sacrament is a usual part of the feast. (See also SACRAMENT, THE BLESSED.) The special mass for the feast was written in 1264 by St. Thomas Aquinas (1225–1274) at the request of Pope Urban IV.

The feast of Corpus Christi was initiated by the bishop of Liege in 1246 on the basis of a vision seen by a nun, Juliana of Mont Cornelion. She saw the moon shining except in one spot, which she interpreted as the absence of a feast in honor of the Blessed Sacrament. Her own feast day is April 5 and her vision was sanctioned in 1869.

corruptible (L., *corrumpere,* "to corrupt"). Capable of being spiritually and morally tainted, contaminated, bribed, or changed from the love of God, the faith, and a state of righteousness or truth, to the impure state of unrighteousness. Opposite of *incorruptible.*

council (L., *concilium,* from *con,* "with," and *calare,* "to call"). Also SYNOD. An assembly of ecclesiastical authorities convened to consider matters of faith, liturgy, morals, doctrine, discipline, policy, administration, legislation. In churches that have bishops, the meeting is of bishops.

Some Christians hold that the first Christian council was held by the Apostles at Jerusalem in 51, under the authority of St. Peter (Acts 15). Christian bishops held councils during the first two centuries of Christianity.

council, ecumenical (L., *concilium,* from *con,* "with," and *calare,* "to call"; Gk., *ὀικουμένη [oikoumenē],* "the inhabited world," from **οικεῖν** *[oikein],* "to inhabit," or *οἰκος [oikos],* "dwelling," "house"). **1.** In general, a council at which a church as a whole is represented, or called, in accordance with the laws governing that church. **2.** Specifically, in the Roman Catholic church, the assembly of bishops which the pope convokes, presides over, confirms, and dismisses, and who are regarded as successors to the Apostles.

What is recognized as the first ecumenical council was convened by Emperor Constantine in 325 at Nicaea. The Roman Catholic church lists twenty-one such councils from the one in Nicaea to VATICAN COUNCIL II (1962–1965). The first eight were officially called together by Roman or Byzantine emperors who were considered to be the guardians of the faith. The other councils were called by the pope of Rome. (The Eastern Orthodox church lists seven councils.)

Council of Trent (1545–1563). Considered to be the nineteenth of the Roman Catholic ecumenical councils, and was a COUNTER-REFORMATION response to the rise of reformed churches and thought. It was held under Popes Paul III, Julius II, and Pius IV. Its sessions took place intermittently in Trent and Bologna. Regarded as the most comprehensive of any ecumenical council.

counsels of perfection. Usually listed as POVERTY, OBEDIENCE, CELIBACY (virginity, chastity), and martyrdom (see also MARTYR).

Counter-Reformation. The period of Roman Catholic reform sparked by the REFORMATION, generally regarded as a period from 1522 to 1648. The Counter-Reformation attempted to restore the doctrinal power and genuineness of the Roman Catholic church and control the growth of Protestantism. This response from the Roman Catholic church resulted in the formation of new holy orders, revitalization of those already in existence, greater missionary activity and service to those of the faith, and more liberalization of the doctrines, policies, and structure of the Church. The COUNCIL OF TRENT (1545–1563) gave the Counter-Reformation its formal and official structure and direction and was one of its consequences.

covenant (L., *convenire,* "to come together," from *con,* "with," and *venire,* "to come"). **1.** In general, an agreement (a compact, a contract, a commitment) that binds one to its stipulations. **2.** Specifically, a solemn contract made among members of a church to hold to the faith, ways, and discipline of the church. **3.** The promise made by God to the Jews (see also COVENANT, THE OLD) and to Christians (see also COVENANT, THE NEW), as revealed in the BIBLE, that they were those specially chosen to fulfill his divine purpose.

Covenant implies "partnership," "testament." But theologically it implies God's complete sovereignty and mastery over mankind.

Covenant, the New. The Christian doctrine of the New Covenant is thought to contrast with the Jewish conception of the COVENANT essentially in this way: In the Jewish Covenant (the "Old" Covenant), the people of Israel offered themselves in allegiance and imperfection to God for his mercy, protection, and promises of future glory and salvation of the race. In the Christian Covenant (the "New" Covenant), those under Christ are accepted, forgiven, and given salvation due to Jesus' supreme sacrifice of himself, thereby reconciling humans (the people) with God, and this is done without humans meriting or deserving such salvation. God grants unconditional and perfect ATONEMENT through Jesus Christ. God is shown to be the God of Pure Love, graciousness, and forgiveness. This establishes a new relationship, or COVENANT, with the God of Israel who now becomes the God for all people through his GOSPELS. See also COVENANT, THE OLD.

At the LAST SUPPER, Jesus alludes to the blood of the New Covenant (Mark 14:24; Matt. 26:28) and to the Paschal Lamb (John 19:36). Paul spoke about Jesus' death as sealing the New Covenant (1 Cor. 11:23–25). See also NEW TESTAMENT, THE.

Covenant, the Old. Used by Christians to refer to Israel's unique and personal relationship with God, as found in the Old Testament, who chose the Israelites as his special, chosen people to fulfill his commands and purpose. This covenant with Israel cannot, and will not be, renounced. Israelites were to be the People of God; God was to be their only ruler; Jews were to remain loyal to God and God to the Jews; Jews were to have complete acceptance of God's way and use of his power.

This covenant was an honor, a privilege—and a burden, a sacrifice. Israelites were to be of service to God's plan of salvation for all people. Israel was to bring knowledge of God to the GENTILES—to all humanity. Israel must preach to the world (at Zach. 8:23, every Jew was to be a priest to ten Gentiles). CIRCUMCISION was one of the signs of the covenant.

This covenant was made with all the great prophets and patriarchs of Israel. It was made with Noah (Gen. 9:8–17), Abraham (Gen. 15:18), with Moses on Mt. Sinai (Exod. 20; 34), with David (2 Samuel 7, where David is promised a descendant who will be God's Son and will ensure the continuation forever of David's house. This for Christians is a portent of the New Covenant in Jesus Christ.)

According to Christianity, the Jewish hope, the Old Covenant, was fulfilled by the coming of Jesus Christ, the Messiah. Jesus' church was a church fulfilling the Old Covenant, the Old Testament prophecies. See also COVENANT, THE NEW.

When the covenants of the Old Testament were declared, usually blood from animals was shed in a sacrifice to God. So too in the New Covenant (Mark 14:24; Luke 22:20; 1 Cor. 11:25) Jesus' blood is shed as a sacrifice to sanction, or seal, the New Covenant between God and humans. Also see Galatians 4:24; 2 Corinthians 3:6–18.

creatio ex nihilo. Latin, "creation out of nothing." Designates the idea that God created the universe out of nothing—not out of chaos; not out of matter; not out of his own Being, but out of Absolute Nothingness. Reference to this notion does not appear in biblical references to Creation. It is a product of the early Church Fathers.

creationism. **1.** In general, the doctrine that the universe and its life forms were produced (and/or are being produced) by God. **2.** Matter (the universe) was created instantaneously by God out of nothing. See also CREATIO EX NIHILO. **3.** The human soul is separately created and presented by God at birth (or at conception). Opposed to generationism and TRADUCIANISM.

A strong creationist tradition in Roman Catholic theology: Every individual soul is created out of nothing by God who combines this soul at conception with the physical cells of the parents to form a human being. The soul does not exist before its fusion with the parents' cells. This position is opposed to preexistentialism and TRANSMIGRATION, both of which accept the existence of the soul in some way, at some place before union with a body. Another tradition in Catholic theology: The soul enters the body (the embryo) at the moment of the first breath.

creation, the doctrine of God's. God imposes an order upon chaos. The earth is separated from the waters. Animals are named and their relationships to each other are ordered. Humans are given dominion over all things. Adam dwells in the Garden of Eden and is seduced by Eve away from total obedience to and dependency upon God. Humans then lead an independent, free-willed existence, able to break away from God and live a life unlike that desired by God. Humans are thrown out of PARADISE and must learn to struggle and survive. Two differing creation stories can be found in the first two chapters of Genesis.

creatures, the four living. Also referred to as *beasts*. The four creatures revealed to John in Revelation 4:6–8: "And out of the throne proceeded lightnings and thunderings and voices: and *there were* seven lamps of fire burning before the throne, which are the seven Spirits of God. And before the throne *there was* a sea of glass like unto crystal: and in the midst of the throne, and round about the throne, *were* four beasts full of eyes before and behind. And the first beast *was* like a lion, and the second beast like a calf, and the third beast had a face as a man, and the fourth beast *was* like a flying eagle. And the four beasts had each of them six wings about *him;* and *they were* full of eyes within: and they rest not day and night, saying, Holy, holy, holy, Lord God Almighty, which was, and is, and is to come." (Most translations have "ox" rather than "calf.")

In Christian art, these four creatures have come to symbolize the four evangelists. The LION symbolizes SAINT MARK. The voice of the lion symbolizes the roaring of St. Mark; the lion itself, Jesus' Resurrection. The ox (sometimes a calf) symbolizes SAINT LUKE, who begins his Gospel with Zacharius the priest at the altar. The ox (and calf) are symbols of sacrifice—the sacrifice of Jesus. The man symbolizes SAINT MATTHEW, who beings his Gospel with the human ancestry of Jesus back to David and beyond. This man becoming angel symbolizes Jesus' humanity and Incarnation. The EAGLE symbolizes the messenger SAINT JOHN, who speaks of the Word of God and of the Holy Spirit; the eagle symbolizes the divinity and Ascension of Jesus.

Especially in medieval art, the lion was regarded as the king of beasts, the ox (see OX, WINGED) as the king of domestic animals, the eagle as the king of birds, and man as king of the earth. They all attended upon Jesus Christ who is the king of all that is visible and invisible.

creed (L., *credo,* "I believe," from *credere,* "to believe"). **1.** An official, formal, and authoritative statement of the essential beliefs of a faith. **2.** The *Creed* usually refers to the APOSTLES' CREED.

Creed, Apostles'. See APOSTLES' CREED.

Creed, Athanasian. See ATHANASIAN CREED.

creed, baptismal. The earliest creeds of Christianity were baptismal creeds that affirmed a personal confession of faith and began with "I believe . . . " in contrast to other creeds that usually begin with "We believe . . . . "

creed, conciliar. A creed produced by a church or ecumenical council to serve as guidelines or doctrine for adherents and oppose any heresy.

Creed, Nicene. See NICENE CREED.

Creed, Niceno-Constantinopolitan. See NICENO-CONSTANTINOPOLITAN CREED.

cremation (L., *crematus,* from *cremare,* "to burn"). The incinerating of a corpse. Cremation was a common method of disposing of dead bodies during Roman times. Christian belief, such as in St. Augustine, (354–430) which believed in the literal resurrection of the body, opposed cremation.

crosier. Also *crozier* (L., *crocia,* "cross"). The PASTORAL STAFF of church officials such as bishops or abbots that serves as the symbol of their office, representing them as shepherds of the flock of God and the church or faith. It resembles and is a symbol of a shepherd's crook. It is tall, made of wood (sometimes metal), ornamented, usually curved at the top and pointed at the lower end. The crosier together with items such as a pectoral cross (see also CROSS, PECTORAL), a ring, and a MITRE symbolize the high distinction of a BISHOP or ABBOT.

cross, the (L., *crux,* "cross"). The Greek word for cross is *σταυρός (stavros),* which means "a stake." The Romans used four kinds of crosses in punishment: **1.** the *crux simplex* (a stake); **2.** the *crux decussata,* two stakes intersecting or crossing each other in the form of an X (believed to be the method by which St. Andrew was martyred and has been called the St. Andrew's cross); **3.** the *crux immissa* (†); and the **4.** *crux commissa* (T). There is dispute as to the actual method of Jesus' CRUCIFIXION.

The cross is an emblem of that on which Christ died and of the church he founded. The cross is the principal instrument of the PASSION OF CHRIST and is a sign of his suffering and laying down his life in sacrifice, by means of which humans have been given redemption and salvation. There are over two dozen shapes and names of crosses used in Christianity as an emblem.

Tradition has it that Emperor Constantine, on the eve of a battle, saw a luminous cross in the heavens bearing the words *In hoc signo vinces* (In this sign conquer). He ordered this sign to be placed on the imperial standard and with it won a victory over Maxentius at the Milvian Bridge on October 27, 312.

Cross, adoration of the. Also *veneration of the Cross.* The part of the GOOD FRIDAY service in some Roman Catholic and Eastern Orthodox churches during which a CROSS of Jesus is uncovered by the priest and adored by the clergy and people. The faithful approach the cross (or crawl or creep to it) in reverence, prostrate themselves before it, kiss it, utter prayers, and sing hymns to it. A similar rite occurs that commemorates the finding of the true cross by St. Helena. See also CROSS, EXALTATION OF THE HOLY.

Cross, Exaltation of the Holy. Also known as feast of Holy Cross Day, September 14, in honor of the cross of Jesus Christ. The feast is specifically connected with the finding of the cross by Empress Helena (see also CROSS, INVENTION OF THE HOLY).

Cross, Invention of the Holy. Christian tradition has it that in the early fourth century, about 326, Empress Helena, mother of Emperor Constantine, traveled from Rome to Jerusalem to find and visit the holy places in Jesus' life. She found at GOLGOTHA three crosses, one of which was the cross upon which Christ was crucified. This has been known as the *Invention of the Cross,* from the Latin *inventio,* meaning "to find," "to come upon." Jesus' cross was identified as the True Cross by raising a dead man back to life and restoring a sick woman to health, and, in general, by its miraculous powers to heal. Much of the True Cross is said to have been given in small pieces as relics to churches and dignitaries throughout Europe. A large portion is believed to have been lost in battle. See also CROSS, EXALTATION OF THE HOLY.

cross, pectoral (L., *pectoralis,* "pertaining to the breast"). A small cross worn by bishops and abbots as a sign of their office. It is suspended from the neck and lies on the breast. An insignia or emblem of their office.

cross, sign of the. **1.** The forming of a cross over something by the use of the hands or breath. It was an early belief that evil demons could be repelled or exorcized by making the sign of the cross. **2.** The forming of a cross across one's body from head to chest or heart, side of shoulder to side of shoulder, ending upon the chest. In the Roman Catholic church, the open palm with all fingers extended together, from left shoulder to right, is used. In the Eastern Orthodox church, the thumb and the first two fingers are grouped together to symbolize the Father, Son, and Holy Spirit, with the remaining two fingers tucked in, and the sign of the cross extending from right shoulder to left. (In early Christianity, the sign of the cross was performed on the forehead only.)

The purpose of the sign of the cross upon one's body is ritualistic, as a response in the liturgy, to consecrate, sanctify, dedicate actions, to serve as an encouragement in terms of fright, temptation, etc.; at the recognition of holy things, as a sign of reverence, to call upon the Holy Spirit, to praise God, etc. The sign of the cross has liturgical uses when made upon persons or things such as in blessings, baptism, confirmation, and sanctifying, consecrating, making oil holy, etc.

Cross, the Stations of the. Also the *Way of the Cross.* The fourteen representations (pictures, points, images) of the successive stages of the PASSION OF CHRIST and his death, depicting the major incidents happening to Jesus from Pilate's house to the burial of Jesus at Calvary. This route or way in Jerusalem is called the VIA DOLOROSA. These representations are created for purposes of devotion and veneration. They may be found in churches, or outdoors leading to churches or shrines, and be simple, such as a mere cross, or complex, such as sculptures or engravings on walls. The Franciscans developed this as a devotion. The believer meditates at each station, in succession. The stations: **1.** Jesus is condemned to death by Pilate; **2.** Jesus receives and carries his Cross; **3.** Jesus falls the first time under the Cross; **4.** Jesus meets his Mother Mary; **5.** Simon of Cyrene helps Jesus carry the Cross; **6.** Veronica wipes the face of Jesus; **7.** Jesus falls the second time; **8.** Jesus speaks to the women of Jerusalem; **9.** Jesus falls the third time; **10.** Jesus is stripped of his clothing; **11.** Jesus is nailed to the Cross; **12.** Jesus dies on the Cross; **13.** Jesus is taken down from the Cross; **14.** Jesus is buried in a tomb.

crown of thorns (L., *corona,* "a crown," "a wreath"). A crown has been the symbol of royalty, honor, dignity, and victory. It has been worn by emperors, kings, queens. In Christian art, a crown is worn by God the Father, Christ, and the Blessed Virgin Mary as a symbol of their authority, royalty, sovereignty, and power over all the earth and the kingdom of heaven. Popes, patriarchs, archbishops, bishops wear crowns. (For example, the papal TIARA is a triple crown representing the Trinity, with a cross at the center.) At Matthew 27:27–30 a crown of thorns was put on Jesus' head in mockery of his claim to kingship. (Also see Mark 15:16–19; John 19:1–5.) The crown of thorns is a symbol of Jesus' suffering and of his victory over death, and is used as such in Christian art. Also in Christian art, martyrs are often depicted carrying or wearing crowns as a symbol of their sacrifice and their having conquered death.

crucifix (L., *crucifixus,* "fastened to a cross"). An image of Jesus Christ crucified on a cross.

crucifixion (L., *crux, crucis,* "cross" and *figere, fixum,* "to fix"). The act of crucifying or putting to death by nailing to a cross. Crucifixion is believed to have been a Roman rather than a Jewish form of punishment. The method used was of impaling a body on a stake and publicly exhibiting it in order to serve as a deterrent.

Most Jews denied Jesus as the Messiah (see also MESSIAH, CHRIST AS THE) because of his crucifixion. Jesus' crucifixion is interpreted by Christians not as a denial or defeat of the Messiah, or the Christ, but as a victory of life over death, of the power of light over darkness. Scriptural references to Jesus' crucifixion: Matthew 27:32–56; Mark 8:31; 15:21–41; Luke 23:26–49; John 19:17–37. See also entries at CROSS.

At Romans 5:9ff.; Colossians 1:20; Ephesians 2:13; 1 John 5:6; Revelation 1:5; Christ's death is associated with sacrifice. At Matthew 26:28; Mark 14:24; Luke 22:20; 1 Corinthians 11:25; Hebrews 9:15, Christ's crucifixion is related to the giving up of the blood necessary for a New Covenant with God.

Christian art portrays Christ nailed to a CROSS with either four nails (or spikes), one in each hand and one in each foot, or three nails, one in each hand one piercing Jesus' overlapping feet. See also PASSION, INSTRUMENTS OF THE.

cult (L., *cultus,* "worship," from *colo,* "to till, cultivate the earth," "to worship"). Used to refer to the rituals, rites, practices, ceremonies, celebrations pertaining to worship of a deity.

cup of wine (L., *cuppa,* "a cup"). At Matthew 26:28, during the LAST SUPPER Jesus gave the cup of wine to his disciples and said: "For this is my blood of the new testament, which is shed for many for the remission of sins." The cup of suffering is also mentioned by Christ during his agony in the garden of Gethsemane. At Matthew 26:39, Jesus' inevitable, predestined sacrificial suffering and death is alluded to in the symbol of the cup: "And he went a little farther, and fell on his face, and prayed, saying, O my Father, if it be possible, let this cup pass from me: nevertheless not as I will, but as thou *wilt.*"

curacy. The office, status, authority of a CURATE.

curate (L., *cura,* "care," and *curatus,* "one having the care of souls"). **1.** As used in the past: any clergyman or ordained person. **2.** As used presently: an assistant to a RECTOR, or VICAR. A clerk in holy orders or an assistant to such a clerk.

curia. Latin, "court." In general, an ecclesiastical court. Used specifically to refer to the papal court, which acts from delegated authority from the pope.

D

damn (L., *damnare,* "to condemn," or *damnum,* "penalty," "damage"). Usually used with "to." **1.** To sentence, to doom, to condemn, to judge as guilty. **2.** To condemn as BLASPHEMY, wicked, sinful, false, invalid. **3.** To curse, to bring ruin upon. See also ANATHEMA.

damnation. Condemnation to eternal punishment. Some Christian faiths hold that all those who are ignorant of the Gospel of Jesus Christ—and/or all those who do not accept it—are doomed to eternal damnation.

deacon/deaconess (Gk., διάκονος *[diakonos],* "minister," "servant"). An officer in a church usually below the level of a PRIEST, PASTOR, MINISTER, or CLERGY.

death. **1.** In general, the cessation of life qualities. The cessation of all brain function without the possibility of resuscitation. **2.** Specifically, the cessation of the Christian spiritual life—of the faith or church. **3.** The life of SIN (see also FREEDOM FROM BONDAGE).

dedicate (L., *dedicare,* "to declare," "to dedicate," from *de,* "from," "down," "away," and *dicare,* "to declare"). **1.** To single out with solemn devotion and consecrate (see also CONSECRATION). **2.** To devote oneself to a religious or sacred task (duty, labor, service). See also DEVOTION. **3.** To commit oneself totally in body, mind, spirit to the Lord Jesus Christ.

dedication. The ceremony of dedicating oneself, or someone, or something to Jesus Christ, as in *dedication ceremony, dedication service.* One of the essential features of BAPTISM. Often used interchangeably with CONFIRMATION; CONSECRATION; INITIATION. See also DEDICATE.

deference (L., *deferre,* "to bring down"). The emotion of complete regard for God's wishes and will. *Deference* implies a voluntary and courteous submission of one's own wishes, will, judgments, opinions, and preferences to those of God.

Deism (originally from Gk., *θεός [theos],* "God," transliterated into Latin as *Deus).* In general, the belief in the existence of God. The term *Deism* was first used in Christianity during the latter part of the sixteenth century; in England, it appeared during the early seventeenth century. Deism is associated with the period of the Enlightenment or the "Age of Reason." For the most part, Deism holds to the following beliefs: **1.** God as the FIRST CAUSE created the universe *ex nihilo.* **2.** God created the unchangeable laws by which the universe is governed. **3.** God is in no way immanent in his creation, but totally different from it, transcending it as, for example, a watchmaker transcends the watch he has made and set in motion. **4.** God occasionally suspends the laws of the universe and history in order to perform a beneficent event. **5.** God personally intervenes in the lives of humans and in providing grace and/or moral guidance. **6.** Reason is in harmony with revelation (or revelation must conform to reason). **7.** In general, Deists held that divine revelation was not necessary in proving the existence of God or knowing his characteristics. Reason and reason alone could demonstrate the existence of a creator who was thought of as "the Intelligent Author of Nature," "the Mathematical Genius Behind the Order of Nature," "the Moral Ruler or Governor of Nature." **8.** The Bible must be analyzed according to reason and its doctrines should not be made into mysteries. **9.** God has a preordained plan for the universe; all things are predetermined. **10.** The highest duty and sole aim of human life is to fulfill God's purpose and destiny.

Deists (American). American Deists of the 1700s held to the superiority and supremacy of human reason over faith, revelation, miracles, prophecy. They opposed any established church as the true and only source of religious knowledge and supported individualism, religious freedom, and the separation of church and state.

American Deists (such as Thomas Jefferson [1743–1826], Thomas Paine [1737–1809], Ethan Allen [1738–1789]) rejected the Calvinist notion accepted by American Puritans, that man was inherently sinful, partaking of the original sin of Adam. They believed that each and every event is determined by the natural laws that God as the FIRST CAUSE laid down and by which the universe was governed. All things—including humans—are manifestations of an omnibenevolent God. A human is too good to be sent to hell. Humans are capable of achieving a good life here on earth by the use of their reason; they need not wait for the heavenly kingdom of God.

demon (L., *daemon,* "evil spirit," "spirit," and Gk., *δαίμων [daimōn],* "a divinity"). An evil spirit or a DEVIL, of supernatural nature and intermediate somewhere between a human and God. Often referred to as *unclean spirits.* Jesus cast out demons. At Mark 1:24, demons blurt out the secret of who Jesus is. (Refer also to 1 Cor. 10:20ff.; Matt. 8:31; 12:28; Mark 1:23ff., 3:11, 22; 5:1ff.; 9:17ff.)

ANGELS are friendly toward humans, whereas demons are hostile and cause disease, strange behavior, misfortune, catastrophes. See also EVIL POWERS.

demonology. Also *daemonology* (Gk., *δαίμων [daimōn],* "a god," "a deity," "a divine being," sometimes "an inferior deity" or "evil spirit," and *λόγος [logos],* "the rational account of," "the study of"). **1.** In general, the study of hostile or evil spirits (demons). **2.** Specifically, ascribing to evil spirits that occasionally inhabit human bodies such things as evil, bad fortune, satanic behavior, multiple personalities, aberrant conduct, mental derangement, even physical disease. See also DEMONS; DEVIL, THE; EXORCISM; SATAN.

depravity (L., *depravare,* "to be wicked," "to be perverse," "to be crooked"). The general theological term that designates the state of humans after the FALL. Characterized by corruption, debasement, sin, deterioration, degeneration, evil, perversity, loss of purity, alienation, estrangement. Every human faculty or function is regarded as having an innate possibility for sin (see also SIN, ORIGINAL).

The traditional belief as in St. Augustine (354–430) has been that depravity is inherited materially (by means of sexual union) through the parents.

descent into Hell, Jesus'. Also *Harrowing of Hell.* Controversy exists in the Christian tradition as to whether Jesus, during the period between his entombment and resurrection, descended into HELL, SHEOL, HADES, PURGATORY, or LIMBO. Some references in the New Testament on Jesus' descent into Hell (or his presence among the dead): 1 Peter 3:19ff; 4:6. Revelation 5:13; Philippians 2:10; In Acts 2:27–31, St. Peter speaks of the descent of Christ into "Hell" and of his subsequent resurrection or separation from it. In Ephesians 4:9, St. Paul writes about "the lower parts of the earth" where departed spirits exist in the unseen regions.

A variety of analyses exist on this topic. **1.** Jesus did indeed enter for a period of time a region to be thought of as hell (Hades, Sheol). This region is where the spirits of those already dead await to be resurrected, and Jesus' presence there was for this purpose. Specifically, Jesus' presence there was to baptize, and thus assure resurrection to, the just and the saints of the Old Dispensation. They had slept in righteousness without the seal of baptism. Jesus proclaimed the victory of his BASILEIA to the powers of the underworld.

According to Justin Martyr (100–165) in *Dialogues Against Trypho,* Jesus remembered the dead and "descended to them to preach the glad tidings of salvation." Also Irenaeus (ca. 115–202), in his *Against Heresies,* writes that Jesus preached in Hades "to the righteous men, the prophets and the patriarchs." (Many Church Fathers refer in a similar vein to this descent of Jesus into Hell. This view persists throughout Church history to modern times. The APOSTLES' CREED [370] as well as other creeds affirm this descent.)

Apart from the intent to resurrect all those who died before the INCARNATION or the RESURRECTION, Jesus' descent gives all those who died before Jesus the chance to hear the GOSPELS, the EVANGELION, the only means of salvation, and thus also be saved. God's justice and redemptive will require this. (The Apostles and early Church Fathers were concerned with the question "And what of those who died before hearing of the good news?")

2. Jesus' descent into hell presents the human reality of Jesus' death—the reality that like all humans, Jesus too gave up his spirit, as we all must do. Jesus obediently, and in the embodiment of a human, accepts death, realizes the powers of death (impotence, immobility, insentience, inactivity, helplessness), and overcomes these powers by means of his redemptive submission to his Father's plans. By dying, and then descending into death (hell), Jesus associated himself with all those who had died before him and united all humanity in a spiritual oneness, sharing with them his message, hope, and eternality. **3.** Jesus's descent into hell shows that Jesus, as flesh, was not loath to experience the moral punishment of all humans, of all sinners—death—and to mercifully sympathize with them in love and acceptance. **4.** Jesus' descent illustrates his complete victory over all the universe, over all the levels and powers of Being. No region is untouched by Jesus' spirit and power.

deus absconditus. Latin, "the hidden God." See THEOLOGY OF THE CROSS.

Deus a Se. Latin, "God as he is in himself." Usually refers to the inner, mysterious, private nature of God that can never be penetrated by the finite reason of humans. Contrast with DEUS PRO NOBIS.

Deus est suum esse. Latin, "God is his own being." Refers to the concept of GOD AS NECESSARY BEING as, for example, held by St. Thomas Aquinas. What God's being is, is nothing else than that by which he exists—the pure act of existing.

Deus incognitus. Latin "the unknown, unknowable God." See also AGNOSTICISM.

Deus pro nobis. Latin, "God as he has revealed himself to us," or "God on our own behalf." **1.** Refers to those aspects and manifestations of God available to human finite minds—both by means of reason and revelation. **2.** Specifically, has been used to refer to God's directly relating himself through Jesus Christ to humanity in order to allow humanity to atone for its DEPRAVITY, to redeem itself and attain a higher state of being (close to that before the FALL). Contrast with *Deus a Se.*

Devil, the (Gk., διάβολος *[diabolos]*, "slanderer," "liar," or "to throw across," from διά *[dia]*, "across," and βάλλειν *[ballein]*, "to throw"). Also SATAN. **1.** The ultimate, supreme evil spirit. **2.** A DEMON, evil spirit, or power for unrighteousness.

The Devil is spoken of as a spirit (Eph. 2:2) who has fallen angels under his control. At 1 Timothy 3:6 the Devil is one who fell through pride. (Also see Rev. 12:9; John 8:44). The Devil is also referred to in the New Testament as Beelzebub (lord of the flies). In Mark 3:22–26, devils form a kingdom of their own and are opposed to Jesus BASILEIA. They are manifested in the act of possessing humans. (Also Luke 10:18; Matt. 12:28.)

Christians have believed in preter-human, evil powers, diabolic forces, satanic principalities, demons, devils, etc., which operate in the world. Some scriptural references: Luke 13:16; 1 Thessalonians 2:18; Hebrews 2:14. It has also been a traditional belief among Christians that death, illness, misfortune, pain, suffering, destructive and self-destructive forces are expressions of the power of the Devil (devils, demonic powers). The principal method of manifesting these evils is by POSSESSION. The principal method of relieving, or exorcising, these devils or demonic spirits is by EXORCISM and by prayers to God or Jesus for protection from malign, diabolic powers. See also EVIL POWERS.

devote (L., *devovere* "to vow"). **1.** Often used interchangeably with some meanings of consecrate and DEDICATE. (See also CONSECRATION.) **2.** To give up one's earthly ways and attachments and commit oneself to a spiritual life, as, for example, by a vow.

devotion. **1.** To DEDICATE oneself wholly, exclusively, and solemnly to the Word of God. **2.** The state of being devoted to God. **3.** The act of prayer or worship. **4.** The piety, devoutness, zeal, love, and feelings toward God as expressed, for example, in worship, prayer, the religious experience. Implies feelings such as earnestness, attachment, respect, devotedness, reverence, humility, humbleness, religiousness.

devotions, liturgical. The rituals, feasts, and religious acts that express spiritual feelings toward God in worship of him, such as the ANGELUS, the BENEDICTION, THE STATIONS OF THE CROSS, the ROSARY, the Veneration of Relics (see also VENERATION; CROSS, ADORATION OF THE), Novenas, the

Poor Souls in PURGATORY, the Five Wounds (see also WOUNDS OF CHRIST, THE FIVE), the Seven Sorrows (see also SORROWS OF MARY, THE SEVEN).

diocese (Gk., διοίκησις *[dioikēsis]*, "housekeeping," "province," from διά *[dia]*, "through," and οἰκεῖν *[oikein]*, "to manage a household"). The district or territory of a church over which a bishop has jurisdiction.

disciple (L., *discipulus*, "learner," "disciple," from *discere*, "to learn"). **1.** In general, understood as a pupil, follower, believer in the beliefs of a teacher or master. Implies a personal adherence to and veneration of a wise person's doctrines. **2.** Specifically, one who followed Jesus Christ as one of the twelve apostles (see also APOSTLES, THE TWELVE). Used synonymously with APOSTLE.

Disciples, Jesus' Twelve. Also *Jesus' Twelve Apostles; Those of the Way.* At Matthew 10:1–4: "And when he had called unto him his twelve disciples, he gave them power against unclean spirits, to cast them out, and to heal all manner of sickness and all manner of disease. Now the names of the twelve apostles are these: The first, Simon, who is called Peter, and Andrew his brother; James, the son of Zebedee, and John his brother; Philip, and Bartholomew; Thomas, and Matthew the publican; James, the son of Alphaeus, and Lebbaeus, whose surname was Thaddaeus; Simon the Canaanite, and Judas Iscariot, who also betrayed him." (Also refer to Luke 6:13–16.)

According to the Gospels, the disciples were endowed with extraordinary, miraculous powers such as healing the sick, powers of prophecy, speaking in tongues, raising humans from the dead, etc. See also APOSTLES, THE TWELVE.

The twelve disciples (whom Jesus also called "apostles") may symbolize or designate the twelve tribes of Israel, which Jesus claimed as his people—the very people Jesus wanted them to preach to about the kingdom of God: "These twelve Jesus sent forth, and commanded them, saying, 'Go not into the way of the Gentiles, and into any city of the Samaritans enter ye not. But go rather to the lost sheep of the house of Israel. And as ye go, preach, saying, the kingdom of heaven is at hand' " (Matt. 10:5–7.)

disciplina arcani. Latin, "arcane discipline." Refers to keeping the rituals and doctrines of the Church secret and accessible only to those fully initiated (communicants, participants) and not to be divulged, for example, to pagans, atheists, or even catechumens.

discipline (L., *disciplina*, from *discipulus*, "disciple"). **1.** The Christian way of life as prescribed by the church or faith. **2.** The rules, regulations, practices, duties, and way of life of a holy order or tradition.

Discipline implies concepts such as discipleship, learner, faithfulness, education, training, service, mission, believer, subjection to rule and authority, obedience, reverence, devotion, dedication, and commitment.

dispensation (L., *dispendere*, "to weigh out," "to dispense," from *dis,* "away," "apart," "between," "asunder," and *pendere," "to weigh").* **1.** The distribution of good and evil by God to humans (see also GRACE). **2.** The method, such as the COVENANT, by which God controls and regulates loyalty and obedience from humans. **3.** The system of rules, principles, creeds, sanctioned and administered by a Christian church. The origin of this system is God who by this means instructs humans in the ways of morality, obedience, and worship of him. Examples: "the Mosaic dispensation"; "the dispensation of the Old Covenant (. . . the Law)"; "the dispensation of the New Covenant of Jesus Christ (. . . Grace)." **4.** The exemption from or the dispensing with something such as an obligation, promise, canon, or ecclesiastical law. This implies a relaxation of ecclesiastical rules or laws, and/or a permission to do something that would ordinarily be illegal under such laws. Ecclesiastical laws, as all laws, run up against exceptions—or exceptions are deemed wise. Dispensation to ecclesiastical law or canons has been practiced since the fifth century, by bishops and other ecclesiastical authorities. At the COUNCIL OF TRENT (1545–1563) it was formally decreed that the pope would hold such power of dispensation. (He had in practice exercised this power throughout the Middle Ages, often giving the privilege of dispensation to papal legates.) In the Church of England, the power of dispensation resides in the archbishop of Canterbury, who previous to 1534 was the pope's legate for dispensation. (The pope's power of dispensation was legally terminated in 1534.) Bishops in the Church of England have some power of dispensation, and the registrars of marriages, for example, have the power of dispensation with respect to the granting of marriage licenses without the necessary prerequisites.

dispensation of grace. Refers to the New Covenant of Jesus. See also COVENANT, THE NEW.

dispensation of the law. Refers to the Mosaic Dispensation, or the Old Covenant. See also COVENANT, THE OLD.

ditheism (Gk., δίς *[dis],* "twice," "double," and ϑεός *[theos],* "God"). Belief in the existence of two gods, one good and one evil, struggling for control of the universe. See also DUALISM, THEOLOGICAL.

divination (L., *divinatio,* from *divinare,* "to foresee," "to foretell," "to prophecize," or from *divinus,* "divine"). Prophesying, foretelling, or foreseeing future events. Often derogatively equated with *augury.*

divine (L., *divinus,* "divine," "divinely inspired," from *divus, dius,* "of a deity"). **1.** Having to do with God. **2.** That which proceeds from God, as, for example, his (divine) power or as in the divine rights of a king or leader. **3.** That which is given up to God, as in a divine worship service. **4.** That individual authorized by the church to represent or speak for God such as a priest, clergyman, theologian, saint, holy man.

Related to concepts such as godlike, pious, sacred, holy, ethereal, ephemeral, spiritual, unearthly, celestial, supernatural, supranatural, immutable, immaterial. See also CHRIST, THE.

divine afflatus (L., *affare,* "to breathe," "to blow on"). **1.** The impartation of knowledge (insight, wisdom, prophecy) by God. **2.** Being stimulated, controlled, and inspired by God's spirit and power. See also INSPIRATION.

divine monarchy. The doctrine especially as found in the HOLY TRINITY whereby God the Father is regarded as the ontological source of the other two members of the Trinity. See also MONARCHIANISM. Compare with COMMUNICATIO ESSENTIAE. Contrast with COINHERENCE.

divine names. The names, or characteristics, that can rightly (correctly, properly) be applied to God in His majesty, grandeur, and unity. See also GOD, THE ATTRIBUTES OF.

divine rights of the king. Based on the concept that **1.** some humans in a society are sacred, special, designated apart as rightful rulers and governors of other humans; **2.** secular, profane authority was granted its status and powers by divine sanction and permission; **3.** monarchs (especially those hereditarily entrenched) represent God—to their people—stand for, and act out God's will; **4.** those governed have no occasion, or right, to resist the wishes of a monarch; **5.** (in the concept of an absolute monarch) the monarch was subject only to God, to the laws of God—not the pope, or any religious authority or power; **6.** (in some early cases) the king had, or could receive, supernatural powers to do such things as heal, perform miracles, give pardon, override secular laws, etc.

divinitatis sensus. Latin. Refers to a sense or awareness of God (divinity) and his presence in all things. This *sensus* is usually regarded as potentially natural to man's mind.

docetism (Gk., δόκειν *[dokein],* "to appear," "to seem"). The belief that Jesus Christ was a divine being who did not really become flesh (see FLESH, JESUS AS) but walked the earth in the disguise of one of his creatures (the human). The INCARNATION is a form of THEOPHANY. Docetism is based on assumptions such as: **1.** God being divine and perfect could not in any fully real sense enter the realm of the flesh with its imperfection, corruption, limitations, and incontinence; **2.** God in delivering us from acts of the flesh could not himself have done it through flesh, but only through some divine level of being and Jesus Christ was that divine means. Jesus Christ as flesh was only an appearance of flesh. Jesus Christ was the ideal for flesh but was not of flesh. **3.** God himself, being eternal and "all-in-all," could not be born, or suffer, or be a human, or die. All these events in Jesus' life, including his crucifixion and resurrection, were mere appearances of a more fundamental reality. (Docetists hold that there are allusions to their position in texts such as St. John's First and Second Epistles: I John 4:2 and II John 7.)

Doctors of the Church. See FATHERS, THE FOUR GREEK; FATHERS, THE FOUR LATIN.

doctrine (L., *doctrina,* from *doctor,* "teacher," from *docere,* "to teach"). That which is taught as a formal belief (faith, tenet, body of knowledge) by a church.

dogma (Gk., *δόγμα [dogma],* "that which seems to one," "an opinion," "a belief,"). **1.** In general, a DOCTRINE (belief, ideology, tenet, authoritative opinion, principle) that has been formally stated and authoritatively proclaimed (decreed) by a Christian church. See also CREED; DOGMATICS; FAITH; THEOLOGY, DOGMATIC; THEOLOGY, DOCTRINAL. **2.** Specifically, in Acts 16:4; 17:7, the principles (ordinances, decrees, beliefs) impressed by apostolic authority. Also in Colossians 2:14; Ephesians 2:15. **3.** The decrees of the ecumenical councils of the church for the purpose of systematizing Christian belief, defining and imparting its knowledge, and correcting HERESY.

The Reformation churches do not promulgate dogmas, but present *confessions* of faith (see also CONFESSION) as in the Augsburg Confession (1530) Westminster Confession (1643), *doctrines,* or *creeds.* Since the REFORMATION and the Age of Enlightenment, the word *dogma* has had a pejorative connotation, suggesting intolerance, narrowness, repression of thought, and especially authoritarianism as opposed to individual reasoning about the Bible. For example, *dogmatic* came to mean fervently holding to a doctrine in the face of equally good or better alternatives; *dogmatism* connoted unmerited positiveness in asserting the truth of a doctrine or belief. Immanuel Kant (1724–1804) applied the term *dogmatists* to thinkers who believed **(a)** that the nature of the universe could be known by means of inferences derived from a few self-evident principles without recourse to observation, control, experimentation, and testing, and **(b)** that finite humans have the ability to transcend ordinary sense-experience and independently of that sense-experience arrive at truths about the universe on the basis of speculative beliefs (dogmas).

dogmatics (Gk., *δόγμα [dogma],* "dogma," from *δοκεῖν [dokein],* "to think," "to appear"). **1.** The formal study of Christian DOGMA, DOCTRINE, faith). Assumes the Bible as the divinely revealed word of God. **2.** The attempt to systematize and put into doctrinal form, or dogma, the revealed truths of Scripture. **3.** That branch of theology that presents the tenets (doctrines, dogmas) of its institutionalized, formal Christian faith. See also HERMENEUTICS; THEOLOGY, DOGMATIC; THEOLOGY, DOCTRINAL.

Dolours of Mary, the Seven. See SORROWS OF MARY, THE SEVEN.

dominical (L., *dominus,* "master," "Lord"). God's or Jesus' domain or wishes, as in *dominical doctrines, dominical sacraments* (those sacraments originated by Jesus himself such as BAPTISM and the LORD'S SUPPER).

donkey, the. Used in Christian art as a symbol of humility, obedience, and dedication, usually depicted carrying Mary to Bethlehem or the Holy Family into Egypt.

donum superadditum. Latin, "super-additional capacity or endowment from God." Refers to those gifts humans lost at the FALL. Some: eternal life; eternal harmony and obedience to God's will; eternal and complete happiness; freedom from pain, misery, and suffering; the ability to know —have a vision of—God's nature and being and be one with him in companionship and love.

double procession of the Holy Spirit. The Western Christian church's interpretation of the Holy Trinity as propounded principally by St. Augustine (354–430), who held that the HOLY SPIRIT proceeded from (both) the Father *and* the Son. The Eastern Orthodox church accepts the doctrine of the *single procession* of the Holy Spirit *from* the Father (in order to preserve the Singularity, Unity, and Monism of God's substance), *through* the Son. See also TRINITY, THE HOLY.

douleia. Greek, *δουλεία*, "servitude" from *δοῦλος (doulos),* "slave." A lower level of veneration than LATREIA. Specifically in the Roman Catholic church, regarded as that kind of respect given to saints (and angels).

dove, the. Used as a symbol or emblem of the HOLY SPIRIT—the third person of the Holy Trinity. Doves were made of gold and/or silver and suspended above the fonts of early Christian churches to symbolize the Holy Spirit. The dove was used in Christian art, especially to depict the Holy Spirit as it descends during Jesus' baptism (Matt. 3:16; Mark 1:10; Luke 3:22). The dove (as well as sheep and the fish) symbolize a Christian (see Matt. 10:16). Symbols of a dove are found on many Roman catacombs. The poetic and symbolic meaning of the dove date back to Noah. See also INCARNATION, THE.

doxology (Gk., *δοξολογία [doxologia],* from *δόξα [doxa],* "opinion," "praise," "glory," and *λέγειν [legein],* "to speak"). **1.** The study of the means, or methods, by which God is glorified. **2.** A hymn, or other means, of expressing praise to God. The *Gloria in Excelsis* is referred to as the greater doxology; the *Gloria Patri,* the lesser doxology. A common doxological form: "Praise God, from whom all blessings flow."

dualism, theological (L., *duo,* "two"). The belief that two gods exist, vying for control of the universe. Also referred to as DITHEISM.

duty (L., *debere,* "to owe," "to be in debt"). **1.** In general, that which one is obliged and expected to do (or not to do) in reference to God's will and commands (and/or the strictures of a Christian church). **2.** Specifically, a responsibility, an obligation, an act decreed by God that when not fulfilled renders one punishable by God. Examples: the celebration of the MASS; PRAYER; FORGIVENESS; LOVE; CHARITY; SACRIFICE; participation in the sacraments.

dyophysitism (Gk., δύο *[duo]*, "two," and φύσις *[physis]*, "nature"). The belief that there are two separate natures, the human and the divine, inextricably united in the person of Jesus Christ. Contrasted with MONOPHYSITISM.

dyotheletism (Gk., δύο *[duo]*, "two," and θέλησις *[thelēsis]*, "will"). The doctrine that there are two natures, two wills in Jesus: the human and the divine. The human is always subordinate to the divine. Dyotheletism was adopted at the Third Council of Constantinople (681). Contrasted with monothelitism, which holds to the identity of Jesus' will, it being divine and human at the same time but manifested as human or divine according to historical or supernatural activity. See also DYOPHYSITISM.

E

eagle, the **1.** In general, a Christian symbol of nobility. **2.** The symbol or emblem associated with St. John the Evangelist (see also CREATURES, THE FOUR LIVING). **3.** A symbol of spiritual power and spiritual aspiration.

The eagle was regarded as the king of the birds and was believed to be able to look straight into the sun without damage to its eyes and to cure itself of blindness by soaring upwards toward heaven.

Easter. Also *Easter Sunday* (The name may be from that of a Teutonic goddess as in Anglo-Saxon *Eastre,* and German *Ostern,* having some linguistic connection with the Roman Astarte or Venus). The yearly Christian festival that commemorates Christ's RESURRECTION from the dead, on the third day after his CRUCIFIXION. The Sunday following GOOD FRIDAY. Corresponds to the Jewish Passover (see also PASCHA). Celebrated on the first Sunday after the full moon that falls on or next after March 21, the vernal equinox—thus between March 22 and April 25. The Council of Nicaea (325) arrived at this method of determining the date. It is difficult to ascertain the correct day and month in which Jesus Christ was crucified and resurrected. The year of 29 A.D. has been given as the most probable, together with March 18, 21, and April 7 and 9.

Eastern church, the. Also *the Eastern Orthodox church.* Used in contrast to the Western church or churches, or the Roman Catholic church or Latin church. In 1054 Christianity divided into eastern and western portions, an event that has been called the Great Schism. The eastern emperors of

Constantinople supported the patriarchs; the western emperors of Rome supported the popes. The western section of the church became known as the Roman Catholic, with its center at Rome. The eastern section became known as the Greek or Eastern Orthodox church, with its center at Constantinople, the seat of the Byzantine Empire. The Eastern church regards itself as the original Christian Church, or Church of Christ, and an uninterrupted continuation of it. It considers the Roman church as a separation from the true historical procession of Christ's message.

Several bodies exist, mostly of national origin, in the Eastern Orthodox church: the Albanian Orthodox church, the Bulgarian, the Rumanian, the Russian, Polish, Finnish, etc. Most have their own patriarch. The five original Patriarchates of the Eastern Orthodox church were Constantinople, Alexandria, Antioch, Jerusalem, and Cyprus. They claim origination respectively by Andrew, Mark, Paul, Peter and James, and Paul and Barnabas. The patriarch of Constantinople is recognized as the leader of the other patriarchs but is only "the first among equals" and not supreme over the others. He holds the title of "Archbishop of Constantinople, the New Rome, and Ecumenical Patriarch."

Some of the major differences between Eastern Orthodox churches and the Roman Catholic church: **1.** The Eastern church does not recognize the Roman pope as infallible, or of supreme authority. **2.** It believes that the Holy Spirit proceeds directly, and only, from the Father. (Whereas the Roman Catholic church has added a FILIOQUE clause to the Nicene Creed, holding that the Holy Spirit also proceeds "from the Son." **3.** The Eastern Orthodox church does not believe in PURGATORY or LIMBO, only in heaven and hell. **4.** It does not believe in the Immaculate Conception of the Blessed Virgin Mary. Mary was born with original sin but was purged of it on Annunciation Day. **5.** There was no physical assumption of the Blessed Virgin Mary at which Mary was also "resurrected." **6.** CELIBACY is not required of priests unless they choose to advance beyond parish priests in the ecclesiastical hierarchy. **7.** Both the wine and leavened bread are partaken of by the laity during Holy Communion.

Ebionites (Heb., *ebyonim,* "poor people"). An Early heretical Jewish Christian sect that originated in the first century and persisted until the seventh century (see Rom. 15:26: "The poor saints which are at Jerusalem"). They held to the following beliefs: **1.** A rigid obedience by Christians to the Law of Moses. **2.** Jesus Christ was a human being, a Jewish child of Joseph and Mary. **3.** Jesus was the awaited Messiah but he was not God. The Holy Spirit descended on Jesus at his baptism at which time Jesus' Messiahship was revealed to Jesus by Elijah in the form of John the Baptist.

ecclēsia. Greek ἐκκλησία, from ἔκ *(ek),* "out," and καλεῖν *(kalein),* "to call," "to welcome out," "to request to come out". The church building itself and the assembly of believers. In ancient Greek times, a political gathering of citizens for decision making who were called out by the town crier.

ecclesiastic (Gk., ἐκκλησιαστικός *[ekklēsiastikos],* "preacher," from ἐκκλησία *[ekklēsia],* "church," from ἐκ *[ek],* "out," and καλεῖν *[kalein],* "to call"). A clergyperson, minister, priest, reverend, divine.

ecclesiastical (Gk., ἐκκλησία *[ekklēsia],* "an assembly of citizens called out by the crier"; also refers to the "church"; from ἐκ *[ek],* "out," and καλεῖν *[kalein],* "to call"). Pertaining to the clergy, the priestly, the ministry, or to their church organization, administration, and government. The contrasting term to SECULAR.

ecclesiolatry (Gk., ἐκκλησία *[ekklēsia],* "church," and λατρεία *[latreia],* "worship of," "devotion to," "service to"). Devotion to the church. Often used pejoratively to denote excessive obedience, subjection, and devotion to the ceremonies, traditions, dictates, and authority of a church.

ecclesiology (Gk., ἐκκλησία *[ekklēsia],* "church," and λόγος *[logos],* "the study of," "a rational account of"). The study of the church in all its components: as an institution, its functions, hierarchy, doctrines, history, buildings, rituals, decorations, important personages, theological changes, etc.

ecstasy (Gk., ἔκστασις *[ektasis],* "being out of place," "displacement," "entrancement," "astonishment," "a trance," from ἐκ *[ek],* "out," and ἱστάναι *[istanai],* "to set," "to stand," "to stand outside oneself"). **1.** The state of joy, rapture, exaltation in realizing the love, beauty, and perfection of God. **2.** The ineffable emotion when feeling the presence of, or being overpowered by God—an emotion beyond the realm of reason and even self-control. **3.** The spiritual happiness and contentment felt in the awareness of God's unqualified love for one's existence. **4.** A mystical and/or prophetic vision or trance. See also HOLY SPIRIT, MYSTICISM; MYSTICAL EXPERIENCE, NUMINOUS, THE. **5.** A state of rapture (joy, exaltation) overwhelming one's awareness. Ecstasy has been related to the feeling of not being in control, not being the cause of the emotion, of its having a divine source or reason. Ecstasy has been regarded as beyond all reason—cannot be rationally described and has no rational basis for its inception. Ecstasy has been associated with the overpowering feelings of the mystic, the prophet, religious seer, and poet. The feelings in ecstasy are of intense and complete mental, spiritual, and physical elation, euphoria, and bliss.

The feeling involved in ecstasy is so intense and overwhelming that it is interpreted **(a)** as being "*extra*ordinary," of divine origin, **(b)** as an experience of "standing outside of" one's ordinary consciousness,

(c) as a climactic focus of absorption of all the faculties into an undifferentiated unity, the unity of God, in which there are no distinctions among things such as body, spirit, mind, thought, will, desires, drives, needs, emotions.

ecumenical. Also *oecumenical* (Gk. **οἰκουμενικός** *[oikoumenikos]*, from **οἰκουμένη** *[oikoumenē]*, "the inhabited world," from **οἰκεῖν** *[oikein]* "house," "dwelling"). One of the New Testament words used to refer to the world, or to the inhabitants of the world. Now used to refer to the church as a whole—to Christianity as a community—to the Christian inhabitants of the world. An *ecumenical conference* refers to a general conference of Christian faiths or churches. Specifically, an ecumenical council in the Roman Catholic church is a council of the Roman hierarchy, summoned by the pope who presides over the council, at which matters of faith and policy are discussed. Its decrees are binding on the whole Roman Catholic church. See also COUNCIL, ECUMENICAL.

ecumenical movement. Also *ecumenism.* Refers to the desire and commitment among Christians to attain a unity in Jesus Christ of all Christian faiths and churches. As a specific movement, it had its official beginning at the Missionary Conference at Edinburgh, Scotland in 1910. Holds to the ideal of one Church of Jesus Christ united in faith, aims, and spirit.

elder. **1.** Sometimes synonymous with PRESBYTER. **2.** In most cases, used to refer to a layperson (sometimes ordained) who assists the presbyter, or MINISTER, in governing the church, and who may represent him at meetings or at other churches whenever requested.

Calvin distinguished two kinds of elders: **(a)** presbyters, ordained ministers who taught and conducted services, and **(b)** ruling elders who functioned as administrators.

election. St. Paul interprets a passage in Genesis in which Abraham is blessed by God to mean that God's blessing achieves culmination in the life of Jesus Christ, and through Jesus Christ all men too are blessed (see also BLESSING) in Christ (Gal. 3:8ff.; Rom. 6:4ff.). We meet this same form of thought in Hebrews 6:17, in Acts 3:25, and in Matthew's tracing of Jesus' genealogy back to Abraham (Matt. 1:1ff.). This form of thought is the foundation of APOSTOLIC SUCCESSION and the concept of the ELECT.

God's BLESSING is the method (or symbol) of election. For Christians, God's plan finds fruition in Jesus Christ. A new community of the elected (the chosen) arises in a common spirit that will share in the promised blessings of the messianic age (Eph. 1:3,14) and that is God's means by which the blessings of God are revealed to all and made available for all men (Eph. 1:10). For Calvin, election was a mystery involving repentance, faith, and sanctification.

elect, the. Those chosen by God's divine grace to be eternally saved. In

Ephesians 5:25–27 and Romans 8:29–34, the work of God's salvation is limited to the elect, to the justified, to the sanctified, to those of the Church. In John 3:16, there is salvation for "whosoever believeth." In 2 Corinthians 5:14ff., the universal "all" is used (but may refer to only all those who die in Christ). Atonement, salvation are offered freely to all without distinction—provided they freely choose to follow Christ's way, but the theory of the elect stresses a mystery of divine election (or selection). God is the only Being that can ultimately restrict and exclude. All that humans can do is declare endlessly the love, goodness, and mercy of God, especially as found in the redeeming atoning work of Christ.

St. Augustine (354–430) toward the end of his life preached a doctrine of the elect: There was a predestined number of the elect, chosen by God and only known by him, who would constitute the heavenly or invisible Church (see also CHURCH, THE INVISIBLE). According to Calvin (1509–1564), there could be those elected (selected) by God—graced by God—who were outside any organized Christian church body. Calvin in the *Institutes,* iv. 1:2: "only to God is knowledge of his Church to be allowed, a Church whose foundation is his *hidden* election." See also INFRALAPSARIANISM.

emanation theory of creation (L., *emanare,* "to flow out of," from *e,* "out," and *manare* "to flow"). A creation theory with Neo-Platonic foundations, upon which some Christian thinkers looked with favor, that states that all reality (all being, all the universe) proceeds by necessity from God, the one perfect, eternal, central principle. Opposed to CREATIO EX NIHILO. The emanation conception of creation uses the analogy of the sun and the light it radiates. The sun is the source of the light; God is the source of all existence. Light "emanates" from the sun and is totally dependent upon it (but is not identical with it); the universe (matter, being, reality) "emanates" from the One Perfect God and is utterly dependent upon God (and the universe is not identical with God). Take away the sun, you then take away light; take away God, you then take away the universe. The further you are from the sun, the less bright the light; the further away from God a thing is, the less spirituality and perfection it possesses. (Pure matter, according to the emanation theory, is the furthest away from God—hence the most evil. Pure bodiless souls [psyches, spirits] are closest to God, followed by bodily intelligences.)

The emanation theory of creation (sometimes referred to as *emanationism)* was (erroneously) regarded as a form of PANTHEISM and mainly for this reason was condemned by the first Vatican Council (1804) since it was thought to deny Christian concepts such as: **1.** CREATIONISM, **2.** the immutability of God, **3.** the simplicity, and **4.** the transcendence of God.

encyclical (Gk., ἐνκύκλιος *[enkyklios],* from ἔν *[en],* "in," and κύκλος *[kyklos],* "circle"). **1.** In general, an ecclesiastical letter sent to churches, places, or persons. **2.** Specifically in the Roman Catholic church, a papal encyclical is a letter from the pope to all Roman Catholic bishops, pointing out errors of faith, giving encouragement to the work of the church, etc.

enhypostasia. Greek, from *ἔν (en),* "in," and *ὑπόστασις (hypostasis),* "substance." The belief that the person (the HYPOSTASIS) of God, which became incarnate in Jesus, contained all the properties of human nature in a perfect state. The person of Christ is thus divine, and yet wholly human. A common position in *enhypostasia* is that God became incarnate in Jesus Christ by means of the activity of the LOGOS whereby Jesus received a human personality, or a personage. Compare with ANHYPOSTASIA.

enthronization. **1.** The solemn rite of placing a bishop on his throne. **2.** Also refers to the enthroning of relics of a saint in the altar of a church at its CONSECRATION. **3.** Sometimes refers to the installation of a presbyter (priests, clergy) to their assigned churches.

enthusiasm (Gk., *ἐνθουσιασμός [enthousiasmos],* from *ἐνθουσιάζειν [enthousiazein],* "to be inspired by the god," from *ἔνθεος [entheos],* "inspired," from *ἔν [en],* "in," and *θεός [theos],* "God"). **1.** Divine inspiration or possession. **2.** Impassioned rapture or emotion about God, or the divine. **3.** ECSTASY or exaltation of the spirit. **4.** Fervor or eagerness to forward the spirit of Jesus Christ as Savior and Lord and Master.

eon. See AEON.

epiclesis. Greek *ἐπίκλεσις.* The prayer in the ANAPHORAS of the Eastern Orthodox church asking for the descent of the HOLY SPIRIT upon the bread and wine at the EUCHARIST to change them into the body and blood of Christ.

Epiphany, the (Gk., *ἐπιφάνεια [epiphaneia],* "appearance," from *ἐπί [epi],* "upon," "on," "to," and *φαίνειν [phanein],* "to show," "to appear"). Also TWELFTHIDE, which designated the beginning of the carnival season preceding LENT. **1.** A church celebration (festival, service) celebrated on January 6 that commemorates the coming of the MAGI to Jesus to proclaim him King at his birth at Bethlehem (see also ADORATION OF THE MAGI). **2.** Also celebrated as the day of Christ's divine appearance to humankind at his baptism, at which a voice from heaven announces Jesus as God's only begotten son. **3.** It has been, in its long history from the third century, also celebrated in connection with Jesus' miracle of the wine at the marriage feast in Cana.

For Christians, the supreme epiphany is the INCARNATION. Christianity also holds that there will be a final epiphany of Christ at the SECOND COMING, at the end of fulfilled history. See LIGHT.

episcopacy. **1.** The office, or diocese, of a bishop. **2.** The church structure that includes the bishop, priests, and deacon. **3.** The method of governing of the church by bishops, priests, and deacons.

Episcopalianism. The theology of the Protestant Episcopal church. It adheres to EPISCOPALISM.

Episcopalism (Gk., ἐπίσκοπος *[episkopos]*, "a bishop"). The concept that in the governance of the church, supreme, ultimate authority should reside in a body of bishops, not in the membership as such, and not in any one individual such as the pope or a patriarch. This view was officially rejected by the Roman Catholic church at the Vatican Council (1869–1870). See also COLLEGIALITY.

episcopi vagantes. Latin, "wandering bishops." For some Christians, the CHARACTER of HOLY ORDERS is indelible, unerasable, permanent, unchangeable, and never lost. For example, excommunicated bishop continues to have a divine, supernatural sign or mark and can thereby continue to ordain priests.

epistle (Gk., ἐπιστολή *[epistolē]*, "a letter," "a message," from ἐπιστέλλειν *[epistellein]*, "to send to"). **1.** In general, a letter or a writing directed to a person. **2.** Specifically, one of the Epistles (letters) of the New Testament such as St. Paul's Epistle to Timothy. **3.** A selection from the Epistles of the New Testament that is read or sung during the communion services of many churches.

eschatology (Gk., ἔσχατος *[eschatos]*, "the last," "the furthest," "the outermost," "the last time," and λόγος *[logos]*, "the study of," "a rational account of"). **1.** In general, the study of those beliefs associated with last or final events such as death, immortality, a judgment day, heaven and hell, the end of the earth (or an AEON), the final cataclysmic moment of human history, and our human destiny in relationship to them. See also APOCALYPTIC. Roman Catholic theology also includes the study of PURGATORY and LIMBO. **2.** The study basically of three aspects of Jesus' knowledge or prophecies, revealed to humans: **(a)** Mark 9:1ff., at which reference is made to Jesus' prophecies in regard to his presence with the Church from the time of the PENTECOST; **(b)** Luke 21:20, at which the fall of Jerusalem is prophesied; **(c)** Matthew 24:37ff., at which Jesus refers to his final coming (PAROUSIA) in glory. See also KINGDOM OF GOD, THE. **3.** The field of theology that systematically studies **1.** with special reference to **2.**

Some of the basic problems of eschatology: **(a)** Did Jesus expect to appear imminently in full glory after his death or resurrection? **(b)** When will the Second Coming of Jesus occur? Can we determine how soon it will occur? **(c)** Did Jesus himself believe his death would bring the world to its end and immediately lead us to the New Age? See also ADVENTISM; CHILIASM. **(d)** Is the forthcoming reappearance, or PAROUSIA, of Jesus merely a symbolic expression of the cycle of individual and world history?

esoteric (Gk., ἐσωτερικός *[esōterikos]*, "inner," "interior"). Refers to private or secret doctrines (beliefs, rituals) understood and shared only by those initiated into the church. Opposed to EXOTERIC.

Essenes, the. An ascetic Jewish religious, monastic brotherhood that existed at the time of Jesus in Qumran, near the Dead Sea. They are believed to be the authors of the Dead Sea Scrolls. They are believed to have had influence upon John the Baptist, upon Jesus, and upon the Fourth Gospel. Their sect has been traced to a period 200 years before Christ and 200 years after. They practiced a strict form of ASCETICISM, CELIBACY, abstention from marriage, observance of the Sabbath, the Jewish rites of purification.

essentia nec generat nec generatur. Latin. A Scholastic notion based on Aristotelian concepts that "an essence can neither generate another essence nor be generated by another essence." This was used to deny those concepts of the Holy Trinity that stressed that each of the three members was essence but could generate or produce the others.

estrangement (L., *extraneus,* "strange," from *extraneare,* "to treat or regard something as a stranger," sometimes an unwanted and unknown stranger). The act of **1.** being, or keeping oneself at, a distance or **2.** withdrawing and withholding one's commitment and emotions from God's loving Spirit. See also ALIENATION.

eternity/eternal (L., *aeternus,* from *aevum,* "age"). **1.** Everlasting. Of infinite duration. Endless continuation in time without beginning or end. Sempiternal. **2.** Sometimes: having no succession, but existing all at once, referring to an unchanging, timelessly present God.

Eucharist, the (Gr., *εὐχαριστεῖν [eucharistein],* "to give thanks," "to give thanks for a good gift," from *εὐ [eu],* "well," "good," and *χάρις [charis],* "favor," "thanks," "love'; the act of giving thanks or gratitude for gifts given; the feeling of thankfulness). **1.** The SACRAMENT OF THE LORD'S SUPPER (see also AGAPE). Often referred to as the Blessed Sacrament (see SACRAMENT, THE BLESSED). **2.** The consecrated bread a wine that has become the body and blood of Jesus Christ. (Matt. 26:26–28: "And as they were eating, Jesus took bread, and blessed it, and broke it, and gave it to the disciples, and said, 'Take, eat; this is my body.' And he took the cup, and gave thanks, and gave it to them, saying, 'Drink ye all of it; for this is my blood of the new testament, which is shed for many for the remission of sins.' ")

The rite of the Eucharist also has as its scriptural basis the Last Supper of Jesus as found in 1 Corinthians 10:16ff.; 11:23ff.; Luke 22:19ff.; Mark 8:6, 19; 14:22ff.; Matthew 14:19; 15:26; John 6:11, 23, 54–58; 1 John 1:7; Hebrews 7:24–25; 9:11–14; 10:19–22; 12:22–24.

Jesus declares that the bread was his body, that the wine was his blood for the new DISPENSATION (COVENANT). He instructs his disciples to continue this tradition of thanksgiving and blessing the bread and wine as his memorial and in his remembrance (ANAMNĒSIS). In these passages, Jesus gives his "body" and "blood" as food and drink to be eaten and drunk under the appearances of bread and wine. Jesus, in dying, giving up his blood as a suffering servant of God, establishes God's New Covenant. Jesus accepts his violent death as necessary, inevitable, and in complete free obedience to God's command. See also COMMUNION, HOLY; CONCOMITANCE; CONSECRATION; MASS; TRANSUBSTANTIATION.

The Lord's Last Supper has been related to the Jewish custom at a meal—specifically the Passover meal—at which the food and drink were blessed by giving thanks to God the maker, for their presence. (References to the "breaking of bread" can be found in the Old Testament, for example, Isa. 58:7; Lam. 4:4. The father, or most important member of the family, would "break bread" and give up a blessing, gratitude, and thanksgiving to God.) The food and drink were offered as gifts by God to his people and only after an expression of gratitude was the food and drink to be taken. The Passover meal expressed a special gratitude and thankfulness for God's deliverance of his people out of Egypt. In Christian theology, the Eucharist is celebrated, among other things, in thankfulness for Jesus' offering himself up (a gift from God) to deliver his people from evil as Moses had delivered his people from Egypt (and false gods). The Passover meal commemorated the Exodus from Egypt; Jesus' meal commemorated the new spiritual deliverance of God's people through his spirit and remembrance of him. The Passover meal gave thanks to God's redemptive power by which he brought the Jews out of bondage, made them his chosen people, sealed with them a covenant and gave them through Moses a law by which they were to live; Jesus' meal was to be repeated as remembrance of his bringing his people out of a spiritual bondage, showing them the only way to God through him, giving them the message of redemption. The Eucharist has been seen in the context of a religious evolution from Moses' time: In Exodus 24, Moses offers himself as a sacrifice, his blood, for a new covenant of love and the awaited New Age. Jesus also has been seen as fulfilling the prophecy found in Jeremiah 31:31ff., Isaiah 42:6; 49:8, by preparing at the Last Supper for his own death and obediently allowing it as the ultimate sacrifice. Jesus becomes the true paschal lamb, whose blood would save the people of God.

Two polar attitudes toward the Eucharist exist in Christian theology: **1.** The Eucharist is to be taken only as an offering of thanksgiving, a communion service, for our redemption by Christ's sacrifice on the Cross—a praise of gratitude for Jesus' propitiatory sacrifice. The Eucharist is a symbolic gesture and no holy consecration of the bread and wine occurs. **2.** The Eucharist is a SACRAMENT, and as a sacrament has supernatural and spiritual efficacy: When it is eaten, not only are the death and resurrection of Jesus proclaimed, not only is this done in remembrance of him, but the person is spiritually changed and united into the community of Jesus' spirit and body—the Church. When the bread and wine (body and blood of Jesus) are taken, the death of Jesus is proclaimed and accepted as providing salvation. At that moment of partaking, the individual is united as one in the community of one spiritual body of Jesus Christ. Christ himself is present whenever the Eucharist is celebrated. The Eucharist enables the person to receive spiritual grace by means of which he/she can share in the life of Jesus, thereby coming closer to the ideals of Jesus, such as love, forgiveness, obedience, thankfulness, hope, faith, and patience.

The Eucharistic rite is presently, and has been in its long Church history, expressed in a variety of ways. In general, though, its central form remains: **(a)** The OFFERTORY (the offering of the bread and wine; see also BREAD; WAFER); **(b)** the CANON (the blessing of the bread and wine); **(c)** the FRACTION (the breaking of the bread); **(d)** the communion (the giving or distributing of the bread and wine to members of the church community).

In 1 Corinthians 11:23ff. and Luke 22:19, Jesus is said to have requested that the Eucharist be performed for his ANAMNESIS (remembrance). The Eucharist is performed both as a spiritual remembrance of Jesus and as a ceremony commemorating the event. The attempt is to bring into a present reality a past event, "recalling" it, with all its original power and reality. It is the risen Jesus (the Risen Lord) who is the host at each Eucharist (see also HOST, THE SACRED), and the BLESSING is Christ's word showing power and the miracle of feeding (plenty).

evangel (Gk., *εὐαγγέλιον [evangelion],* "glad tidings," "good news," from *εὖ [eu],* "good," "well," and *ἀγγέλλειν [angellein],* "to bear a message"). **1.** The good news ("good message") of SALVATION through Christ. **2.** Any one of the four Gospels of the New Testament. **3.** Sometimes used interchangeably with EVANGELIST.

evangelical. **1.** That which is contained in, or relates to, the four Gospels. **2.** Those beliefs that are in conformity with the Gospels, as in *evangelical beliefs, evangelical doctrines.*

Some of the major tenets of evangelical Christianity: Humans are sinful due to Adam's FALL; Christ atones for the sin of humans; Christ is the only redeemer and savior, Lord and Master; all humans require a new birth, or rebirth, in Jesus Christ; redemption is possible through faith in Jesus Christ; Christ will come again.

Evangelical proclaims a pure loyalty to the gospels of Jesus Christ and stresses the spirit of Jesus working in one's life, in contrast to the ritualism and authority of an institutionalized, historical church.

evangelion. Greek *εὐαγγέλιον.* Used in the New Testament for **1.** the good news (good message, good tidings) of the kingdom of God as, for example, proclaimed by Jesus in Mark 1:15; and **2.** the proclaiming by the Apostles of the good news regarding Jesus' RESURRECTION from the dead at Romans 1:1–5. See also GOSPELS, THE FOUR.

evangelism. Actively preaching or promulgating the GOSPELS—the word of Jesus Christ—usually in the hope of conversion of others or revitalization of the HOLY SPIRIT.

evangelist. **1.** One who brings (proclaims, preaches, teaches, disseminates) the good news of the Gospels of Christ. Usually thought of as one who travels on a mission of preaching and teaching the Gospels, or in general, the Bible. Also usually thought of as one who preaches to convert others to the Christian faith or to be reborn. **2.** The writer of any of the four Gospels; the four evangelists.

evangelists, the four. The authors of the four Gospels of the New Testament: SAINT MATTHEW; SAINT MARK; SAINT LUKE; SAINT JOHN. See also CREATURES, THE FOUR LIVING.

Eve (From the Heb. *hawwah,* derived from *hayah,* "to live"). The wife of Adam, created by God as a helper to the first male and created from Adam's rib, regarded as the completion of the male (Gen. 2:23).

evil powers. Jesus and others in the New Testament speak of evil powers that lie in wait to inflict evil on humans. These powers or spirits are called by many names: DEVIL, DEMON, Prince of the World, Prince of the Power, Prince of Darkness, powers, the Beast, etc. Refer, for example, to Matthew 4:1–11; John 12:31, 16:11; Ephesians 2:1ff., 6:12; 1 Peter 5:8; 1 John 3:8–10; Revelation 13:1ff.

evil, the theological problem of. Stems from assuming three things, only two of which are compatible (sometimes called the *Incompatible Triad):* **1.** the omnipotence of God, **2.** the omnibenevolence of God, and **3.** the existence of evil.

Epicurus (342–270 B.C.) presented the problem this way:

Is God willing to prevent evil, but is *not able* to prevent evil?
Then He is not Omnipotent.
Is God able to prevent evil, but is *not willing* to prevent evil?
Then He is not Omnibenevolent.
Is God *both* willing and able to prevent evil?
Then why does evil exist?

David Hume (1711–1776) presented the same problem:

If evil in the world is the intention of the Deity, then He is not Benevolent.
If evil in the world is contrary to his intention, then He is not Omnipotent.
But it is either in accordance with His intention or contrary to it.
Therefore, either the Deity is not Benevolent, or He is not Omnipotent.

ex cathedra. Latin, "from the chair." In general, acting with authority by virtue of one's position or office. Specifically, refers to the pope's defining or explicating a dogma regarding the faith or morals to be accepted by the Roman Catholic church. See also INFALLIBILITY OF THE POPE.

excommunication (L., *excommunicare,* "to excommunicate," "to cut off communication"). An ecclesiastical censure against a believer whereby the believer no longer has the privileges, rights, and sanction of the church. Excommunication may take a variety of forms such as exclusion from the EUCHARIST (or some of the other SACRAMENTS), preventing a person from worshipping, etc. (see also ANATHEMA). Excommunication is decreed for sins such as idolatry, murder, impurity, loss of faith, denunciation of church doctrine, etc.

exegesis (Gk., ἐξήγησις *[exēgēsis]*, "interpretation," from ἔξ *[ex]*, "out," and ἡγεῖσθαι *[hēgeisthai]*, "to guide"). **1.** In general, a commentary upon, an interpretation, an exposition, an explanation of the Scriptures. **2.** Specifically, that field in theology of systematic study and analysis of the Bible in which specific principles of interpretation (see also HERMENEUTICS) are actually applied to the texts. An *exegete* is one who does exegesis.

Exegesis is closely allied with fields such as theology, biblical history and criticism, archeology, and philosophy. Apart from examining texts for their authorship and authenticity, exegesis aims for consistency of Christian belief and to elicit the true KĒRYGMA of the texts.

Since the early Church, there have been several positions taken in exegesis: The Scriptures are to be interpreted **(a)** literally, as absolute, certain, indubitable fact revealed by God; **(b)** figuratively, as allegories (see ALLEGORY) conveying undeniable truths about human nature and reality; **(c)** anagogically (mystically, spiritually, morally; see also ANAGŌGĒ); **(d)** by *communis sensus* (communal sense of a church); **(e)** by the history and tradition—the "mind" of the church; **(f)** by allowing Scripture to be interpreted by itself: *scripta interpres scripturae* (scripture should interpret scripture)—a position characterizing the REFORMATION; **(g)** by relating the Bible to its historical, sociological, religious, and philosophical setting in order to find its relative truths, as opposed to accepting it as literal truth or as revelation.

exemplarism (L., *exemplar*, "an ideal model"). A view of ATONEMENT held from medieval times that believes that Christ as a perfect, exemplary person serves as a model, stimulus, and inspiration to the minds and wills of human beings so that they are motivated to love, holiness, repentance, salvation.

ex opere operantis. Latin, "out of the work," "the one performing." Refers to the grace of the sacraments coming only from the goodness of the ordained person administering them.

ex opere operato. Latin, "out of the operation of the work." Refers to the efficacy, or grace, of the sacraments when given by an ordained minister of the church, even if his nature is depraved or evil.

exorcism (Gk., ἐξορκόω *[exorkoō]*, from ἔξ *[ex]*, "out," and ὁρκίζειν *[horkizein]*, "to bind by an oath"). The rite (ritual, act) of driving evil DEMONS or spirits out of the body that they inhabit, usually by adjuration, religious commands, spiritual entreaties, and/or a LITURGY. An *ex-*

orcist is one who performs this rite. Exorcists are included in the minor holy orders. There is a book of exorcisms. The content is learned by heart, and through the bishop, an exorcist can receive the power, or gift, of laying hands on the possessed. Exorcism can be used over both animate and inanimate objects. In the Gospels, Christ drove out demons. Christ also transferred this power to his disciples. Exorcism is a fundamental part, for example, of BAPTISM, of the blessing of Holy Water and Holy Oil, etc.

exoteric (Gk., ἐξωτερικός *[exōterikos],* "outer," "exterior"). The public or popular presentation of doctrines (beliefs, rituals) easily understood by laypersons or noninitiates. Opposed to ESOTERIC.

exousiai. Greek ἐξουσίαι, "the powers." **1.** At Romans 13:1–7 and Titus 3:1, used to refer to the external political powers or authorities of the Roman Empire. **2.** The supernatural powers that God has appointed to govern the universe. Originally they were good but became evil and now work against God and entice humans to work against God. (Col. 1:13; 2:15; Rom. 8:39; Eph. 1:21; 6:12).

expiation (L., *expiatus,* from *ex,* "out," and *piare,* "to seek to appease or purify by means of pious or sacred rites"). **1.** The means by which one finds ATONEMENT for sin. **2.** The actual cleansed state of such an atonement for things such as sin, guilt, greed, disobedience, hatred.

Extreme Unction. See UNCTION, EXTREME.

F

faith (L., *fides,* "faith," "trust," "loyalty"). **1.** Loyalty, being faithful, having fidelity. **2.** That which is believed in—the set of doctrines adhered to as in the Christian "faith." **3.** Acceptance of a system of belief(s) as true. **4.** Belief in something despite evidence against it. **5.** Belief in something that cannot be defended by reason but that is accepted even though it is absurd or contrary to reason. **6.** Belief in something even though there is an absence of evidence for it. **7.** Trust in something because of past experience in or evidence for it. Confidence based on reliability. **8.** Trust in the truth or correctness of something that cannot be rationally or empirically supported by that is indicated or presupposed by some form of empirical knowledge. **9.** Complete trust or firm belief in God (or in a person, doctrine, institution). **10.** The awareness and acceptance of a spiritual reality transcending this reality, regarded as supreme, ultimate, and moral. Specifically in Christian theology: **11.** The steadfast belief and trust in God who has revealed himself and can be known. Belief in the revelation of the Bible and the truthfulness, authority, and powers of Jesus and of biblical teachings. For example, it is by an act of faith, imbued with God's Grace (or the HOLY SPIRIT) whereby humans believe that the Bible is divinely revealed, that redemption occurs through Jesus Christ, that God forgives sins, etc. **12.** The wholehearted acceptance by the intellectual and emotional faculties that God extends his love and favor to humans through Jesus Christ Lord and Master. **13.** Hope. "Now faith is the substance of things hoped for, the evidence of things not seen" (Heb. 11:1).

The foundation for Christian faith may be found in references such as: Hebrews 1:1; John 1:14, 3:16, 5:24, 31–47; 6:29; 8:51; 10:38; 11:25ff.; 13:34ff.; 17:26; 20:31; James 2:19; Romans 1:4–5; 3:21–31; 4:24, 25; 6:4–15; 10:3–10, 17; 12:6; Galatians 2:15ff.; 3:2, 5, 26; 5:5ff.; Acts 6:7; 1 Corinthians 15:3ff.; Mark 9:31ff.; 11:22ff.

Some of the variety of interpretations of "faith" in Christian theology: **(a)** A revelation (see REVELATION, DIVINE) has been made of God's will and purpose in the Scriptures. Normally the individual does not receive this revelation directly. The Christian church is the custodian of this revelation, continues it in its heritage and tradition, and interprets it. Faith is the voluntary acceptance of this revelation and the church's proper care of it; faith is manifesting in one's person the WORD OF GOD as seen incarnate in Jesus Christ as revealed in the Gospels. **(b)** The "act of faith" is caused by the supernatural infusion of God or Jesus Christ (see also INFUSION) and/or by God's GRACE. This "act of faith" implies **(i)** acceptance of God's revelation *in toto,* as absolute truth; **(ii)** total submission of a person's will to the will and Word of God; and **(iii)** being inspired by the presence of God (Jesus, the Holy Spirit). **(c)** Faith may be directed toward many things: **(i)** the system of beliefs (doctrines, customs, traditions) of the Christian church; **(ii)** God as an object of worship, loyalty, and obedience; **(iii)** the personality of God as revealed through the person of Jesus Christ; **(iv)** the work of God (Jesus Christ, the Holy Spirit) in history, in miracles, and in a person's everyday experiences; **(v)** the trust that a person's hope(s) will be fulfilled as the will of God.

faith, autopistic (Gk., *αὐτό [auto],* "self-same," and *πίστις [pistis],* "faith"). FAITH that is self-substantiating, self-evident, and intuitively true and certain. No higher authority, experience, or perspective can, or need, corroborate it. The power of revelation (see also REVELATION, DIVINE) is necessary (such as Jesus as the True Light) in order to receive autopistic faith, since man alone is unable to perceive the truth of faith by means of his own natural capacities. According to Christian faith, both revelation and autopistic faith are gifts of God; both are due to the GRACE of God; both happen in a miraculous way. See also FAITH, FIDUCIAL.

faith, fiducial (L., *fiducia,* "trust," "confidence"). Used in APOLOGETICS for that specific kind of Christian faith propounded by the REFORMATION. Faith is the *fiducia,* confidence, trust persons feel in their hearts when being aware of God's forgiveness, through Jesus Christ, of their sins and their continuing sinfulness. The Reformation wanted to put less emphasis on faith as a voluntary, mental affirmation or assent to doctrine and more on individual ways of salvation; less adherence to doctrine and performance of rites, and more on the persons own ability for JUSTIFICATION. See also FAITH, AUTOPISTIC.

Fall, the. The doctrine that ADAM disobeyed God's command and was tempted to eat the forbidden fruit from the Tree of Knowledge. This act of disobedience (see also SIN, ORIGINAL) lost Adam, and all humans succeeding him, a perfect state of existence that God had originally created. God originally created a Garden of Eden, or Paradise, of good, loving, obedient, righteous creatures, all living an immortal life in harmony and love of God. In disobeying God, Adam was expelled from the Garden of Eden and condemned to a life of struggle, regret, sorrow, pain, and death. Once the Tree of Knowledge was eaten from, then Adam and his descendants were to be like God in respect to judging between good and evil but were to have the power to act according to base human will as opposed to God's will. Humans have the faculty of free will whereby they may choose between good and evil, God's commands or Satan's.

Because of Adam's disobedience, humans are liable to temptation—their main limitation; humans have lost their perfection and righteousness; humans have lost eternal life; humans have lost their capacity to attain SALVATION on their own. The restoration of humans was given by God to Jesus Christ, his Son (see also ADAM, THE NEW), who descended from heaven and became human like those for whom he had come to be a ransom and serve as a sacrifice upon the cross, thereby granting eternal life and salvation to humans. See also CHRISTOLOGY.

Humans lost many gifts (endowments, capacities, powers, states) because of the Fall (see also DONUM SUPERADDITUM). But some humans retained the ability to have a conscience; the use of reason, intelligence and intuition; the limited capacity for pleasure, happiness, hope, faith, mercy, compassion, love, and charity. These are often referred to as *natural gifts* (powers, capacities, endowments) that are still present, but in reduced strength, from before the Fall, and are basically related to the natural and moral capacities in humans for fairness, courage, temperance, self-control, justice, prudence, friendship, goodness. See also SACRAMENT; SPIRITUAL GIFTS.

At Genesis 3:1–6, EVE is tempted by the serpent (SATAN) in the Garden of Eden to eat the fruit from the Tree of Knowledge of Good and Evil—fruit that God had forbidden to be eaten. After eating of the fruit, Eve gave Adam some to eat (Genesis does not specify the fruit, although it is usually represented as an apple). At Genesis 3:7, they hereafter realize their nakedness and cover their nakedness with fig leaves: "the eyes of them both were opened, and they knew that they were naked; and they sewed fig leaves together and made themselves aprons."

Fall, the Premundane. **1.** The belief held by Christian theologians such as Ireneaeus (ca. 115–202), Origen (185–254), Athanasius (293–373), Augustine (354–430), Anselm (1033–1109), and Aquinas (1225–1274) that some of the angels fell from God's grace before Adam's fall and due to the same reasons, the main one being pride. **2.** The belief that Satan (Lucifer, the Devil) organized other angels created by God like himself to revolt against God. The revolt failed and Satan and his followers were banished from God's paradise.

fatalism (L., *fatum,* "an oracle," "that which is ordained to happen by the gods," from *fari,* "to speak"). **1.** The belief that God, as all-knowing (omniscient) and all-powerful (omnipotent), foresees and necessitates (causes) according to his FOREKNOWLEDGE (see also FOREKNOWLEDGE, DIVINE) how every event in a person's life and in the universe will occur. See also OMNIPOTENCE, PARADOX OF GOD'S; OMNISCIENCE, PARADOX OF GOD'S; OMNIPOTENT; OMNISCIENT. **2.** All that a person is and becomes is caused by God's rational power (see also LOGOS) operating in conformity with his divine will. Nothing that a person can do will alter that fixed plan. Only that which God has decreed to happen happens, and that which happens is that which God has decreed to happen. **3.** God causes certain events to happen to a person according to his foreknowledge of his/her faith and merit as a believer. These events can then be said to be "fated" to occur. **4.** In general, common sense fatalism asserts that a person cannot in any way direct his/her behavior or destiny, nor that of history. Kismet: "What will be will be." A person cannot help being what he/she is and acting as he/she does. Even attempts to countermand fate are irrevocably set. Salvation thus as a free act of faith is not possible.

Christian theology in general tends to avoid the word *fatalism* because of its pejorative connotations, preferring to use words such as foreknowledge; predestination (see PREDESTINATION, DIVINE); predetermination; preordination. Fatalism connotes to many natural fate (as opposed to God's control).

fates, the. Personified destinies, or powers (such as **Μοῖραι** *[Moirai],* **Κλωθώ** *[Klōthō],* **Λάγεσις** *[Lagesis],* **Ἄτροπος** *[Atropos]* in Greek mythology), or superior, arbitrary, capricious, unfriendly, impersonal, or menacing forces—elements contrary to Christian theology.

fate (L., *fatum,* "an oracle," "fate," "that which is ordained by the gods," from *fari,* "to speak"). The necessary destiny for humans determined by God. Usually a disastrous event.

At 2 Thessalonians 2:8–12, the fate of humans who refuse Christ's offer of salvation is total annihilation and no chance of entering HEAVEN:

"And then shall that Wicked be revealed, whom the Lord shall consume with the spirit of his mouth, and shall destroy with the brightness of his coming: *Even him,* whose coming is after the working of Satan with all power and signs and lying wonders, And with all deceivableness of unrighteousness in them that perish; because they received not the love of the truth, that they might be saved. And for this cause God shall send them strong delusion, that they should believe a lie: That they all might be damned who believed not the truth, but had pleasure in unrighteousness. But we are bound to give thanks always to God for you, brethren beloved of the Lord, because God hath from the beginning chosen you to salvation through sanctification of the Spirit and belief of the truth: Whereunto he called you by our gospel, to the obtaining of the glory of our Lord Jesus Christ. Therefore, brethren, stand fast, and hold the traditions which ye have been taught, whether by word, or our epistle. Now our Lord Jesus Christ himself, and God, even our Father, which hath loved us, and hath given *us* everlasting consolation and good hope through grace."

Fathers, the Four Greek. The Eastern Orthodox church venerates St. Athanasius (293–373), St. Gregory of Nazianzus (329–389), St. Basil the Great (330–379), and St. John Chrysostomos (347–394) as the leading early teachers and scholars of the Christian Church. See also FATHERS, THE FOUR LATIN.

Fathers, the Four Latin. Also the *Doctors of the Church.* St. Ambrose (ca. 334–397), whose emblem in Christian art is a beehive or a scourge; St. Jerome (ca. 342–430), whose emblems are an inkhorn and a lion; St. Augustine of Hippo (ca. 354–430), whose emblem is usually a heart; and St. Gregory (ca. 540–604), whose symbols are a cross and a dove.

Others are classified as Fathers, or Doctors, of the Latin or Roman church. These are the traditional and standard four. (St. Teresa of Avila [1515–1582] is included as the first woman Doctor of the Church.) These four Fathers of the Church were regarded as the foremost teachers and scholars of Christianity and represented Christ's Earthly Church, and are often grouped in Christian art with the four evangelists (see also EVANGELISTS, THE FOUR), who represented Christ's Spiritual Church. The sculptor Bernini surrounds the throne of St. Peter in the Vatican with four Fathers of the Church—two Latin Fathers, St. Ambrose and St. Augustine, and two Greek Fathers, St. Athanasius (293–373) and St. John Chrysostomos (347–394).

fideism (L., *fides,* "faith"). **1.** The doctrine that Christian truth (REVELATION, DIVINE; the WORD OF GOD, SCRIPTURE) is founded on FAITH and not on reason or empirical evidence. **2.** The method of faith is superior to reason (or science) in establishing Christian truth and knowledge. Where reason denies faith, it must be rejected; where reason supports faith, it must be accepted. **3.** All other sources of knowledge, such as philosophy and science, must conform to and support knowledge obtained by faith—they are handmaidens of faith (theology). **4.** The belief that only faith, not reason or intuition or revelation, can prove the existence of God and the divine truths of Scripture.

fides quaerens intellectum. Latin, "faith preceeds the intellect." Best exemplified by St. Anselm (1033–1109) in his *Proslogion:* "I do not seek to understand in order that I may believe. I believe in order that I may understand. For this too I believe: that unless I believe, I shall not understand." Faith is the master; reason the servant.

fiducia. Latin, "trust." In medieval theology and philosophy, an essential item in FAITH, together with ASSENSUS (assent) and NOTITIA (understanding). Specifically used to emphasize the trust one must have that the church is teaching the revealed word of God.

filioque. Latin, from *filius* "a son." The word inserted by Western Christianity into the NICENO-CONSTANTINOPOLITAN CREED in order to support the belief in the Double Procession of the HOLY SPIRIT: "Who proceedeth from the Father *and the* Son." See also HOLY SPIRIT, THE DOUBLE PROCESSION OF THE.

finitum non capax infiniti. Latin, "the finite cannot contain the infinite." This was used to deny the possibility that Jesus as a human finite person could ever express the full capacity of the Deity such as Omnipotence, Omniscience, Complete Perfection, Infallibility.

First Cause. **1.** God, the uncaused being that is the initial cause of the universe's existence. Before this first event, there was either **(a)** no universe, no matter in existence, and God created the universe out of nothing (see also CREATIO EX NIHILO), or **(b)** the universe existed statically without any causal series or interrelationships activating it, or **(c)** the universe was in a state of CHAOS, not infused with his Spirit, Purpose, Will, Goodness, and Love. **2.** God, the uncaused being that is the continual causal ground for any particular cause-effect patterns that occur at any given time in the universe—the cause of the causes operating in the universe. God may be as in **1.**, or he may be involved infinitely in an infinite regress of causal support for all events—the eternally existing ultimate ground of an infinite series.

First Mover. Also *Prime Mover, Unmoved Mover.* **1.** That being (God) that although unmoved by anything else, initially sets the universe in motion. Before this event, no motion existed in the universe. **2.** That being that initiates not only the absolute first movement of the universe but who also supports and maintains all the subsequent motions in the universe at any given moment. See also FIRST CAUSE.

Fish. See ΙΧΘΥΣ

Five Wounds of Christ, the. See WOUNDS OF CHRIST, THE FIVE.

flagellants. Those who flagellate themselves, originally using a flagella, lashing their bare arms and shoulders (also calves, thighs, and buttocks).

This activity is based on the belief that by such scourging of one's body for the world's sins—often done on Good Friday—God's wrath will be appeased. Some flagellants also practice mutual flagellation.

flagellation of Christ, the. Also *scourging of Christ.* A favorite representation of Christ's passion (see PASSION OF CHRIST, THE) in Christian art, based on scriptural references such as Matthew 27:26; Mark 15:15; John 19:1. Pilate had his Roman soldiers scourge and crucify Christ; Christ is depicted naked except for a loincloth, bound usually to a column, while being lashed.

flesh, Jesus as. The concept that JESUS was God become flesh or human is found, for example, at John 1:14: "And the Word (LOGOS) was made flesh, and dwelt among us (and we beheld his glory, the glory as of the only begotten of the Father), full of grace and truth." At I John 4:1–3, there is reference to those who refused to confess that Jesus Christ has come in the flesh. "Beloved, believe not every spirit, but try the spirits whether they are of God: because many false prophets are gone out into the world. Hereby know ye the Spirit of God: Every spirit that confesseth that Jesus Christ is come in the flesh is of God; And every spirit that confesseth not that Jesus Christ is come in the flesh is not of God: and this is that *spirit* of antichrist, whereof ye have heard that it should come; and even now already is it in the world." A twofold implication may be involved here: **((a)** a refusal to admit that the CHRIST or Messiah (see MESSIAH, CHRIST AS THE) has actually arrived to bring in the new age, and/or **(b)** a refusal that Jesus Christ is the deity (God, the divine) become flesh, become as human.

The immanentist concept of Jesus as flesh: God entered into Jesus to the highest extent possible for God to enter any human. (This approach had the effect of understanding the Holy Trinity much as ARIANISM did: Jesus was intermediate between God and Humans (see also LOGOS); Jesus was divine—but of a secondary order; Jesus was a created being and in this sense not identical with, not "one with," God. These doctrines tended to make Jesus superior to humans but inferior to, or less than, God.

The incarnational concept of Jesus as flesh (see also INCARNATION, THE): Jesus was the Son of God and as such was distinct from God the Father. But though distinct, Jesus as Son is *eternally begotten* of God and HOMOOUSIOS ("the same in essence and being") with God. See also CHRIST, THE; DOCETISM; EBIONITES.

flesh, the. **1.** The human corporeal (material) body as distinct from the spirit or soul. **2.** The carnal, sensual, passionate, desiring aspect of human nature. St. Paul at 1 Corinthians 15:50: "flesh and blood cannot inherit the kingdom of God." See also FLESH, JESUS AS.

foot washing (pedilavium). A ritual practiced in the Roman Catholic church, based on Jesus' washing of his disciples' feet (John 13:1–17). Takes place on MAUNDY THURSDAY of Holy Week. Examples: The priest or bishop of the church washes the feet of twelve poor men. The pope washes the feet of thirteen priests (or poor men). Variations occur.

After the meal, Jesus rose from the table at the LAST SUPPER and, as a symbol of humility, washed the feet of the disciples, and at John 13:14 says, "If I then, your Lord and Master, have washed your feet; ye also ought to wash another's feet."

foreknowledge, divine. God's knowledge of everything that will occur in the future of the universe. Traditional Christian theology assumed that during his life on earth, Jesus had divine foreknowledge of all events in history and the universe. Intimations of Jesus' divine foreknowledge is exemplified in events in the Gospels such as his prophecies (e.g., Mark 9:1ff.); his references to the fall of Jerusalem (e.g., Luke 21:20); his prediction of his final coming, the KINGDOM OF GOD (e.g., Matthew 24:36ff.).

Divine foreknowledge is implied by the belief in God's being OMNISCIENT: God knows everything that will happen prior to its happening. God thus knows the results of every choice humans will ever make. See also FREE WILL, THE THEOLOGICAL PROBLEM OF.

foreordination. The belief that all events in human life, and in the universe, are preordained by God. Sometimes referred to as God's *foreknowledge* or *prescience*. See also FATALISM; FOREKNOWLEDGE, DIVINE; PREDISTINATION, DIVINE.

forgiveness. In general, the situation in which someone who has been treated unfairly allows (excuses, pardons) the offender to go free without punishment. This implies overcoming resentment or any claim to retribution. See also ABSOLUTION.

The Old Testament showed the forgiveness of God. The New Testament, according to Christianity, purifies that forgiveness and adds the concept of JUSTIFICATION. Forgiveness is one of the prime characteristics of God in Christian theology. According to St. Paul, God asks for no reparation for the injustices done to him, but instead takes upon himself the responsibility of offering reparation (Jesus' death) in order to have humans return back to him in atoning love and acceptance.

Christian trdition believes that Christ gave his disciples (his Church) the power of forgiveness—the power to forgive sins or to refuse to forgive sins, at Matthew 16:19; 18:18; John 20:21ff. See also PENANCE.

fraction (L., *fractio,* 'a breaking," from *fragere,* "to break"). The breaking of the bread in the EUCHARIST. Perpetuates liturgically Jesus' act at the LAST SUPPER. (Different Christian churches have different methods for fraction.)

Franciscans. Those who are members of the Roman Catholic church holy order (the Order of St. Francis) founded in 1209 by St. Francis of Assisi. The theology of Johannes Duns Scotus serves as the basis of their doctrines.

freedom from bondage. Reference in Romans 5–8 to St. Paul's freedom from the bondage of four tyrants: freedom from the WRATH OF GOD; freedom from SIN; freedom from law (see LAW, NATURAL AND LAW, REVEALED); freedom from DEATH. Paul argues that God has set humans at peace with him through his Son God, and that they no longer need feel or fear the WRATH OF GOD. In this new reborn relationship with God through Christ, humans can perceive that wrath as love.

The bondage of death can be overcome through acceptance of Jesus Christ. As in Christ, so men are adopted sons of God and will never face death, but be in eternal glory in one with Christ. Death cannot separate humans from the love of God experienced in accepting Christ. Just as Christ's love and Spirit are eternal, so we too become eternal through identification with him.

To be free from the bondage of sin means for St. Paul to be a servant of Christ (as Christ was a complete servant of God; see also CHRISTOLOGY), in a life of righteousness. This service to Christ replaces the service to sin; this service to Christ frees whereas the service to sin enslaves.

St. Paul also argues for GRACE that delivers one from bondage to the Law. The Law is the Old Covenant; the New Covenant is that of grace. The Law can never be met; the Law is externally enforced and externally compelling. Grace is a freedom of the Spirit to willingly do the righteous and the good in the name and Spirit of Christ.

free will, the theological problem of. Three ways in which this problem has been stated in Christian theology: **1.** God is all-knowing (omniscient) and therefore knows beforehand as an eternal truth each choice that each person will decide upon, each action that each person will perform. If this is the case, then persons cannot "freely" choose or act otherwise than the way in which God knows they will (and if they do choose or act contrary to God's perfect knowledge, then God cannot be all-knowing). If God knows a person's sins before he/she commits them, and they must occur according to his knowledge, then how can a person avoid those sins (how can a person be said to have free will)? See also FOREKNOWLEDGE, DIVINE; PREDESTINATION, DIVINE; PROVIDENCE. **2.** If God has complete, perfect foreknowledge of everything that will happen, and if he is also all-powerful (omnipotent), then he must have organized with his power all things to happen the way in which he has foreknowledge of them happening. If this is the case, then how can it be maintained that persons have free will and that evil is not caused by God? See also EVIL, THE THEOLOGICAL PROBLEM OF. **3.** If God is all-powerful, all-knowing, and all-present (OMNIPRESENT: present everywhere), then in what way is a person free, and/or the cause of his/her sins? God is all-powerful in the sense that he has control of everything in the universe, is using that power to cause all things—he has the world in his hands. He uses his presence in all things to utilize his power. Nothing goes against his foreknowledge since he is omniscient. He must thus have used his power and presence in things to so order the universe as to have it conform to and confirm his divine foreknowledge. If this is the case, then how can we be said to be responsible and accountable for our sins?

Friends, Society of. See QUAKERS.

fundamentalism. A Christian faith that holds to beliefs such as: **1.** The inerrancy and literal interpretation of the Bible. **2.** The Bible as the complete and revealed Word of God. **3.** The return of Christ at the Second Coming (for some, this is imminent). **4.** Eternal punishment of sinners in hell by God. **5.** Salvation in this life and for the afterlife can only take place by means of accepting the Spirit of Jesus Christ—accepting irrevocably Jesus Christ as one's Lord and Master. **6.** Conversion, as, for example, by baptism, is a necessity in being reborn into the New World of Christ. See also GOSPELS, THE FOUR.

G

Gehenna. Also *Gehenna of Fire* (Gk., *Γέεννα [Geenna],* from Hebrew, *Gē Hinnōm,* referring to the Valley of Hinnōm outside Jerusalem that was used as a refuse dump and kept continually burning in order to prevent pestilence). Refers to HELL, SHEOL—a place of punishment after death for sins committed.

generation (L., *generatus,* "generate," from *genus,* "birth"). The relationship of Jesus as the Son of God to God the Father, and how this proceeds in the context of the Holy Trinity.

Genesis (Gk., *γένεσις,* "birth," "beginning"). The name for the first book of the Pentateuch of the Bible in which God's creation of the world is narrated.

gentile (L., *gentilis,* "of the same birth or race"). **1.** Among Jews, one who is not Jewish. **2.** Among Christians, one who is neither a Jew nor a Christian, that is, a HEATHEN, or a PAGAN.

genuflexion (L., *genuflexion,* from *genu,* "knee," and *flexio,* "a bending"). A temporary bending of the right knee in the act of worship. In some forms of genuflexion, the right knee touches the floor. In Roman Catholicism, genuflexion is made, for example, toward the sacred altar in order to adore Jesus Christ who is present in the consecrated Host, before the cross in certain religious ceremonies, at the *Incarnatus est* when the *Credo* is spoken during the mass. A double genuflexion is often made on entering or leaving a church where the Blessed Sacrament of the Eucharist is present. Genuflexion is a symbol of homage given to the pope, cardinal, or bishop.

Gethsemane, the Agony at. Gethsemane is the garden referred to in Matthew 26:36; Mark 14:32, outside the walls of Jerusalem where Jesus went with his disciples after eating the LAST SUPPER with them. The agony refers to the suffering Jesus was feeling when he took St. Peter, St. James, and St. John aside and said: " 'My soul is exceeding sorrowful, even unto death: Tarry ye here, and watch with me.' And he went a litle farther, and fell on his face, and prayed, saying, 'O my Father, if it be possible, let this cup pass from me. Nevertheless, not as I will, but as thou *wilt*' " (Matt. 26:38–39).

This scene is richly depicted in Christian art and often, following Luke (22:43, 44), an angel is included in the scene: "And there appeared an angel unto him from heaven, strengthening him. And being in an agony he prayed more earnestly: and his sweat was as it were great drops of blood falling down to the ground." The three disciples are usually shown asleep. According to Matthew 26:45, Jesus finds them asleep a second time upon his return to them and says: "Sleep on now, and take *your* rest: behold, the hour is at hand, and the Son of man is betrayed into the hands of sinners."

Gifts of the Holy Spirit. See SPIRIT, THE SEVEN GIFTS OF THE HOLY.

Gifts of the Magi. See MAGI, THE.

Gloria. See DOXOLOGY.

glossolalia. (Gk., γλώσσα *[glossa]*, "tongue," and λαλία *[lalia]*, "chatter"). Commonly referred to as *speaking in tongues*. The exclamations or sounds uttered when under the influence of strong religious impulses (or in REVIVALISM, which encourages this, when overcome by the power of the HOLY SPIRIT). Glossolalia has been part of Christianity since the time of St. Paul, who refers to those who speak in an unknown tongue at 1 Corinthians 14:2. Mention is also made of the "gift of tongues" at Acts 2:4–13. Accepted by some in the Christian tradition as a spiritual gift from God and a mark of CHARISMA. See also PENTECOST.

Gnosticism (Gk., γνῶσις *[gnōsis]*, "knowledge," "wisdom," "insight." When used in the context of Gnosticism, *gnosis* implies a meditative [mystical, contemplative, intuitive] and/or a revelatory [supernatural] knowledge in contrast to knowledge derived from reason and observation). A first and second century A.D. system basically of Neo-Platonic thought based in the Middle East that claimed knowledge *(gnosis)* of the whole of reality and God, a knowledge availale only to its initiated disciples and necessary for anyone's salvation. Regarded as an early competitor of Christianity and in its Christian form considered as one of the early Christian heresies. Some of its basic tenets: **1.** God can be known although God is completely transcendent outside the realm of nature and of ordinary human experience and knowledge. **2.** God's nature can be known by means of a unique knowledge obtained through mystical initiation, revelation, rites, beliefs, practices, discipline. **3.** God is perfect and perfectly good. Matter is perfectly evil. **4.** The world was made by the demiurge, God's created spirit. **5.** There is a hierarchy of powers between God and matter that creates and rules this world since its fall from perfection. (The demiurge is the principal power that is all-good, but not all-powerful.) **6.** The universe's creation is a series of emanations or effluxes from the Perfect God, and humans are one of these emanations, as are angels, creatures, and all existing objects. **7.** God is now totally alien to this world, yet perfectly good, pure spirit, and pure life—states of being innately desired by humans that can be attained through salvation. **8.** Salvation and immortality are received by knowing, through revelation, the true being of this alienated God and the divine source and reason for all things. **9.** A mediator exists (in Christian Gnosticism it is Jesus Christ) between God and humans, who serves as our deliverer out of darkness into the light of the divine.

God. That Being that is considered to be the fundamental initiating and sustaining source for all existence and values. In Christian theology, God is a living, personal, loving, and merciful God, who is master and ruler of history (John 3:16; Rom. 5:8; 8:32; Eph. 2:4ff.; 1 John 4:9ff.). God's purpose is to recreate through Christ a New Israel for God's victory and use. See also GOD, THE ATTRIBUTES OF.

God as necessary being. God's existence cannot have its source in, or be reduced to, any other being or cause. All things in the universe depend upon God for their existence, but God's existence depends upon nothing else for its existence. God's existence is necessary and self-sufficient.

God, the attributes of. Some of the attributes given to God in Christian theology: Father, Creator, Sustainer, Destroyer, Redeemer, Transcendent (and also Immanent), Perfect, Personal, Loving, Merciful, Just, All-Good (Omnibenevolent), All-Powerful (Omnipotent), All-Knowing (Omniscient), All-Present (Omnipresent), Infinite, Limitless, Eternal, Timeless, Immaterial, One, Pure Spirit, Cosmic Mind, Pure Being, Ultimate Being, Being-in-Itself, Being-as-Being, the Absolute, the Highest Good, First Cause, Uncaused Cause, Prime Mover, Unmoved Mover, Immutable, Supernatural, Supranatural.

Golden Rule, the. **1.** Do to others as you would want others to do to you. **2.** Do not do to others what you would not want done to you. Found, for example, in the New Testament at Matthew 7:12: "Therefore all things whatsoever ye would have men should do to you, do ye even so to them: for this is the law and the prophets."

Golgotha (Gk., *γολγοθά [Golgotha],* and Heb., gulgōleth, "skull"). "The place of the skull," referring to Calvary (John 19:17), or Jesus' burial place.

In Christian art, a skull sometimes is shown at the base of the CROSS upon which Jesus was crucified. This signifies Golgotha, which according to biblical tradition was the place that Adam was buried. The skull is Adam's skull, whose sin is now washed away by the blood trickling upon it from the wounds of Christ (see WOUNDS OF CHRIST, THE FIVE).

goldfinch, the. A Christian symbol of Christ's CROWN OF THORNS (the goldfinch eats thorny plants) and his PASSION.

Good Friday. Commemorates the crucifixion of Christ—the day of the Great Atonement.

Gospels. (Probably of Anglo-Saxon origin "godspell" from gōd "god" or "good" and "spell" "a story", "a tale.") **1.** The word of Jesus Christ. **2.** The good news concerning the Christ, belief in him, his Resurrection and Second Coming and salvation for all who believe in him. **3.** The teachings of Christ and the apostles as found in the New Testament. **4.** The history of Christ's life, ways and beliefs as found in the New Testament.

Gospels, apocryphal. The many writings other than the canonical Gospels, Acts, and EPISTLES of the NEW TESTAMENT. They were written during early Christian activity by sects such as the Christian Gnostics. Many of the early CHURCH FATHERS referred to, and freely used, what we now regard as apocryphal writings about Jesus. Apocryphal sayings of Jesus were also accepted.

Gospels, the Four (Anglo-Saxon, *godspell,* from *god,* "God" or "good," and *spell,* "story," "tale"). Good news or tidings concerning the Christ, the kingdom of God and Christ's salvation for all, contained in the New Testament narratives of Jesus' life and beliefs, Matthew, Mark, Luke, and John (see also EVANGELION). A prevalent belief among Christians is that these four gospels cohere brilliantly to present a oneness about the personality of Jesus and the major events in his life and are thus the only Gospels to be regarded as canonical.

The traditional attitude, what has been called the "fundamentalist" (see also FUNDAMENTALISM) attitude toward the four Gospels, and the Bible in general, has been that the Christian faith is unchanging, based on the Gospels that themselves are unchanging and unerring. Practices and the times may change for humans, but the Gospels remain the true font of faith for all times and are relevant in their pristine state for all times.

Gospels, the synoptic. The three Gospels of Mark, Matthew, and Luke (which excludes John). They are referred to as *synoptic* because of their several common narratives of Jesus' life. The Gospel according to John is thought by scholars to have been written probably in the second century, after the other three, and is considered to be more philosophical, spiritual, and aimed at presenting Christ's message to Greek thought of the time.

grace (Gk., χάρις [CHARIS], "graceful," "agreeable," connected with χαίρω *[chairō],* "I rejoice," and from L., *gracia,* from *gratus,* "beloved," "agreeable"). In general: **1.** the forgiveness or mercy of God; **2.** the blessing or enjoyment of God's favor; **3.** a Christian virtue or quality such as the graces of meekness, love, humbleness, forgiveness, humility, charity, tolerance. Specifically: **4.** the love (kindness, favor, blessing) of God unconditionally given to humans as illustrated in the INCARNATION and ATONEMENT (death and RESURRECTION) of his Son, Jesus Christ. John 3:16 ff.; 1 Corinthians 15:10; 2 Corinthians 5:18ff.; 8:9; Philemon 2:6ff., are some of the passages that refer to redemptive divine love, i.e., grace. (See also LOVE.) Christian theology stresses features about grace such as: **(a)** God's love of even the ungodly—those resisting the spirit of Godliness, his will and purpose. **(b)** God's unconditional acceptance and forgiveness of all our sins. **(c)** God's REDEMPTION of us sinful, finite creatures by means of the acceptance of the Gospels and the sacrifice of his only Son. **(d)** God's ultimate restoration of all sinners into his spiritual realm.

Roman Catholicism views grace as an actual supernatural force (power; spirit), obtained from God primarily through participation in the SACRAMENTS. Roman Catholicism connects both faith and works with the receiving of grace (by faith, grace is received and/or by work, grace is merited and graciously bestowed), whereas for most Protestants, grace is received through faith alone (by faith, grace is received and good works automatically follow).

When grace is received traditionally, the following occur: **(i)** Our sins are forgiven. **(ii)** We receive JUSTIFICATION—a new relationship with and awareness of God's presence. **(iii)** We receive a spiritual power that activates our very being and conduct. We often act as if not of our will, but of the will of the divine presence. We are being led, directed, counselled. **(iv)** We become sanctified (see SANCTIFY), acting out our lives from a new moral perspective and spirit, embodied in Jesus Christ. **(v)** We perceive the world around us with acceptance, openness, joy, friendliness, and love. **(vi)** We see the world as a manifestation of divine power, of Christ redeeming the world.

The ways by which one is "graced" by God vary in Christian theology: **(a)** Following the way of Jesus Christ as Lord and Master as found in the Gospels. **(b)** Performing the sacraments. **(c)** Doing good works. **(d)** Living the contemplative life. **(e)** Believing and keeping the faith. **(f)** Receiving grace directly, and unmerited, from God in accordance with his mysterious ways—mysterious to our finite minds. **(g)** A mixture of the preceding.

Some of the "kinds" of grace: **(i)** *Sanctifying Grace.* The supernatural power (specifically the work of the HOLY SPIRIT) imbuing the human soul, bringing it into union with the will of God and Christ, thereby justifying (see also JUSTIFICATION) it and making it favorable for God's acceptance. This grace produces a CONVERSION, a transformation of one's predispositions whereby the one being infused (see also INFUSION) with the spirit of God and righteousness becomes a different person whose personality expresses God's work automatically as a habit (sometimes called *habitual* grace: through this kind of grace, good actions become a habit). **(ii)** *Efficacious grace.* The power, or powers, given to us by God that we make use of in expressing and fulfilling the Word of God. **(iii)** *Sufficient grace.* The power, or powers, given to us by God but which are not being used to manifest the spirit of God. Sufficient grace is given to all humans, even the worst sinners and nonbelievers, in whom lie dormant the powers of repenting and accepting the faith and being saved. **(iv)** *Actual grace.* The power, or powers, bestowed by God to enable a person to perform special activities or meet special situations that contribute to the person's salvation such as: overcoming a particular temptation; making the right spiritual and moral choice; avoiding an evil or sin; loving another in spite of receiving a specific hurt. (The sacraments are especially important in this kind of grace as vehicles for the regeneration of souls.) **(v)** *Prevenient grace.* Grace bestowed on those who are unaware of the Word of God, such as in infants (see also BAPTISM), primitive peoples. **(vi)** *Irresistible grace.* Grace working in a person producing such conditions as good works, faith, righteousness but which do not necessitate the person's final salvation. That final salvation is confined to an elite, or elect, who are predestined by God to a blessed, eternal life with him. See also entries under PERSEVERANCE.

A traditional view of grace (one held, for example, in Roman Catholicism) is that humans can act to ready themselves for the entrance of God's grace. Once having received grace, they then can perform good deeds, or works, that qualify them to receive more grace until, with enough grace, an eternal, blessed life in heaven is achieved. Good deeds must be done with the end in view of attaining God's state of bliss in heaven. With the help of grace, humans can receive by MERIT even more grace. Grace leads to more grace. Grace perfects human nature. Without grace, perfection and completeness of the person cannot be attained.

graces, Christian. Christian virtues such as love, meekness, temperance, forgiveness, discipline, patience, humbleness, humility, charity, tolerance. See also VIRTUES, THE THEOLOGICAL.

Greek church, the. In contrast to the Latin church, or Roman church (Roman Catholic church). Also referred to as the Eastern Orthodox church, or the EASTERN CHURCH.

Greek Orthodox church, the. The national church of Greece, but sometimes used in general to refer to the Eastern Orthodox churches, or the EASTERN CHURCH.

guilt (Anglo-Saxon, *gylt,* "crime"). **1.** The feeling associated with, or that may lead to ESTRANGEMENT; the feeling that one has committed a breach of conduct and violated God's wishes. **2.** The emotion felt in the state of being alienated or separated from God's love, support, and righteousness—the knowledge that one is offending God and is not worthy of his caring love. In Christianity, guilt can only be removed once one realizes that God grants unconditional love and forgiveness through Jesus Christ.

H

hagiography. (Gk., ἅγιος *[hagios]*, "a saint," "holy," and γράφειν *[graphein]*, "to write"). Writing about the lives of the saints (for purposes of reverence, veneration, and prayer).

hagiolatry (Gk., ἅγιος *[hagios]*, "holy," "a saint," and λατρεία *[latreia]*, "service," "worship of," "reverence toward"). **1.** The worship of holy persons or saints. **2.** The invocation of saints to act as mediators with the divine in order to receive favors or blessings.

hagiology (Gk., ἅγιος *[hagios]*, "holy," "a saint," and λόγος *[logos]*, "the study of"). **1.** The study of the lives of the saints. **2.** The study of the history and sources of holy or sacred writings. **3.** A list or catalogue of saints or sacred persons. **4.** A story or narrative about a holy person.

halleluia. Also *hallelujah, alleluia.* Latin from the Greek and Hebrew, *hallelu-yah.* Used as an exclamation or song of praise, happiness, joy, thanksgiving, gratitude, and hope, and can be translated as: "O Lord, save me," or "Praise ye the Lord," or "Praise ye Jehovah."

hallow (Anglo-Saxon, *halig,* "holy"). **1.** Consecrate (see also CONSECRATION.) **2.** To single out for a HOLY, spiritual, sacred, or religious use. Allhallows is another name for ALL SAINTS' DAY. The evening preceding Allhallows (October 31) is Halloween.

halo (Gk., ἅλως *[halōs]*, "the circle of light surrounding the sun or moon"). Also *glory, nimbus, aureole, corona.* A circle (usually) of colored, radiant light surrounding the body and/or head. In Christian art, for example, a round halo is painted around the heads of saints, symbolizing their holiness and attainment of heaven. Christ is often given a cruciform halo as a symbol of his crucifixion. Representations of the Holy Trinity often receive a triangular halo. See also MANDORLA.

hamartia. Greek, ἁμαρτία, meaning a failure, fault, guilt, error, or a serious mistake. Translated as *sin.*

heathen (Anglo-Saxon, supposedly referring to one who lived on the *heaths,* or wastelands). **1.** One who is not converted to Christianity and does not acknowledge Jesus and the biblical God. Used interchangeably with *idolater* (see also IDOLATRY) and PAGAN. **2.** In general, one who is irreligious or nonreligious or one who practices non-Christian customs.

heaven (Anglo-Saxon, *heofon,* "heaven"). **1.** The holy place beyond the earth where God dwells. **2.** The holy place beyond the earth for the blessed dead, who receive immortal life through Jesus Christ.

Jewish thought at the time of Christ believed in several heavens above the earth. At 2 Corinthians 12:2, St. Paul refers to "the third heaven." In Ephesians 4:10, Christ is described as having risen "far above all heavens." At Ephesians 2:6, believers in Jesus Christ do (and will) sit "in the heavenly places." (Also see Luke 16:26; 23:43; Matt. 25:1.) In the New Testament, heaven is a final consummation and state for the Christian.

Heaven is traditionally regarded as a PARADISE, where sin and evil are not present. The soul is blessed and in blissful rest, completely in accord with God's will. God is praised and honored for his ways.

Disagreement exists as to when the soul enters heaven. Some hold that this will come about at the Second Coming (see PAROUSIA). (For example, Augustine [354–430] in *The City of God* holds to the notion of "secret heavens and abodes" where souls await the last judgment.) Medieval theology believed that souls first are cleansed of sin in PURGATORY and then enter heaven awaiting their bodies. Others have held the direct entry at death into heaven (or HELL).

heilsgeschichte. German, "holy history," "holy events." In Christianity, this includes the major commemorations: The INCARNATION, Jesus' birth, his BAPTISM, his EPIPHANY, his fasting in the desert, his overcoming temptation, his suffering for humankind (see PASSIONTIDE), his death (see GOOD FRIDAY), his RESURRECTION, the giving of the HOLY SPIRIT (see also PENTECOST), his SECOND COMING.

These commemorations are based upon historical incidents in the life of Christ in contrast with commemorations having to do with harvesting, solstices, the rhythms of nature (fall, winter, spring, summer), the phases of the moon or the cycles of life and death. Commemorations of important or sacred historical events are traditional also to Judaism as in the Passover (the Exodus from Egypt), the Receiving of God's Commandments, the Sojournings in the Desert, etc. But holy commemorations are often directly dated in relationship to natural events. For example, the occurrence of the Passover, EASTER, the PENTECOST are standardized by the phases of the moon.

hell (Probably N. Ger., *hel,* "realm of the dead"). **1.** Place of the dead after death, where sinners are punished in pain and misery for an eternity. **2.** A world for departed souls. **3.** Place of lost souls. **4.** The underworld.

Hell is variously referred to as Hades, the GEHENNA OF FIRE, SHEOL,

Tartarus. Augustine (354–430) in *the City of God* declares that hell is composed of physical fire. (Hell-fire, worms, grinding of teeth are common inducements in traditional Christianity for CONVERSION.)

Some of the New Testament scriptural references: Matthew 10:28; 16:18; 25:46; Luke 12:5; 16:23; Revelation 1:18; 20:13–15; 2 Peter 2:4; Jude 6, 7.

A commonly believed concept held in the Christian tradition is that the everlasting punishment of sinners in hell begins immediately at death and does not await the Last Judgment or the Second Coming of Christ (see PAROUSIA). Hell has also been interpreted symbolically to mean such things as alienation from God or the way of Jesus Christ, the failure to be saved, the bad results of living a life of sin.

hēnosis. Greek, ἥνοσις, "union." Refers to the union of the two natures, the human and the divine, found in Jesus Christ. Compare with SYNAPHEIA.

heresy (Gk., *αἵρεσις [hairesis],* "a taking," "a sect," "a choosing"). **1.** An error in matters of faith. **2.** The denial of a DOGMA. **3.** An unorthodox religious position that tends to produce SCHISM, conflict, division, or dissension. **4.** A religious belief opposed to that commonly accepted as part of the faith.

Dozens of formal heresies exist in the Christian tradition. Some of the primary ones that have lost out to the present Christian heritage: APOLLINARIANISM, ARIANISM, collyridianism, DOCETISM, eutychianism, GNOSTICISM, macedonianism, manichaeism, monothelitism, montanism, NESTORIANISM, photinianism, priscillianism, SABELLIANISM.

hermeneutics (Gk., *ἑρμηνευτικός [hermēneutikos],* "interpretation," related to *ἑρμενέος [hermeneos],* "messenger," as in Hermes, the Greek god who served as the messenger for the other gods and also symbolized eloquence). **1.** That branch of theology that prescribes the rules by which the Bible is to be explained, interpreted, and understood. Compare with EXEGESIS. **2.** In general, the interpretation and communication of sacred texts, mostly of ancient origin, that appear to be divinely revealed or inspired.

heterodox (Gk., *ἑτερόδοξος [heterodoxos],* from *ἕτερος [heteros],* "other," and *δόξα [doxa],* "opinion," "belief"). **1.** In general, that which is against commonly held beliefs. Often used synonymously with UNORTHODOX. **2.** That which differs from the Bible, or Christian doctrine or faith, hence not orthodox but heretical.

hierarchy (Gk., *ἱεράχης [hierachēs],* "a chief priest," from *ἱερός [hieros],* "sacred," and *ἀρχός [archos],* "ruler," from *ἄρχειν [archein],* "to rule"). **1.** A ranking or ordering of holy beings such as angels. **2.** The organized and structured levels of power (authority, privileges) of a church such as bishops, priests, deacons—the episcopates. When prefixed with *papal* or *the,* refers to the highest levels of authority in the Roman Catholic church such as the pope, cardinals, legates, vicars, and all the sublevels within each.

hiereus. Greek, ἱερεύς "priest."

historical method. Also *critico-historical method.* **1.** The attempt to understand what the authors of the Bible were saying in the context of the ideologies, culture, and imagery common at their time, which were preconditioning them to view and state things as they did. **2.** The attempt to understand Christian beliefs, institutions, practices—in short, the Christian faith—in terms of how they came to be what they were at their time and for their time.

hoc est Christum cognoscere, beneficia eius cognoscere. Latin, "to know Christ is to know his benefits (blessings)." Found, for example, in Melanchon and typical of much of Pre-Reformation and Reformation theology.

holy (Anglo-Saxon, *hal,* "well," "whole"). **1.** Those elements of a religious experience that stem from, or produce, a sense of the NUMINOUS, the SACRED, REVERENCE, VENERATION, AWE, MYSTERY, etc. **2.** Sacred. Opposite of PROFANE. Hallowed (see HALLOW). **3.** That which is singled out to serve God's will. **4.** Spiritually perfect (whole, well, pure, sound). Godlike.

Holy Communion. See COMMUNION, HOLY.

holy days. Also *holydays.* Feast days on which Roman Catholics are bound to attend mass unless excused for a legitimate reason. (In the United States, the six holy days prescribed are: **1.** the Feast of the Immaculate Conception of the Blessed Virgin Mary, December 8; **2.** the Feast of the Nativity of Jesus—Christmas Day—December 25; **3.** the Octave Day of Christmas—New Year's Day—January 1; **4.** Ascension Day, forty days after Easter; **5.** the Feast of the Assumption of the Blessed Virgin Mary, August 15; and **6.** the Feast of All Saints, November 1.)

Holy Father. A title of the POPE.

Holy Ghost (Anglo-Saxon, *gast,* "breath," "spirit," "soul"; also Ger., *geist,* "spirit"). Synonymous with the more current and favored HOLY SPIRIT, the third member of the Holy Trinity.

holy order. See ORDER, HOLY.

Holy Saturday. The Saturday immediately preceding EASTER Sunday. One of the rituals on Holy Saturday: the lighting of the Paschal Candle from the "new fire," symbolizing the new light and new life given by Jesus' RESURRECTION. Often referred to as the *Vigil of Easter,* LENT ends at noon on Holy Saturday.

Holy Scripture. Another name for the BIBLE.

Holy See, the. The SEE of the pope.

Holy Spirit. The third person of the Holy Trinity. A special expression of God's supernatural power that enables a person, for example, to be inspired toward God's purpose, to speak in tongues, to prophesy, to heal, to work miracles, to be reborn, to receive GRACE and CHARISMA, to feel an ecstasy about living, to accept the Word of Jesus and see Him as Lord and Master over all things, etc. See also SPIRIT, THE SEVEN GIFTS OF THE HOLY; TRINITY, THE HOLY.

Holy Spirit, the double procession of the. An interpretation of the Holy Trinity that holds that the HOLY SPIRIT proceeds (derives, originates, emanates) from *both* the Father *and* the Son (see also FILIOQUE). Western Christianity following St. Augustine (354–430) accepted this position, as opposed to the single procession of the Holy Spirit from the Father, which the Eastern Christians accepted.

Holy Spirit, the single procession of the. An interpretation of the Holy Trinity that holds that the HOLY SPIRIT proceeds directly from the Father (and if from the Son, this is qualified by *from* the Father and *through* the Son).

Holy Thursday. In the Roman Catholic church, the Thursday in HOLY WEEK—the Thursday before EASTER. Also referred to as MAUNDY THURSDAY.

Holy Trinity. See TRINITY, THE HOLY.

Holy Water. Blessing of the Holy Water by the priest takes place in a ritual with lighted candles. He forms the sign of the cross several times over salt and water in the name of the true God, the living God, and the Holy God, who is beseeched to banish all demons and evil spirits from the salt and water. The salt and water are mixed. The mixture is used to banish evil spirits from houses and other places. Bottles of Holy Water are blessed on WHITSUNDAY and are kept and used as a cure for diseases and a preventive against evil (spirits).

Holy Week. Also *Paschal Week, Passion Week.* The week before EASTER, beginning with PALM SUNDAY, which commemorates the many events of the last days in Jesus' life. A few of the forms of celebration in the Roman Catholic tradition during Holy Week: **1.** Blessing of Palms, during which palms or olive branches are blessed by the priest and given to the congregation; **2.** the Tenebrae, at which fifteen lighted candles are placed on a triangular candelabrum, and at the end of each psalm one is put out until only one candle is left lighted at the top of the triangle; **3.** the Adoration of the Cross (see CROSS, THE ADORATION OF); **4.** the Blessing of the Paschal Candle, at which a candle is blessed by the deacon or priest, who adds five grains of incense in memory of the five wounds of Christ and of the five spices used at Christ's burial.

Holy Writ. The SCRIPTURE; the BIBLE.

homage (L., *homo,* "a man"). The ceremony (ritual, rite, service) by which a person reverentially acknowledges his/her loyalty and submission to God.

homilaria (Gk., *ὁμιλία* "sermon"). The name given to the many ancient and medieval collections of sermons or homilies (see also HOMILY), for example, those read at MATINS, and the *Book of Homilies* published by the Church of England in 1547 (and a second part in 1562).

homiletics (Gk., ὁμιλητικός *[homilētikos]*, from ὁμιλεῖν *[homilein]*, "to accompany," "to deal with others"). **1.** The area of theology that deals with the methods for constructing, preparing, and presenting a sermon. **2.** The study of preaching—its art and techniques (see also HOMILARIA, HOMILY). **3.** An exposition or commentary upon (discussion of, conversation about, extrapolation upon) a passage read from the Bible. Often thought of as a less rigid form of speaking than a SERMON.

homily (Gk., ὁμιλία *[homilia]*, "converse," "sermon," "an assembly," from ὁμος *[homos]*, "same," and ἴλη *[ilē]*, "crowd"). A sermon (discourse, lecture, speech) given to an audience assembled for that purpose.

homoios. Greek, ὁμοῖος *(homoios)*, "like." Refers to Jesus Christ as Son of God who was *like* God the Father, but not of the same essence, substance, or being with God the Father. A contrast to HOMOOUSIOS.

This view of the Holy Trinity was accepted by the church during the time of Emperor Constantine in the fourth century.

homoousios. Greek, ὁμοούσιος *[homoousios]*, from ὁμος *[homos]*, "same" and οὐσία *[ousia]* "essence," "substance," "being." Refers to Jesus Christ as the Son of God who was *like* God the Father in the sense of being identical in essence, substance, and being with him; Jesus is consubstantial with God.

This view of the Holy Trinity was proposed by Basil of Aneyra and is in accordance with the NICENE CREED. A contrast to HOMOIOS.

honor. The esteem, glory, RESPECT, and worship owed to God as creator and sustainer.

hope, Christian. **1.** Life after death, based on the belief that Christ rose from the dead and that this was a sign (and promise) of immortality for all humans faithful to Christ. 1 Corinthians 15:19: "If in this life only we have hope in Christ, we are of all men most miserable." **2.** RESURRECTION (see also RESURRECTION, HUMAN) of the dead.

Host, the Sacred (L., *hostia*, "sacrifice"). **1.** The consecrated wafer used in the Roman Catholic mass. **2.** The bread before its consecration.

There is a solemn procession of the Sacred Host, for example, at the feast of CORPUS CHRISTI.

hylotheism (Gk., ὕλο *[hylo]*, "matter," and ϑεὄς *[theos]*, "God"). The belief that matter, the physical substance of the universe, is divine; God is material.

hymn (Gk., ὕμνος *[hymnos]*, "hymn," "an ode or song of praise"). A sacred song (poem, ode, lyric) of praise and adoration of God. Hymns have been sung by Christians from earliest times: Mark 14:26; Ephesians 5:19. A *hymnist* is a writer of hymns.

hymnal. Also HYMNOLOGY. Sometimes *hymnary*. A collection, or book of hymns.

hymnarium. The liturgical book of the Western church that contained the hymns of the divine office, prepared for the different rites of the liturgical year.

hymnology. **1.** The study of the content, religious nature, and history of hymns. **2.** Hymns in a collected form, as a book of hymns. **3.** Sometimes, the composition of hymns.

hyperdouleia. Greek, *ὑπέρ [hyper],* "above," "over," "over-and-above," and *δουλεία [douleia],* "servitude," from *δοῦλος [doulos],* "slave." **1.** In the Roman Catholic church, the veneration or adoration given to the Blessed Virgin Mary as the most exalted of all creatures. **2.** A higher and more special level of veneration than DOULEIA (but lower than LATREIA).

hypostasia. Greek, *ὑποστασία* "self-subsistance," "that which gives support to something, "substance." **1.** The position such as in the NICENE CREED that holds that the substance *(hypostasia) and* the essence *(ousia)* of God the Father and Jesus Christ the Son of the TRINITY are one and the same. **2.** The substance *(hypostasia) and* the essence *(ousia)* of the three personalities in the Holy Trinity are one and the same—identical.

This is in opposition to ARIANISM in which God the Father and Jesus the Son were one in *hypostasia* (substance) but different in *ousia* (essence).

hypostasis. Greek, *ὑπόστασις [hypostasis],* "substance," "substratum," "that which stands on its own, or supports itself," "that which is the fundamental ground of something," from *ὕπο [hypo],* "under," and *ἵστασθαι [istasthai],* "to stand," or *ἵσταναι [istanai],* "to cause to stand." The entire unity of Jesus Christ **1.** as three personalities of the Godhead, Father, Son, and HOLY SPIRIT, or **2.** as both human and divine.

I

icon. Also *ikon* (Gk., *εἰκών [eikōn],* "image," "representation"). An image or representation of one who is venerated, such as a saint, Jesus, the Blessed Virgin Mary, etc. Often icons are revered as sacred, and many are produced by monks.

iconoclast (Gk., *εἰκών [eikōn],* "image," and *κλᾶν [klan],* "to break"). **1.** One who is against the worship of images of God or Christ or the saints. **2.** One who attacks ("breaks") the use of any kind of images in depicting and worshipping God or Christ. **3.** One who in general opposes the religious use of images, paintings, sculpture, icons, or any form of art. See also IDOLATRY.

Iconoclasm is the belief that the creation of concrete objects such as paintings or carvings in VENERATION of God must be abolished. (The reverence of icons or artistic objects representing the divine has been, and is, a constant feature in both the Eastern and Western church. The Second Ecumenical Council of Nicea (787) officially proclaimed the right to the use of art in portraying the SACRED, the HOLY.)

idol (Gk., εἴδωλον *[eidōlon]*, "image," "appearance," "idol," "phantom," from εἶδος *[eidos]*, "that which is imaged or seen," "form," "shape," from ἰδεῖν *[idein]*, "to see"). **1.** A HEATHEN or PAGAN god, and thereby a false god or deity. **2.** A representation of **1.** that is worshipped.

idolatry (Gk., εἰδωλολατρεία *[eidōlolatreia]*, from εἴδωλον *[eidōlon]*, "image," "phantom," and λατρεία *[latreia]*, "worship of," "service," "revenue toward"). **1.** Worship of false gods (or a false god meaning not the Christian God). **2.** Worship of idols, icons, representations, graven (carved) images of gods, or of anything not truly God. Also *Idolism*. **3.** In general, excessive devotion to or veneration of representations of God or Jesus Christ. See also ICONOCLAST. **4.** Respect for, and/or the practice of, heathen worship.

A worshipper in any of these senses is called an "idolater." See also HEATHEN; PAGAN. PRIDE is regarded in the Christian tradition as a form of idolatry. Idolatry of one form or another has been recognized as sinful from early Christian times. (See St. Paul in 1 Cor. 5:11; 10:7, 14; Col. 2:18; 3:5; Acts 17:16; Gal. 5:20.)

images, Christian. Traditional Eastern and Western churches believe that religious images (icons, art in general) are important and useful in helping to raise the minds of believers (and nonbelievers) to the spiritual level of that represented by the images. The grave sin is to worship the images themselves rather than allowing them to lead you into an embrace of the highest in humans and of the divine. See also ICON; ICONOCLAST; IDOLATRY.

imago Dei. Latin, "image of God." Refers to man's being created in the image of God as in Genesis 1:27. Contrasted with VESTIGIUM DEI. Luther held that the image of God had been lost in the Fall.

imitation of Christ. See CHRIST, IMITATION OF.

Immaculate Conception of the Blessed Virgin Mary, the Mother of God. The bull *Ineffabilis Deus* presented on December 8, 1854 by Pope Pius IX officially defines this doctrine: "that the Blessed Virgin Mary, at the very moment of her being conceived, received immunity from all stain of original sin, due to the merits of Jesus Christ the Savior of humanity. . . ."

This position was in some fashion or other popularly held during medieval times, although most major medieval theologians, with the exception of Duns Scotus, held that she was conceived in original sin, as all natural procreation is, but was relieved of original sin sometime before her birth. These interpretations suggest that the Virgin Mary had the graces normally received at baptism (and the other SACRAMENTS) imbued in her at conception (or as an embryo). She is the child of St. Joachim and St. Anne.

The Blessed Virgin Mary becomes the new EVE, the mother of the sinless New Adam and thereby is immune from the law of Original Sin (see SIN, ORIGINAL). The feast day in celebration of this is December 8 and is a Holy Day.

The perfect, sinless, pure nature of the Virgin Mary has been held in the Eastern churches since the seventh century.

immersion. (L. *immergere* "to immerse" from *im,* "in" and *mergere,* "to dip".) BAPTISM by submersion, or plunging of the person into water. A method of baptism practiced, for example, by the Eastern Orthodox churches, and some Protestant sects. Contrasted with AFFUSION.

immolation (L., *im,* "in," "on," and *mola,* "meal mixed with salt"). **1.** The coating of a sacrifice with sacrificial meal before its slaying. **2.** The act of killing of a sacrificial victim in a ritual offering. See also MACTATIO. **3.** In Christian usage, the death of Jesus Christ upon the Cross—the CRUCIFIXION. **4.** In the Roman Catholic church, the offering of Jesus Christ in the EUCHARIST.

immortality (L., *im,* "not," and *mortis,* "death," or *mori,* "to die"). The state of not being mortal, hence undying, deathless, and everlasting. Unending life or existence offered to humans by God through Jesus Christ at the RESURRECTION. Before the coming of the MESSIAH and the Resurrection, human souls entered SHEOL (Hades) where they remained in a semiconscious, groggy state awaiting their savior.

Christian faith does not accept that God, who reveals himself, has kept promises to humanity, has made covenants with humanity, has love for humanity . . . would ever allow humans to be annihilated at DEATH, to leave them eternally dead.

impanation (L., *im,* "in," and *panis,* "bread"). The belief that Christ's material body is present in the bread (and the wine) of the EUCHARIST without any change in the nature and substance of that bread. See also CONSUBSTANTIATION.

imputation (L., *imputare,* "to reckon in," from *in,* "in," and *putare,* "to think," "to reckon"). An attribution, implication or ascription. In St. Paul: just as Abraham's faith was imputed to him as the way of righteousness (Gen. 15:6), so the Christians' faith is imputed to them (Rom. 4:3; 9:22ff.; Gal. 3:6). At Romans 4:6, 11: God imputes righteousness. At Romans 4:7ff.; 2 Corinthians 5:19: God does not impute sin but forgives it.

Incarnation, the (L., *in,* "in," and *caro,* "flesh"). God, as Christ, became flesh. According to Christian tradition, God becomes human for the purpose of humanizing mankind with the Christ-Spirit. Also according to Christian tradition, God fulfills his dispensation of sacrificing in

Christ. One of the many scriptural references: Hebrews 1. See also SACRIFICE.

God was made flesh as Jesus Christ, the second member of the Holy Trinity, on the day of the INCARNATION when the Archangel Gabriel appeared to the Virgin Mary and announced that she had been chosen to bear the Son of God (Luke 1:26–38; Matt. 1:18–25). See also IMMACULATE CONCEPTION OF THE BLESSED VIRGIN MARY, THE MOTHER OF GOD.

In the history of Christian art, a DOVE is often depicted hovering over Mary, indicating the moment of Incarnation by the HOLY SPIRIT. See also ADAM, THE NEW; ANNUNCIATION OF THE BLESSED VIRGIN MARY.

Index Librorum Prohibitorium. Latin, "the index of prohibited books." Sometimes referred to simply as the *Index*. The list of books, or general areas, that should not be read by members of the Roman Catholic Church. The Index first appeared in 1557 and is a product of the COUNCIL OF TRENT.

indulgence (L., *indulgere,* "to be indulgent," "to gratify," "to grant a favor or privilege"). A method of remitting temporal punishment due to one's sins, but after sincere repentance. The giving of indulgences as a system of commuting, or remitting, punishments or penalties, allowed in conjunction with CONFESSION and ABSOLUTION. It was interpreted in medieval times as a method of absolving one from guilt or penalty—a way of purification and remission of sins.

Indulgences were often letters of pardon sold by priests absolving the purchaser of sins. The sale of indulgences was criticized and rejected by Roman Catholics who looked upon this as blasphemous even before the Reformers. Martin Luther was critical of the effect the selling of indulgences had upon the everyday lives of his parishioners. He felt this kind of easy pardon, commercially paid for, prevented humans from changing their lives, made them less contrite, and contributed to more sinning.

The COUNCIL OF TRENT reformed the sale of indulgences. Where indulgences are still obtainable today, some criteria such as the following are applied: the sinner must be graced by the SACRAMENTS; the sinner must do specified tasks (labors, works); the sinner must have a true intention to be absolved of sin and guilt.

infallibility (L., *in,* "not," and *fallere,* "to deceive"). **1.** Inerrancy. Being incapable of making a mistake. **2.** Exempt from error (by divine authority, power, or connection). The Roman Catholic and Eastern Orthodox churches have accepted the notion of infallibility in regard to the proclamations of doctrine or dogmas by their Councils or other authorized institutional appointments. Christian tradition holds to the infallible authority of the Bible; Scripture is incapable of error.

infallibility of the pope. At the First Vatican Council of the Roman Catholic church (1870), the infallibility of the pope was equated with the infallibility of the Roman Catholic church: when the pope speaks EX CATHEDRA, "from the chair" of St. Peter, then he is "endowed with that infallibility with which the Divine Redeemer has willed that his Church should be equipped." When the pope speaks *ex cathedra,* what he says is regarded as certain, infallible, and irreformable.

infant baptism. Also PAEDOBAPTISM. The practice of baptizing infants began during the third century and was held until the REFORMATION when sects such as the ANABAPTISTS and BAPTISTS rejected infant baptism and adopted a believer's BAPTISM. (Protestants such as Lutherans and Presbyterians accept infant baptism as do the Eastern Orthodox churches.)

infralapsarianism (L., *infra,* "below," "lower than," and *lapsus,* "a falling," "fall"). Also SUBLAPSARIANISM. Held by CALVINISM: God's decree of election contemplated the FALL as a past event and the elect as already being fallen and guilty when elected. God decreed election (selection) of those to be graced or saved, based upon God's will, wish, and pleasure and not upon a human's faith. Jesus' redemptive powers, his atonement of humans, applies only to the ELECT. Humans are so corrupted that only by the grace of God's election can they be saved. (Contrasted with SUPRALAPSARIANISM.)

infusion (L., *infundere,* "to pour into," from *in,* "into," "in" and *fundere,* "to pour"). A pouring in. An animating or inspiring of. An imbuing with. At Acts 2:17, 33, the HOLY SPIRIT himself "pours out" among humans. (Also refer to Rom. 5:5.) Supernatural GRACE is infused, or poured, into human souls. Also sanctifying grace is infused at BAPTISM. See also CHILD OF GOD.

ingeneracy (L., *ingenerare,* "to bear," "to bring forth," "to produce," from *in,* "not," or "in," and *generare,* "to beget"). **1.** A conception of the Holy Trinity (see TRINITY, THE HOLY) whereby none of the three persons of the Godhead are generated one from the other. Contrast with GENERATION. **2.** A conception of the Trinity whereby the Son and the HOLY SPIRIT are innate (generated from within, inborn) in God. **3.** The ungenerated, self-dependent quality of God the Father in his unique particularity that differentiates him from the other two members of the Trinity. For example, ARIANISM rejects the complete divinity of Jesus basically on the grounds that God the Father could be said to be *unbegotten* (whereas Jesus was begotten), yet both were *uncreated.*

initiation (L., *initiare,* "to begin," or *initium,* "beginning"). The formal rites, celebrations, ceremonies, or teachings with which one becomes a member of the Christian faith and begins the process toward SALVATION. See also CONFIRMATION.

inner light. **1.** Illumination. Enlightenment. Regarded as a result of BAPTISM and/or a MYSTICAL EXPERIENCE. **2.** A feeling that one is saved or on the right path toward salvation. **3.** Belief that humans can have a direct kowledge of God by means other than those of our sense organs. Oftentimes connected to phrases such as "the divine spark," "the divine presence."

This phrase has been used especially by the Society of Friends, or QUAKERS.

in patria. Latin, "in one's fatherland." In HEAVEN. Pertains, for example, to the joys, insights, and blessings to be found in heaven in contrast to those IN VIA (found in life, on the road to heaven). See also BEATIFIC VISION.

inspiration (L., *inspirare,* "to breathe in," from *in,* "in," and *spirare,* "to breathe"). **1.** The divine or supernatural influence upon humans that causes them to receive divine or supernatural truth (see also REVELATION, DIVINE) and qualifies them to communicate it (see also ENTHUSIASM). **2.** The divine or supernatural truth that is received and communicated.

Inspiration implies an awakening, an attentiveness, a quickening of spirit that is unusual and extraordinary. In its totally overwhelming, absorbing, and compelling state, it is often referred to as the DIVINE AFFLATUS.

For example, 2 Timothy 3:16; 2 Peter 1:21 (where "holy men of God spake *as they were* moved by the Holy Ghost").

Instruments of the Passion. See PASSION, INSTRUMENTS OF THE.

insufflation (L., *insufflare,* "to breathe upon," "to blow upon," from *in,* "on," "upon," and *sufflare,* "to blow upon," "to inspire"). The ritual of breathing or blowing upon a person (or thing) to symbolize, or bring into reality: **1.** the INFUSION of the HOLY SPIRIT, or **2.** the INSPIRATION of a new spiritual life, and/or **3.** the expulsion of evil spirits or demons.

Insufflation is practiced at BAPTISM, EXORCISM, blessing of the font, holy oil, and CHRISM.

intercession of the saints (L., *intercessio,* "an intervention"). The belief that the prayers (entreaties, petitioning, mediations) of saints in heaven, or departed souls in heaven, can affect God's judgment upon those alive. Christian tradition has also held that departed souls and/or saints can be prayed to as intercessors, or mediators, for God's forgiveness. See also ANAPHORA; INVOCATION.

Introit (L., *introitus,* from *introire,* "to enter," from *intro,* "into," "within," and *ire,* "to go"). **1.** In the Roman Catholic church, that part of the MASS during which a PSALM with its ANTIPHON is sung while the celebrant(s) and minister approach the altar, and the psalm is read afterwards by the celebrant from the Epistle side of the altar. **2.** In the Anglican churches, an anthem or psalm sung while the clergy enter the sanctuary or approach the altar in celebration of the Eucharist. **3.** Sometimes, a musical composition played and/or sung at the beginning of the Holy Communion service.

in via. Latin, "in or in one's way, path." In life. Pertains for example, to the things obtained in life during one's earthly passage toward that to be obtained IN PATRIA. See also BEATIFIC VISION.

invocation (L., *invocare,* "to invoke," from *in,* "in," "on," and *vocare,* "to call," from *vox,* "voice"). **1.** The practice of invoking the saints (or angels) as intermediaries between humans and God. This was official and popular in the fourth century. (See also INVOCATION OF THE SAINTS.) **2.** The prayers to the Apostles, prophets, saints, martyrs, the Virgin Mary. **3.** Solemn entreaty. The act of calling for (as in prayer) the assistance or presence of God or Jesus Christ. **4.** Also used to refer to conjuring up, or calling forth, demons or evil spirits.

invocation of saints. Prayer to the Saints to intercede on a human's behalf, whether alive or dead, and to thus serve as mediators to God. (See also INTERCESSION OF THE SAINTS). A tradition stemming back to the fourth century of Christian faith. The Reformation criticized this practice because of its belief that Jesus Christ is the only mediator to God or that the individuals can on their own relate directly to the divine without an intermediary.

invocation of the Blessed Virgin Mary. Prayers to Mary can be found in the third century: "Under the shelter of thy mercy we take refuge, o mother of god; lead our prayer not in temptation, but deliver us from evil, thou who alone art chaste and beloved." Invocation to St. Mary can be found in the liturgy during the late fifth century.

ipsum esse. Latin, *ipse,* "itself," and *esse,* "being." Refers to God as Pure Being, Being-in-Itself, in which God's essence is existence and his existence is his essence. Essence and existence are identical in God. God's essence is to exist and to exist is his essence. See also ACTUS PURUS.

isagoge (Gk., *εἰσαγωγή [eisagōgē],* from *εἰσάγειν [eisagein],* "to introduce," from *εἰς [eis],* "into," and *ἄγειν [agein],* "to lead"). The preliminary study of the Bible such as the study of its literary history, before its actual exegesis and defense.

ΙΧΘΥΣ. Greek, *ICHTHYS,* "fish." an important Christian anagram (initialism, acronym, monogram). The initial letters from the Greek phrase: Jesus Christ, Son of God and Savior. Used from early Christian times as an insignia, symbol, or emblem by Christians to designate themselves as Christians (or by non-Christians to designate those who were Christians).

References to fish are found in Christ's parable of the draw-net (Matt. 13:47–49; Luke 5:4–10) and Jesus' calling his disciples to be "fishers of men" (Matt. 4:19).

J

Jerusalem, the New. Also *the Heavenly Jerusalem; the Heavenly City on Earth; the City of God.* Described in the Revelation of St. John, 3:12: "the city of my God, which is the New Jerusalem, which cometh down out of heaven from my God." According to Christian tradition, this new city will be established by Jesus at his Second Coming (see PAROUSIA).

Jesus (Heb., *Yehoshua, Y'shua, Josue,* meaning 'Yahweh is salvation"). Jesus was born a Jew before the year 4 B.C. at Bethlehem in Palestine. He grew up in Nazareth. His mother was MARY. At 27 years of age, he was an itinerant religious teacher in Palestine. Jesus preached that he was the Son of God the Father, that the BASILEIA of God was at hand. This reign of God redeems lost, sinful humans through belief in him. All humans can be converted and saved. The religion that God established in the Old Testament would be fulfilled by Jesus and his church, which is open to all humans. He seems to have preached conversion by faith in him and the gift of God's grace through him. He preached a personal God and one with whom a personal relationship (primarily through Jesus) could be established. God was a God to be loved and completely obeyed in joy and submision. God was a loving and merciful God.

Jesus probably died in the year 30. He regarded his suffering and execution on the cross as a voluntary sacrifice to God for the sins of the world and as a mark of immortality granted thenceforth by God as an expression of his love for all upon receiving the highest sacrifice possible.

On the third day after his violent death, his sealed and guarded tomb was empty. Jesus showed himseslf to his disciples physically alive, although transfigured. It is stated that Jesus also appeared physically after his death to more than 500 people at once.

Jesus left behind him a community of believers who were to constitute his church. His disciples became the bishops of this community, traveling in a missionary fashion, being martyred, and announcing the good news of Jesus, his method of salvation, and the impending kingdom of God. This community is bound together by the belief that Jesus is the Christ, Jesus is the KYRIOS (the Lord), the Redeemer of all humanity by the power of His HOLY SPIRIT.

The Roman Catholic church regards itself as the uninterrupted continuation of this community created by Jesus. Peter was the head of the Apostles and to him Jesus granted the keys to his church. Bishops of Rome since Peter, who is regarded as the first bishop of Rome, carry on the spiritual powers of Peter as popes of the Roman Catholic church—and, according to that church, of all Christianity. This church, founded by Jesus, accepts only Jesus as the Lord, as God, as a Holy Trinity; accepts baptism as initiation into the Church; necessitates the celebration of the Last Supper, the Eucharist, at which Jesus' death is made present physically and spiritually by absorption of his Body and Blood; awaits Jesus' PAROUSIA—the return of Jesus to fully reveal God's judgment, dominion, and salvation for all.

Some of the attributes given to Jesus, and which he seems to give to himself: Jesus has the power to forgive sins (God alone can forgive sins, and since Jesus is God, Jesus can forgive sins); Jesus knows that he is the Master and Lord of all humans and of all divine law; the leader of God's church; the judge of all history; the Lord of all the angels; the only begotten Son of God; the only one eligible to be at the right hand of God. Jesus existed before his earthly life.

The credibility of these attributes given to Jesus is based on his ability to work miracles, on his RESURRECTION, on the incomparable perfection of his life, on his virgin birth, etc. See also BRETHREN OF JESUS; CHRIST, THE, and other entries under JESUS.

Jesus as a Jew. Jesus was born a Jew. Jesus has been considered a Jewish prophet who used the religious thought of his time to proclaim the imminence of the Jewish kingdom of God that had long been anticipated by Jewish culture. Jesus was regarded as a messianic prophet, a teacher, one with characteristics of a rabbi. He healed the sick, cast out demons, related himself to outcasts. Jesus as a Jew grew up obeying the Law. He was a member of the House of David. He worshiped in the Temple. He meditated upon the traditions, theology, and practices of Israel. He was opposed by Jewish officials. (He preached, for example, that the Sabbath was made for humans and not humans for the Sabbath: The Law is relative to what is the highest value to humans.)

Jesus as divine. According to Christian faith, Jesus is diferent from humans not only in degree but also in *kind*. This belief is held for several reasons, including the following: He was born of a Virgin in a supernatural way. He was resurrected. He was chosen to provide atonement. He was proclaimed our Lord and Master. He performed miracles.

Jesus as king. See KING.

Jesus as the Messiah. See MESSIAH, CHRIST AS THE.

Jesus as priest. See PRIEST, CHRIST AS.

Jesus as prophet. At Matthew 21:46, Jesus is popularly seen as a prophet. (At Mark 8:28ff. Jesus is seen through the eyes of the disciples as the Messiah [see also MESSIAH, CHRIST AS THE]). At Acts 3:18–26; 7:37, Peter in his sermon associates Jesus with the prophet of Deuteronomy 18:15. (See also Luke 24:19; John 6:14; 7:40.)

According to Christian tradition, Jesus as a prophet (and PRIEST and KING) fulfilled the New Covenant between God and his people. (PROPHETS, priests, and kings were all embodied with God's Spirit and in many cases were anointed with oil.) Jesus as a prophet epitomizes the highest form of such an office: he brings to humanity the novel, unique, final, and decisive message of God (Acts 3:26). See also CHRIST, THE. (At Hebrews 1:1–3, a difference is made between prophets and the Son, implying a higher rank.)

Jesus of the Gospels. According to Christian faith, the Jesus of the Gospels is not merely a personality in history (contrast with JESUS, THE HISTORICAL), but a divine figure, humanity's Lord and Master, the risen Christ who ascends to God in heaven and has been proclaimed as savior from eternity.

Jesus, the historical. Sometimes *the Jesus of History*. **1.** The attempt to present Jesus as Jesus was apart from the additions, accretions, embellishments of legend, myth, belief, an even later faith. **2.** The attempt to see Jesus by means of the empirical methods of history. **3.** The attempt in addition to **1.** and **2.** to trace extrabiblical references for Jesus, or to his life, and to authenticate Jesus as a historical person.

The many attempts to present a coherent view of Jesus as a human, historical person have taken on a variety of dimensions: Some have stressed explanations for happenings in Jesus' life; others with criticisms of what has been taught about Jesus (especially Jesus as deity or as divine); some with the personage of Jesus; some with his real teaching; others with his inner changes, choices and development; some with his influence upon those around him and upon subsequent history.

The tendency of this quest for a historical Jesus has been to treat him not as an object of faith, not as a member of the Holy Trinity, not as a supernatural agent, but as a human around whom beliefs of divinity grew, and upon whom they were attached. In short, it tended to play down the theological living Christ of the HOLY SPIRIT.

Judgment, the Last. Also *Day of Judgment; Day of the Lord; the Judgment of Christ*. The end (consummation, completion) of the world and of all human history at which all souls will be judged and sentenced by God (or Christ). According to Christian tradition, this end of the world is fixed. God has decreed when it will come. The character of this endpoint, and the fulfillment of the history leading to this endpoint, will be (and has been) determined by the work of Jesus Christ and his redeeming spirit through the HOLY SPIRIT. See also APOCALYPTIC; PAROUSIA.

Scriptural references for the Last Judgment can be found at Matthew 10:15; 18:23–35; 24:43–51; 25:31–46; Mark 14:62; Luke 17:20ff.; John 5:24–35; 1 Thessalonians 5:3; Galatians 5:5; Colossians 3:4; 1 Corinthians 6:1–5; Romans 8:31–39; 1 Peter 1:5ff.

jus divinum. Latin, "divine law." Compare with CANON LAW and JUS NATURAE.

jus naturae. Latin, "natural law." Compare with CANON LAW and JUS DIVINUM.

justification (L., **justificare,** "to justify," from *justus,* "just," and *ficare,* "to make"). **1.** Becoming or being made righteous, just (or in the strong sense saintly), by God. **2.** Setting oneself right or in harmony with God by means of the Christian faith—or the work of the HOLY SPIRIT. **3.** To be unconditionally vindicated or pardoned and accepted by God (by means of his grace). See also SALVATION.

According to Christian tradition, justification produces humans who ally themselves with God; humans who work in a new relationship with the God of righteousness, thereby being absolved from guilt or blame, following the pattern of God made flesh, Christ, in his sinlessness, his total righteousness and obedience to God's will. With justification, God gives a human a share in the divine (2 Pet. 1:4). This occurs when God causes the Holy Spirit to enter a human soul and provide conversion of the human spirit into one that is free, holy, divine, and in essence a new creation (see Rom. 1:4ff.; 8:15; 2 Cor. 3:17). Signs of this rebirth are acceptance of the faith, of Jesus as the only Lord and Master, of baptism and the holy sacraments. (Also see Rom. 1:17; 6:20; 8:10; 1 Cor. 15:17ff.; Gal. 5:5; Eph. 4:24.)

justification by faith alone. Primarily a Protestant view. Often referred to as the SOLA FIDE theory. Good works, merits, penance, indulgences do not produce justification by God. He is influenced by none of these. Held, for example, by Martin Luther (in distinction with SCHOLASTICISM): "faith alone justifies, without any, even the smallest, works." Faith in Jesus Christ alone provided JUSTIFICATION OR SALVATION. Based on the belief in a spiritual relationship or bond between a human and Jesus Christ. God accepts the sinner in sin, while still tainted with sin (not after the sinfulness has been purged). The activity of Jesus through the HOLY SPIRIT begins the katharsis, purging, of sin in the human as a continuing process.

justification by faith formed with love. The Roman Catholic view *(fides caritate formata)*.

justification by grace alone. Primarily a Protestant view. See also ELECT, THE; GRACE.

K

kairos. Greek, καῖρος "time," "the proper, appropriate time." **1.** The appointed time in the purpose of God fulfilled in Jesus Christ. **2.** A significant, critical moment in history. In Christian faith, the presence of Christ in history is the ultimate and unique *kairos*. **3.** The time of salvation chosen and declared by God (Mark 1:15). **4.** The fullness of time (Gal. 4:4). **5.** The final offer of God's loving grace and redemption to all humans through Jesus Christ (Luke 19:44; 2 Cor. 6:2). **6.** The beginning of the Day of Judgment (1 Pet. 4:17; Col. 4:5). **7.** God's complete control over all time and history.

In popular idiom, *kairos* designates a time when conditions are right for the accomplishment of a crucial action: the opportune and decisive moment.

kenōsis. Greek, *κένωσις* "an emptying," from *κένος (kenos),* "empty." Jesus Christ's action of "self-emptying;'; when he became a human—interpreted as his renunciation of his divine nature so as to become flesh (see FLESH, JESUS AS). According to Christian tradition, Jesus "gave up" his place in heaven as God in order to enter human history and save all humans. Refer to 2 Corinthians 8:9; Philippians 2:6ff.

kērygma. Greek, *κήρυγμα,* "that which is preached or proclaimed." **1.** The Word of God as found in the Gospels—Jesus' proclamations to humans that demand absolute obedience. **2.** The preaching of the message of the HOLY SPIRIT. **3.** That which was actually preached about Jesus by the Apostles. A contrast to the quest for the historical Jesus (see JESUS, THE HISTORICAL).

Paul stresses the importance of the *kērygma.* 1 Cor. 1:21; 11:23; 15:3; 2 Cor. 5:19–20). One of the purposes of the *kērygma* is to assist humans in connecting two aspects of Jesus Christ: his Godliness and his flesh; his presence as a Spirit in the here-and-now and his suffering as a human creature.

keys, the power of the. This power includes: **1.** The authority to admit, to initiate into, and to excommunicate from the community of believers in Christ. **2.** The power to remit sin or cause its retention. **3.** The power to admit entrance into God's kingdom. **4.** The authority to use the power of the Christian church as an institution.

According to Christian tradition, Peter is considered the appointed dispenser of Jesus' salvation, the High Steward of the means to salvation that is Christ's church. At Matthew 16:18–20, the keys of the BASILEIA are given to Peter: " 'And I say also unto thee, That thou art Peter, and upon this rock I will build my church; and the gates of hell shall not prevail against it. And I will give unto thee the keys of the kingdom of heaven: and whatsoever thou shalt bind on earth shall be bound in heaven: and whatsoever thou shalt loose on earth shall be loosed in heaven.' Then charged he his disciples that they should tell no man that he was Jesus the Christ." (Refer also to Matt. 10:1ff.; Luke 11:52; 22:29; Rev. 3:7; 9:1; 20:1; John 20:23; 21:15ff.)

The Roman Catholic church believes that since the power of the keys was presented to Peter and Peter was the first bishop of Rome, then this power is passed on in APOSTOLIC SUCCESSION through the popes of Rome. (See also APOSTOLIC COLLEGE.) In contrast, Protestantism holds to the notion that the power of the keys was given by Christ to all the members of the Church and not to a priestly class (see Calvin's *Institutes* iii, 4, 14).

king. Christ as king fulfills the highest expectation of king: He is resurrected in order to rule over humanity; to resurrect them also into a new life of obedience to God (Rom. 6:4–14); to have them share in his reign (1 Pet. 2:9; Rev. 5:10). Christ as king will return in glory to execute a final judgment (Matt. 25:34, 40; Acts 10;42; 17:31). See also JESUS AS PROPHET; MESSIAH, CHRIST AS THE.

kingdom of God, the. God's reign as king over all the world—a world that emulates a HEAVEN, OR PARADISE. Refer to Matthew 5:3; 8:12; 25:34; Luke 12:32; 22:29; John 3:3; 18:36; Romans 14:17; 1 Corinthians 15:24; Colossians 1:13; 2 Titus 4:18; James 2:5; 2 Peter 1:11. See also ESCHATOLOGY; JERUSALEM, THE NEW.

kleronomia. Greek, *κλερονομία*. **1.** The church as the body of Christ. The "inheritance" of Christ. **2.** The general pastoral community over which Christian leaders had jurisdiction. See also CLERGY.

koimēsis. Greek, "a falling asleep." See ASSUMPTION OF THE BLESSED VIRGIN MARY.

koinonia. Greek, *κοινονία*, "communion," "community," "fellowship." The community or fellowship of the HOLY SPIRIT, for example, at 2 Corinthians 13:14.

Kyrie Eleison. Greek, *κύριε ἐλέισον*, "Lord have mercy (upon us)." An expression found in Christian rituals, prayers, and services.

Kyrios. Greek, *κύριος*, "lord," "ruler," "governor." Used interchangeably with the Jewish *Yahweh* (God) in the Greek translation of the Old Testament. Used in the Gospels, by Christians, and as a name of praise, adoration, and ultimate love for Jesus as God.

L

Lady Day. See ANNUNCIATION OF THE BLESSED VIRGIN MARY.

Lady Days, the two. The two feasts: August 15, the date assigned for Mary's entrance into heaven, and September 8, the date celebrating Mary's nativity.

laity (Gk., *λαός* *[laos]*, "people," or *λαϊκός* *[laikos]*, "belonging to the people"). **1.** Used in the New Testament to refer to the adherents, or members, of the Christian community or faith as the people of God. Some Christian faiths accept the function of the whole laity as performing the function of Christ's or the church's ministry. See also LITURGICAL MOVEMENT. **2.** Presently and commonly used to refer to the people of a church, as distinguished from the clergy. **3.** Those who are not members of the priestly class and thus not invested with the jurisdiction of the sacramental powers of Jesus Christ and the Church. Synonyms: *laypeople, laypersons, laymen.*

The distinction between the laity and the clergy can be seen in references to "flock," "sheep," and "shepherd" (Acts 20:28; 1 Pet. 5:34), and "garden" and "gardener" (1 Cor. 3:5–9; 2 Cor. 3:4ff.). The early church fathers reinforced this distinction in their writings, in their preaching, and by their acts.

Last Judgment, the. See JUDGMENT, THE LAST.

Last Supper, the. Also the *Lord's Supper.* The Passover meal, which was the last meal Jesus was to eat together with his disciples (see Matthew 26:17–30; Mark 14:12–26; Luke 22:7–38). Serves as the basis of the sacrament of Holy Communion. (See also COMMUNION, HOLY; EUCHARIST, THE).

latreia. Greek, λατρεία, "worship," "adoration," "servitude," "servantship," from λατρεύειν *(latreuein),* "to serve." A higher level of veneration than DOULEIA and HYPERDOULEIA. Specifically in the Roman Catholic church, regarded as the highest form of worship, paid only to God himself.

law, natural. See NATURAL LAW.

law, revealed. See REVELATION, DIVINE; THEOLOGY, REVEALED.

laying on of hands. The imparting of a special power and gift by putting the hands upon the recipient, to one who is consecrated (see also CONSESCRATION). For example, bishops possess this special power, which they have received in the succession to the Apostles and they can transfer it to those under them who are consecrated. See also APOSTOLIC SUCCESSION. With the laying on of hands, apostolic succession must not break the line of consecrations from the Apostles. The validity of the Roman Catholic church is partly based upon this historical continuity of consecrations. Also used in the rite of CONFIRMATION, in BLESSING, healing, ordination (see also ORDAIN), anointing of the sick, penance, transfer of authority.

Jesus healed the sick by laying his hands on them. So did the disciples. The laying on of hands is associated with prayer (and in some cases also with fasting). Some scriptural references: At Mark 10:16, the laying on of hands is a gesture of blessing. At Acts 6:1–6, it confers the diaconate. At Acts 13:3, it formally dedicates Paul and Barnabas to missionary work (also refer to 1 Tim. 4:14 and 2 Tim. 1:6). At Acts 8:15–17; 19:5ff.; Hebrews 6:2 and elsewhere, the laying on of hands is the rite supplementary to baptism and bestows the HOLY SPIRIT, as in the sacrament of confirmation. At 1 Timothy 4:14 and 2 Timothy 1:6, St. Paul appointed others to take charge of districts by laying on of his hands. At Acts 6:6, the Apostles laid their hands on the "Seven."

lectionary (L., *legere,* "to read"). A book, list, or table of recitations (readings) from the Old and New Testament for each of the days of the year for personal use or to be read at a church service.

Lent (Anglo-Saxon, *lencten,* "spring," or from the Dutch *lenten,* "to make mild," implying the mildness following the harshness of winter). Also *Quadragesima.* **1.** The yearly fasting during the forty days preceding EASTER, the first being ASH WEDNESDAY. Lent is a time of self-denial, penitence, self-appraisal. **2.** Has also been used to refer to Jesus' desert fasting and meditation.

light. At John 8:12, Jesus says "I am the light of the world: he that followeth me shall not walk in darkness, but shall have the light of life." Light is identified with God in a variety of scriptural references such as 1 John 1:5. In Christian tradition, light is a symbol of the removal of darkness and misery. It is also a sign of a divine presence and holiness (see also HALO.). Light is the symbol of goodness, righteousness, and wisdom; darkness of evil, ignorance, and confusion. Light is the central theme at CANDLEMAS. At EPIPHANY, light represents the blessing upon Jerusalem and Christ's Church.

light, inner. See INNER LIGHT.

Limbo (L., *limbus,* "border," "edge," "a fringe"; the Latin *in limbo* means "on the border"). The abode of those unbaptized souls who are excluded from heaven, or from God's kingdom, because they have not partaken of the SACRAMENTS of the Roman Catholic church. In medieval theology, Limbo was a place at the edge of hell. Some views hold that souls committed to Limbo spend an eternity in a state of natural happiness but never attain the beatific vision of God, the highest state desired by humans; the dead deserve neither beatitude nor damnation. (St. Thomas Aquinas [1225–1274], opposing St. Augustine [354–430], believed that the unbaptized dead do not suffer any amount of punishment.)

Limbus Patrum is on the fringe of HELL, at which the saints or the righteous of the Old Dispensation await the Second Coming of Jesus the Redeemer, so that they too may enter HEAVEN. *Limbus Infantium* (or *puerorum*), at the periphery of hell, is assigned to infants who die without baptism.

lion, the. In Christian tradition, a symbol of power and courage. King of the beasts. In Christian art, the lion represents the forces of good, as when a lion is depicted fighting a dragon. The lion represents the forces of evil when seen with a lamb, or human, in his claws or mouth. (The lion has been used to represent the ANTICHRIST.) The winged lion is also a Christian symbol for PRIDE.

The lion, sometimes winged, represents St. Mark (see also CREATURES, THE FOUR LIVING). The lion also is a sign of St. Jerome, having followed him after he extracted a thorn from its paw.

litany, the (Gk., λιτανεία *[litaneia],* from λιτανεύειν *[litaneuein],* "to pray"). The various Christian solemn prayer services. There are special litanies of deprecation, obsecration, intercession, invocation, petition, supplication, joy, exaltation, penitence, etc.

liturgical movement. Began in the Roman Catholic church in the eighteenth century. Its aim is to provide the LAITY an intimate, involved, intelligent, and active role in church worship in general, and in the EUCHARIST in particular. The movement has produced a major change in the vernacularization of the mass and sacred texts. Stresses the nature and value of VENERATION of (worship of and devotion to) God in the spiritual development and growth of humans and humanity.

liturgical worship. Worship in accordance with formal rites or rituals in contrast to worship that does not have a fixed form (such as private prayer).

liturgiology. The theological and historical study of the forms and practices of liturgy.

liturgy, the (Gk., *λειτουργία [leitourgia],* "action of the people," "a public service," "a public worship." In the Epistle to the Hebrews, Jesus Christ is referred to as a **λειτουργός** *(leitourgos),* "a high priest"). **1.** In general, a specific form of public prayer, ritual, or worship service (in distinction from private worship, or less formal meetings such as prayer meetings, etc.). **2.** Specifically, a form of worship for the Holy Communion or EUCHARIST, or mass, or celebration of the Lord's Supper.

Logos. Greek, Λόγος. The doctrine of the *Logos* has its origins in the Greek philosopher Heracleitos and can be found in Platonic, Stoic, and other Greek philosophies. In general, it refers to an immanent, underlying reason or intelligence governing the universe, causing an identity and necessity for all things, which provides the reason for their being the way they are rather than some other way. The *Logos* is expressed especially in the rational faculty of humans.

In Christianity, the word *Logos* has been translated, for example, from John 1:1 as "the Word": "In the beginning was the Word *(Logos),* and the Word was with God, and the Word was God." And at 1:14: "And the Word was made flesh, and dwelt among us . . . ." According to Christianity, Christ was the divine Word dwelling in us through the HOLY SPIRIT (which Spirit inspires us to accept Jesus Christ as Lord and Master). Jesus, like the *Logos,* is the preexistent creator, the incarnated Divine Reason or God, come as the Redeemer of all humanity. (Some, such as Justin Martyr [100–165] believed that the *Logos* was also incarnate in people such as Moses, Socrates, and other great humans prior to Jesus. The early Church Fathers, such as Irenaeus [115–202], Clement [150–220], Origen [185–254], and Eusebius [260–340], prior to the Council of Nicaea in 325, laid great stress upon the doctrine of the *Logos* as being identical with Christ—or another name for Christ. At the Council of Nicaea, the second person of the Holy Trinity was formally proclaimed as the "Son" rather than the *Logos,* and the concept of Jesus' generation from God was decreed.

Lord (Anglo-Saxon, *hlaford,* "bread keeper"). God. The Supreme Being. Jesus Christ, the Savior.

Lord, Jesus as. Paul points out in 1 Corinthians 8:5 that the title of Lord was a common one in the Gentile world. In essence, calling Jesus Lord is equivalent to calling him God. (In John 20:28, Thomas cries out: "My Lord and my God." In Phil. 2:11, there is reference to "Jesus Christ *is* Lord." These and other passages are taken by Christian tradition as affirming the identity of Lord and God, as affirmations of the deity of Christ.)

Lord's Day. Sunday. The Christian Sabbath.

Lord's Prayer. Also *Sermon on the Mount.* The prayer that Jesus taught his disciples and that is used in Christian churches as the ideal and model prayer. At Matthew 6:9–13 Jesus says: "After this manner therefore pray ye: Our Father which art in heaven, hallowed be thy name. Thy kingdom come. Thy will be done in earth, as *it is* in heaven. Give us this day our daily bread. And forgive us our debts, as we forgive our debtors. And lead us not into temptation, but deliver us from evil: For thine is the kingdom, and the power, and the glory, for ever. Amen." (A similar version is found at Luke 11:2–4.)

Lord's Supper. See LAST SUPPER, THE.

love. A feeling of strong, personal affection, the desire for and the promotion of the well-being of others. For the Christian, love is found as the common underlying essential in all other spiritual values (actions, states, feelings) such as hope, repentance, faith, justice, patience, joy, serenity, etc. See also AGAPĒ.

Some New Testament references to love: Matthew 5:44–46: "But I say unto you, Love your enemies, bless them that curse you, do good to them that hate you, and pray for them which despitefully use you, and persecute you; That ye may be the children of your Father which is in heaven: for he maketh his sun to rise on the evil and on the good, and sendeth rain on the just and on the unjust. For if ye love them which love you, what reward have ye? do not even the publicans the same?"; John 15:12, 13: "This is my commandment, That ye love one another, as I have loved you. Greater love hath no man than this, that a man lay down his life for his friends."; Romans 13:8–10: "Owe no man any thing, but to love one another: for he that loveth another hath fulfilled the law. For this, Thou shalt not commit adultery, Thou shalt not kill, Thou shalt not steal, Thou shalt not bear false witness, Thou shalt not covet; and if *there be* any other commandment, it is briefly comprehended in this saying, namely, Thou shalt love thy neighbour as thyself. Love worketh no ill to his neighbor: therefore love *is* the fulfilling of the law."; 1 John 4:7–20: "Beloved, let us love one another: for love is of

God; and every one that loveth is born of God, and knoweth God. He that loveth not knoweth not God; for God is love. In this was manifested the love of God toward us, because that God sent his only begotten Son into the world, that we might live through him. Herein is love, not that we loved God, but that he loved us, and sent his Son *to be* the propitiation for our sins. No man hath seen God at any time. If we love one another, God dwelleth in us, and his love is perfected in us. Hereby know we that we dwell in him, and he in us, because he hath given us of his Spirit. And we have seen and do testify that the Father sent the Son *to be* the Savior of the world. Whosoever shall confess that Jesus is the Son of God, God dwelleth in him, and he God. And we have known and believed the love that God hath to us. God is love; and he that dwelleth in love dwelleth in God, and God in him. Herein is our love made perfect, that we may have boldness in the day of judgment: because as he is, so are we in this world. There is no fear in love; but perfect love casteth out fear: because fear hath torment. He that feareth is not made perfect in love. We love him, because he first loved us. If a man say, I love God, and hateth his brother, he is a liar: for he that loveth not his brother whom he hath seen, how can he love God whom he hath not seen?" Aslo refer to John 13:35; Galatians 5:6, 22; Revelation 3:19.

lumen fidei. Latin, "light of faith." Refers to God's revealing, in a divine revelation, truths of faith that are unobtainable by means of human reason, and/or seem unsupportable by means of the use of reason. Example: the virgin birth, creation *ex nihilo,* the divinity of Christ, the Trinity.

lumen gratiae. Latin, "light of grace." Refers to God's activity of giving humans direct knowledge of the faith that is impossible to obtain by the use of reason.

lumen naturale rationis. Latin, "the natural light of reason," by which humans can gain knowledge of some things around them without the direct assistance of God.

Lutheranism. The theology founded upon the thought and beliefs of Martin Luther (1483–1546), an Augustinian monk in Germany who was excommunicated by the Roman Catholic church in 1520. Some of the principal tenets: **1.** Emphasis on personal faith and a personal, direct involvement with the teachings of the Gospels, as opposed to institutional dogma, tradition, and heritage. **2.** The acceptance of the Apostles' and Nicene creeds. **3.** Recognition of BAPTISM and the Lord's Supper as the two Holy Sacraments of Jesus as means of grace. **4.** Justification by faith. **5.** Salvation as a gift of God. **6.** Belief in CONSUBSTANTIATION.

On October 31, 1517, Luther protested the sale of indulgences by the monk Tetzel and supposedly nailed ninety-five theses to the door of the

Schloss Kirche in Wittenberg. In 1520, Luther burned the pope's bull excommunicating him from the Roman Catholic church. In 1521, Luther appeared at the Diet of Worms and was banned by the Emperor. Luther is considered the first Protestant.

M

mactatio. Latin, "a sacrifice," "a sacrificed victim," from *mactare,* "to sacrifice," "to slay." The act of ritualistically killing a sacrificial victim. In Christian tradition, refers to Jesus' CRUCIFIXION. See also IMMOLATION.

Madonna. Italian, "my lady." Refers to the Virgin Mary. In Christian art, used to refer specifically to the virgin MARY holding the Christ Child, although other motifs can be found with Mary called the "Madonna" such as Mary enthroned as the Queen of Heaven, Mary in the presence of angels, or the Old Testament prophets who prophesied Jesus' coming, or Christian saints, etc.

magic (Gk., *μαγική [magikē],* "magic," from *μαγικός [magikos],* "magician," "sorcerer"). For Christian faith, the word *magic* had derogatory connotations having to do with the seemingly supernatural; SORCERY, conjuration, even NECROMANCY; the arts of invoking the aid of occult powers, demons, or agencies; the illusory and illegitimate use and mastery of secret forces in nature that are not sanctioned by God or the divine.

Magi, the (Gk., *μάγοι [magoi],* "sages," "wise men"). The three wise men who followed the star of Bethlehem to the birthplace of Jesus to proclaim him King (see Matt. 2:1–12). In Christian art, the Magi are represented as kings. They also represent the three ages of humans: Casper (sometimes "Gaspar"), with the long beard, is the oldest; Melchior is represented as middle-aged; Balthasar is a young man (often represented as a black). Christians regard this representation of the Magi as symbolizing reverence for all ages and races. The Magi bring gifts of gold (symbolizing the royalty of Christ as King), frankincense (symbolizing Christ's divinity and priesthood), and myrrh (symbolizing death—his suffering during the PASSION OF CHRIST, and his sacrifice upon the CROSS).

The Magi were probably Jews from other Jewish tribes coming to proclaim Jesus King and offer him the gifts traditionally presented to a king to show allegiance, loyalty, and fidelity. Some Christian traditions believe the Magi were the first Gentiles to accept Jesus as the Christ, the

King. They represent all Gentiles who have faith in Jesus Christ. The Magi were probably Jews of the Dispersion from the East.

Magi, the adoration of the. Celebrated on January 6, by the Feast of the EPIPHANY, when Jesus appeared to the world as the divine Christ.

mandorla. Italian, "almond." In Christian art, the oval HALO that surrounds some representations of God, Christ, or the Virgin Mary. Sometimes it surrounds saints and angels. It is a symbol of divinity, holiness, beatitude.

man, natural. Sinful humans after the FALL who live estranged from the will of God (for which will humans were created by God).

Mardi Gras. See SHROVE TUESDAY.

martyr (Gk., *μάρτυρ [martyr],* "a witness"). One who voluntarily accepts death for refusing to renounce Christ. Martyrdom is usually accompanied by torture, humiliation, mental and physical suffering. At some periods of Christian faith, martyrs were regarded with higher veneration than saints, and those saints who were martyrs, with higher veneration than those who were not. Martyrdom is regarded as the highest form of the imitation of Christ. CELIBACY and virginity rank close to it on the scale. It has from early Christian times been regarded as having the same power to provide JUSTIFICATION and SALVATION as do BAPTISM and the other sacraments. Martyrdom has been referred to as the BAPTISM OF BLOOD. Christian tradition accepts St. Stephen, who died by stoning, as the first martyr (see Acts 7:60). He died praying for his murderers.

martyrology. **1.** The study of martyrs and martyrdom, and/or **2.** the list (record) kept of martyrs and their life.

Mary. In Christian tradition, the virgin mother of Jesus, hence the Mother of God. At Luke 1:43, Mary is the Mother of the Lord (also see Matt. 1:18–25; Luke 1:26–38). Christian tradition regards Mary as The Woman, a Second Eve, at the foot of Jesus' CROSS, which cross is thought of as the tree of Redemption. (It is believed that there are allusions to this concept at places such as John 2:4 and 19:25–27.)

Mary is regard by the Roman Catholic church as the most perfectly redeemed person, the archetype of all those redeemed and of the Church itself. Mary, as perfectly redeemed, has perfection of body and soul. She has perpetual virginity. Pain and injury, which are manifestations of original sin, were absent in Mary during Jesus' birth. Mary was preserved from original sin by means of being given sanctifying grace from the very first moment of her existence (see also IMMACULATE CONCEPTION OF THE BLESSED VIRGIN MARY, THE MOTHER OF GOD). Because of her plenitude of grace, Mary was physically assumed into HEAVEN. She is completely sinless and was never subject to the concupiscence or other forms of sensuous temptation.

The data about Mary's life is sparse but can be found in Scripture at places such as: Matthew, chapters 1 and 2; Mark 3:31–35; Luke 1:26–80;

John 2:1, 12; 19:25–27; Acts 1:14. At Matthew 1:16 ("And Jacob begat Joseph the husband of Mary, of whom was born Jesus, who is called Christ") and at Luke 1:27 ("To a virgin espoused to a man whose name was Joseph, of the house of David; and the virgin's name *was* Mary"), Joseph is the husband of Mary and of royal Davidic heritage. (Some Christian tradition has Mary as a descendent from the house of David and as giving birth to other sons.) No historical or scriptural information refers to her death.

Mary, the Seven Sorrows (Dolours) of. See SORROWS OF MARY, THE SEVEN.

mass (L., *missa,* from *mittere,* "to send"). **1.** The liturgy or worship service of the EUCHARIST; the sacrament of the Lord's Last Supper. **2.** The celebration of the Holy Communion. **3.** Commonly now used to refer to the whole of the Roman Catholic church service of which the Eucharist is the central ceremony. A celebration for and an ANAMNĒSIS of Jesus' life, work, and suffering. A historical event is reenacted representing the belief that once and for all, true salvation can be attained. According to St. Thomas Aquinas (1225–1274), the mass is a representative image of the PASSION OF CHRIST, by which we can participate in, and partake of, the fruits of the Lord's passion.

There are many kinds of Roman Catholic masses: Low Mass (with one priest present), High Mass (with three clergy present: priest, deacon, and subdeacon), Chanted Mass, Presanctified Mass, Dry Mass (or Ship Mass), Requiem Mass, Votive Mass, Pontifical Mass, Private Mass, Parochial Mass, Chance Mass, Mass of the Holy Ghost, Nuptial Mass, etc. The mass, per se, may be separated into forty-one rubrics. The first eighteen are the Order of the Mass. The remainder are the Canon of the Mass. Major periods of devotion are designated by the ringing of bells such as at the close of the Preface (the *Sanctus),* the elevation of the Host, the elevation of the chalice, the Holy Communion, etc.

The mass has two general parts or episodes: the *missa,* the sending out (dismissal) of those such as the catechumens who are not allowed to be present at the consecration of the Eucharist, and *Ite, missa est* ("Go, it is the dismissal"), the dismissal of the faithful.

Scriptural references upon which the mass is based abound. The principal ones: Luke 22:10ff. and 1 Corinthians 11:24ff.

Matins. Also *Mattins* (L., *matutinus,* "of the morning," related to *Matuta,* "goddess of the morning"). Seldom used in the singular form, *matin.* **1.** A service for morning (often held at midnight, sometimes at daybreak). **2.** In Anglican churches, the service of the Morning Prayer. **3.** In the Roman Catholic church, the first of the canonical hours of the Divine Office. Divided into three nocturns composed of three psalms, three lessons, and three responses.

Maundy Thursday. Also *Holy Thursday* (L., *mandatum,* "mandate," from *mandare,* "to commit to one's charge," from *manus,* "hand," and *dare,* "to give"). The Thursday before GOOD FRIDAY, during which the custom is practiced of washing the feet of the poor as a fulfillment of the new commandment, or New Covenant, as found in John 13:5–30. The Last Supper occurs on the evening of Maundy Thursday, the night before Christ died, and is celebrated as a love feast, or a Passover meal. Christ washed the feet of the apostles at the Last Supper (see also EUCHARIST, THE; FOOT WASHING).

mediatrix of all graces. Refers to Mary, in the Roman Catholic tradition, as an expression of reverence for her receptive mediation of intercession and merit. All graces are received through the Blessed Virgin Mary. See also CO-REDEMPTRIX.

meditation. See CONTEMPLATION

millenarianism. See CHILIASM.

meliorism (L., *meliorare,* "to make better"). God is omnibenevolent (all-good) but not ominipotent (all-powerful). Humans must work together with the forces of God in creating a universe with less evil and more good.

mercy (L., *merces,* "hire," "reward," "pay"). Treating the helpless, suffering, and sinful with compassion and forebearing from inflicting due punishment. According to Christian faith, mercy is shown in all God's activities: his creation, his revelation, his redemption of humans, his sacrifice of his only begotten Son. God's mercy is unconditionally given, is undeserved, and is granted through acceptance of the HOLY SPIRIT through Jesus Christ.

merit (L., *meritum,* from *mereri,* "to deserve"). **1.** The punishment or reward that is due to humans in accordance with God's will and plan. **2.** That which humans have earned, or deserve, in accordance with their conduct as appraised by God. **3.** The moral worth put upon a human act by God in accordance with his concept of excellence.

Some Christian faiths put little or no stress upon the notion of merit acquired by good works (see also JUSTIFICATION BY FAITH ALONE). Some also negate any differences in value, or importance, among vocations, professions, or labor (see also GRACE; WORKS, GOOD). The Reformation, for example, did not recognize the notion of merit. The Reformers believed that the goods of God such as SALVATION and eternal life are provided purely from God's own grace and are not earned. As the Reformers interpreted the notion of merit, to earn merit puts an obligation upon God to pay a debt, so to speak, and God owes nothing to anyone or anything.

A traditional Roman Catholic position holds that humans can do nothing on their own to merit redemption, salvation, or eternal life in heaven. The natural powers of humans are helpless in this task without the presence of God—God's grace. It is also believed that meritorious works can produce or earn a growth in God's grace and an integration of the various dimensions of a human life.

Merit, Treasury of. The reservoir of extra merit created by Christ, the saints, and all Catholics upon which the Roman Catholic church may draw in order to benefit those members of the church who may need merit for eternal life.

Messiah, Christ as the (Hebrew, *mashiakh,* "the anointed one," "the expected king and deliverer of the Hebrews"; the CHRIST). Messiah is the title given to a king in the Old Testament. It points to the belief that the king is the blessed and charismatic agent, or presence, of God. God is the only king of Israel, or his people (Judg. 8:22ff.; 1 Sam. 8:7ff.). For example, this title of "messiah" was given to Saul (1 Sam. 12:3ff.), to David (1 Sam. 16:6ff.), and others. It was also given to Cyrus, the Persian king, who for a time was regarded as a means God used to assist Israel (Isa. 45:1). At Leviticus 4:3–5, this designation is given to the High Priest of the Temple. The Jews awaited the promised king whose messianic kingdom would replace the occupying powers and create an independent kingdom of Israel that would rule the whole world. This tendency of thought can also be found in New Testament passages such as Luke 24:21; Acts 1:6. "Messiah" was the Christian Church's early and favorite title for Jesus, as in Acts 2:33–36 (also refer to Jesus' genealogies at Matt. 1:1; Luke 1:32, 69). Another was "Son of David."

Jesus was rejected by most Jews as the Messiah for theological and religious reasons, but Jesus' CRUCIFIXION was the final incident that prevented most Jews from accepting him as their long-awaited Messiah. However, there were early Jewish Christians who considered Jesus as the Messiah, or the Christ, who saw in Jesus the person who would fulfill God's hope and destiny for Israel, and waited for him to do so.

Jesus declares himself to be the Messiah at Mark 14:60ff.: "the High Priest asked him . . . 'Art thou the Christ, the Son of the Blessed?' And Jesus said, 'I am: and ye shall see the Son of Man sitting on the right hand of power, and coming in the clouds of heaven.' " (Also refer to Mark 2:10, 28; 8:29, 38; 13:26. In these passages and others, "Son of Man" is identified with the Christ or the Messiah.) At Luke 24:26, 27 and John 5:37, Jesus appeals to the Old Testament to establish his messiahship. (At Heb. 9:23–38, Jesus is seen in the context of a High Priest in an age of messianic fulfillment and purpose.)

Christians regard Jesus as more than a messiah, more than a prophet, more than a king, more than a (high) priest, more than a perfect human. They believe Jesus also regarded himself as the savior of all humankind, the Son of God, the Redeemer, the judge of the eternal destiny of all humans. See also entries under JESUS.

metanoia. Greek, *μετάνοια*, "change of mind." **1.** CONVERSION to belief in God. **2.** Conversion of a sinner to God through the forgiving powers of Jesus Christ (also translated as REPENTANCE). This conversion is shown in a change of attitude and conduct, and by external indications such as confession of guilt, fasting, works of CHARITY, PENANCE, CONTRITION, etc.

Metanoia is directly related to BAPTISM. John the Baptist preached *metanoia* at Matthew 3:2, 8; Luke 3:7ff. All human beings without exception must experience and practice *metanoia.* At Mark 1:4ff., John the Baptist preaches a "baptism of *metanoia,*" or a "baptism of repentance (contrition; penance)." Also refer to Mark 1:15, where Jesus commands *metanoia* of all: "The time is fulfilled, and the kingdom of God is at hand: repent ye, and believe the gospel."

metaphysics. As commonly understood in theology: **1.** The study of a transcendent reality (God, Pure Being, Being-as-Being, the Being of all beings). **2.** The study of God as that substance (entity, being) that is **(a)** not material and hence has no extension, shape, figure, etc., **(b)** self-sufficient, **(c)** independent of all determination, **d)** completed, and **(e)** the source (cause) of all that is.

metempsychosis (Gk., μετεμψύχωσις *[metempsychōsis],* from μετά *[meta],* "beyond" and ἐμψυχοῦν *[empsychoun],* "to animate' from ἐν *[en],* "in," and ψυχή *[psyche],* soul" The passing of the soul at death into another body. See also REINCARNATION.

Methodism. A religious movement originally within the Church of England, which grew out of a religious club formed at Oxford University in 1729, principally by John Wesley and his brother Charles. (John Wesley believed a Methodist to be "one who lives according to the method laid down in the Bible.")

metropolitan (Gk. μήτηρ *[mētēr],* a "mother," and πόλις *[polis],* "a city"). A bishop who oversees other bishops (also referred to as an ARCHBISHOP or *primate).* In the EASTERN CHURCH, a title given to a major BISHOP in a metropolis, or large city. The name was first used at the Council of Nicaea in 325 and referred to those bishops who were superior to others in dignity, status, and office.

millenarianism. Also *millennialism,* CHILIASM (L., *mille,* "thousand," and *annus,* "year"). A belief held in the early Church that proclaimed that the saints would rule the earth for a thousand years (a millenium) before the Second Coming of Christ. This belief was revived by the ANABAPTISTS and the Adventists (see also ADVENTISM.) Its basis is Revelation 20:1–7.

minister (L., *minister,* "a servant," "an attendant"). **1.** A servant or agent of God. **2.** Used interchangeably with PASTOR, clergyman, clergywoman, REVEREND. One who is duly authorized by a church to conduct religious worship, perpetuate the faith, enforce and administer church policy, and contribute to the spiritual serenity and growth of its adherents.

miracle (L., *miraculum,* from *[mirari],* "to wonder"). **1.** An event brought about by God that is unusual or extraordinary, not like the common events he brings about. **2.** An event brought about by God's suspending, or causing a deviation of, the laws of nature in order to produce some condition beneficial to humans. Miracles have been believed to be essential as evidence of the divine or the supernatural. They have been seen as necessary for religious claims and faith. A religion with miracles in it has been regarded as superior to one without miracles. Miracles coupled with divine revelation have been seen as providing the stamp of divine legitimacy, authority, and sanction.

miracles of Jesus, the. Jesus is connected in the New Testament with the performance of over thirty miracles, all of them designating for Christians his divine powers. (The Apostles are also credited with the ability to perform miracles such as healing. Refer to, for example, Acts 3:6–20 where Peter makes a lame man walk, Acts 6:8 where Stephen performs miracles. Acts 8:6 where Philip performs miracles. At Acts 19:11, "God wrought special miracles by the hands of Paul." At Luke 9:1–2, Jesus gives his disciples power over devils and healing powers: "Then he called his twelve disciples together, and gave them power and authority over all devils, and to cure diseases. And he sent them to preach the kingdom of God, and to heal the sick.")

Jesus' miracles may be classified into seven categories: **1.** *The three miracles of raising the dead.* For example, at John 11:32–44, Jesus raises Lazarus at Bethany, who had been dead for four days; at Luke 7:11–16, Jesus raises the only son of a widow at Nain, at the moment they were putting him in the grave; at Matthew 9:18–26, Mark 5:22–43, and Luke 8:41–56, Jesus raises the daughter of Jairus, the leader of the synagogue at Capernaum. **2.** The four *miracles of exorcising devils.* For example, at Mark 1:23–26 and Luke 4:33–37, Jesus exorcises a man with an unclean spirit. **3.** The seventeen *miracles of healing.* For example, at Matthew 8:2–4, Mark 1:40–45, and Luke 5:13–16, Jesus heals a man of leprosy near Chorazin; at Matthew 9:27–31, Jesus restores sight to two men at Capernaum. **4.** The six *miracles of food,* such as in John 2:1–11 where at Cana, at a marriage feast, Jesus converts the water into wine; Matthew 14:15–21; Mark 6:35–44; Luke 9:12–17; John 6:5–14 where Jesus at Decapolis feeds 5,000 people from a loaf of bread; Luke 5:1–11 where Peter's net is filled with fish; and John 21:6–14 where Jesus appears after his Resurrection at the Sea of Galilee (also referred to as the Sea of Tiberias) and performs a second miraculous draught of fishes. **5.** The two *miracles of judgment,* such as in Matthew 21:18–21 and Mark 11:12–14 where Jesus causes the fig tree to wither. **6.** The three miracles of deliverance such as in Matthew 14:28–33, Mark 6:45–52; and John 6:16–21 where Jesus walks on the sea and saves Peter who tries to do the same; Matthew 8:23–27; Mark 4:37–41, and Luke 8:22–25 where the wind and sea obey Jesus' command. **7.** The seven *miracles attesting to Jesus' divini-*

ty, such as in Matthew 17:1–14, Mark 9:1–14, and Luke 9:28–37 where Jesus is transfigured; Matthew 28:2–10 and Mark 16:4–20 where Jesus is resurrected at the Garden of Joseph; Luke 24:50–51 and Acts 1:6–12 where Jesus ascends into Heaven. (Also refer to: Matt. 2:1–9; 3:16–17; 8:5–13; 9:1–8, 20–23; 12:9–14, 28; 15:17, 27, 21–28, 32–39; 17:14–21; 20:29–34; 27:45–53; Mark 1:9–12; 2:3–12; 3:1–5; 5:1–20, 25–34; 7:24–30, 32–37; 8:1–10, 22–26; 9:14–29, 39; 10:46–52; Luke 3:21–23; 5:17–26; 6:6–10; 7:2–10; 8:26–39; 43–48; 9:37–43; 13:11–17; 14:1–6; 17:11–19; 18:35–43; 22:50–51; 23:8; John 3:2; 4:46–54; 5:1–16, 36; 6:2; 9:1–7; 10:37, 41; 12:28–30; 14:11; Acts 2:22; 4:16; 8:6; 14:3; Rom. 15:19; 1 Cor. 12:10, 29; Gal. 3:5; Heb. 2:4.)

Three Greek words in the New Testament have been translated as "miracle," or put into the context of miraculous activity: **(a)** *δύναμεις (dynameis),* "powers," reflecting the total power of God; **(b)** *τέρατα (terata),* "wonders," reflecting the unusualness of the phenomena; and **(c)** *σημεῖα (sēmeia),* "signs," "indications," reflecting the ability to do extraordinary feats in the name of God (or as in the case of the Disciples, the name of Christ).

Jesus is often reluctant to perform miracles or give signs of his special powers. At Matthew 16:4 (and John 4:48 and other places), Jesus utters a warning against looking for miracles or signs of divinity. "A wicked and adulterous generation seeketh after a sign; and there shall be no sign given unto it, but the sign of the prophet Jonas. And he left them, and departed." At Matthew 24:24, he warns against the pretense of miraculous powers: "For there shall arise false Christs, and false prophets, and shall shew great signs and wonders; insomuch that, if it were possible, they shall deceive the very elect." At Revelation 13:14, miracles are one of the signs of the apocalyptic Beast and at 16:14 the "spirits of devils" work miracles to seduce humans against God.

missal (L., *missalis,* from *missa,* "mass"). The book that contains what is said, sung, or chanted at the mass. There are entries for every day of the year.

mission (L., *missum,* from *mittere,* "to send"). The preaching of the Word of God—the Bible. Often used synonymously with EVANGELISM. Christians regard themselves as God's instruments for his mission, for his preaching, as in John 3:16–18; Acts 2:17; 2 Thessalonians 2:2ff.

missionary movement. Devotes its attention to the ways in which Jesus Christ's saving spirit can bring enlightenment and benefit to all peoples.

mitre. Also *miter* (Gk., *μίτρα [mitra],* "turban," "headband"). The official and formal headdress of a BISHOP, used since about 1000. (In Judaism, it was the headdress of the High Priest.) There are various shapes. Often two long, fringed lappets hang at the back. It is also adorned with gold and precious stones. Used as an insignia of religious rank. See also TIARA.

modalism (l., *modus,* "form," "mode," "manner"). **1.** An early belief about the Holy Trinity that stresses the oneness or unity of the Father, Son, and Holy Spirit. God is one and of one substance. The three names of Father, Son, and Holy Spirit are manifestations of that one, unitary substance; they are adjectives differentiating the one unique being or substance, God. Also referred to as PATRIPASSIANISM. **2.** A belief in the Holy Trinity formulated in the second century that holds: that at the INCARNATION God completely entered into the being of Christ; that God entered the Virgin Mary's womb and appeared as her son; that God himself suffered on the cross and died and resurrected himself.

monarchianism. Also *monarchism.* A heretical Christian group in the second and third centuries who held that the Godhead was composed of two entities: the Father and the Son (the Spirit of Melchizedek). See also BINITARIANISM.

monastery (Gk., *μοναστήριον [monastērion],* "monastery"). The buildings and habitat for men (monks) under religious vows, who practice some form of MONASTICISM.

monasticism. Also *monachism* (Gk., *μοναστής [monastēs],* "monk," "a solitary," from *μονάζειν [monazein],* "to be alone," "to live in solitude," from *μόνος [monos],* "alone"). **1.** The solitary life devoted to God. **2.** The life of poverty devoted to God. **3.** The attempt to imitate the life of Christ (see CHRIST, IMITATION OF). **4.** The surrender of all personality and human will to the personality and will of God. **5.** The surrender of all sexual practices. Seeks liberation from all human life passions. **6.** The attempt to seek perfection and, symbolically, the unity and simplicity of God's being. **7.** The life, practices, and beliefs of the occupants of a MONASTERY who are secluded from temporal, secular affairs and devote themselves communally to spiritual and religious pursuits under a superior such as an ABBOT OR ABBESS. *Monastics* are often thought of as recluses. They are celibates.

monograms of Christ (Gk., *μόνος [monos],* "single," and *γράμμα [gramma],* "letter"). Many characters, ciphers, or abbreviations composed of one or more letters exist to serve as signs of Christ or Christianity. Some: **1.** I.N.R.I. is the initialism for the Latin, *"Iesus Nazarenus Rex Iudaeorum"* ("Jesus of Nazarus, King of the Jews") which, according to John 19:19–22, Pilate had written on Jesus' CROSS. **2.** *IC XC* are the first and last letters of the Greek for Jesus *(IC)* and Christ *(XC)*. (The *C* is the Byzantine way of making the *S* or *σίγμα [sigma].* **3.** *IHS* or *IHC* are the first three letters of the Greek word for Jesus: ΙΗΣOUS *(IHSOUS* or *IHCOUC).* 4. I.H.S., which stands for the Latin, *Iesus Hominum Salvator"* ("Jesus, Savior of Humankind"). **5.** ΙΧΘΥΣ, meaning "fish" in Greek and an anagram for Ἰησούς Χριστός Θεός υἱός Σωτήρ *(Iēsous Christos Theos Sâotâer),* "Jesus Christ Son of God and Savior" (see also ΙΧΘΥΣ). **6.** *XP* are the first two letters of the Greek word for Christ *(XPISTOS)*. This is the CHI-RHO symbol and often combined to form a cross: ☧ **7.** AΩ are the first and last letters of the Greek alphabet, ALPHA AND OMEGA, representing Christ as the beginning and the end of all things (Rev. 1:8: "I am Alpha and Omega, the first and the last. . .").

monophysitism (Gk., *μόνος [monos]*, "one," "single," and *φύσις [physis]*, "nature"). **1.** The belief that the union (see also HĒNOSIS) of Jesus' two natures, the human and the divine, syncretically produced a unique, single divine being or nature. **2.** The belief that Christ had but one united and single nature: divine and human, which constituted one and only one composite nature, or being. Contrasted with DYOPHYSITISM.

monotheism (Gk., *μόνος [monos]*, "one," "single," "alone," "one-and-only," and *Θεός [theos]*, "God"). The belief that there is one and only one God.

monothelitism. See DYOTHELETISM.

mortal sin. See SIN, MORTAL.

mortification (L., *mortificare*, "to mortify," from *mors*, "death" and *ficare*, "to make"). **1.** The subjection of desires, passions, appetites by means of abstinence, penance, renouncement, etc. **2.** The deadening or eliminating of carnality, attachments, affections from one's life by means such as religious discipline. **3.** The state of utter humility and humbleness—to the point of humiliation—in the act of glorifying God. Associated with extreme forms of ASCETISICM; MONASTICISM. **4.** In its strong sense, associated with the torturing of, or injury upon, the body as an illustration of one's religious devotion and subservience.

Mother of God. Refers to the Blessed Virgin Mary as the mother of Jesus Christ, the Son of God. In early Christian tradition, the divine LOGOS was begotten in MARY.

mover, prime. See FIRST MOVER.

mystery (Gk., *μυστήριον [mystērion]*, "mystery," from *μύστης [mystēs]*, "one initiated into the mysteries"). **1.** A religious rite (worship, ritual, ceremony, liturgy) to which only the initiated may be admitted, and of which only the privileged may partake. Regarded as profound, solemn, sacred, and not for public display to nonbelievers or those not confirmed. **2.** A sacrament such as the EUCHARIST, bearing a religious truth basically beyond human comprehension. **3.** The efficacy of the Holy Spirit (or Christian faith, or the liturgy, or sacred objects) upon the human spirit. **4.** The very written words of the Bible and especially the New Testament (in this sense, refers to an ineffable experience and acceptance of God's eternal truths and demands revealed in Scripture).

mystery religions. In Greek religions, a mystery is a secret ritual (rite, initiation, password) by which a person receives a special kind of divine experience and eventually an immortal life as possessed by the gods; one becomes as a god. In the Gospels, Jesus Christ is spoken of as the *mystery* of God—the means, medium, the way to the divine realm of God.

The primary motive of the Greek mystery religions was to release one from mundane existence—from the pain, suffering, and limitations of ordinary human existence—into a divine, euphoric existence of pure bliss, harmony, and immortality. Mystery religions usually contained a long period of initiation that included systems of purification, or katharsis, after which one rose into the sphere of immortal divinity. (Some of the Church Fathers such as Clement of Alexandria [150–220] and Origen [185–254] believed Christianity to be a superior, newer, and ultimate form of earlier mystery religions.)

mystical experience. **1.** The enraptured and ineffable state of union with a higher reality (God). **2.** The ecstatic identification of the self with the totality of all things (God) expressed by such phrases as "The All is One and The One is All." The mystical experience may be a contemplative union or it may be a state of pure overwhelming feeling.

mystical intuition. Where *mystical intuition* is not used synonymously with MYSTICAL EXPERIENCE, it is used to mean that latent or active faculty of the mind by which, and only by which, a knowledge of a higher reality (God) is disclosed (revealed, perceived).

mysticism (Gk., *μυστήριον [mystērion],* from *μύστης [mystēs],* "one initiated in the mysteries or secrets of a truer reality"). **1.** The feeling of utter dependence upon a higher reality that is the source of all things. **2.** The ecstatic feeling of union or oneness with God. **3.** A confrontation with a Divine Presence or the sense of its presence. **4.** The sense that all things are signs (symbols) of the creative activity of a higher reality attempting communication with man's consciousness. **5.** The belief that the divine essence, or God, can be known by means of an immediate intuition or insight (or even revelation) quite different from the knowledge procured by the faculty of reason or ordinary sensation. **6.** Belief in direct communication with the divine reality, or God, and a knowledge of spiritual and godlike things that are unobtainable by any other natural means or powers. **7.** Any apprehension of a transcendent, supernatural, or divine reality. **8.** Any intense religious experience in general during which one feels in contact with the divine. **9.** That aspect of theology that stresses **(a)** the direct apprehension of God, **(b)** the direct communication with, or revelation from, God (with or without sacred texts and accumulated tradition), and **(c)** thereby the attainment of salvation (moral blessedness, beatitude, serenity). **10.** The belief that a knowledge of God's being can be had in an immediate and nonrational way by means of a unity with his existence or an awareness of his presence in all things.

Some of the characteristics of mysticism: (1) A feeling of oneness, total unity, completeness; (2) a feeling of unique joy, euphoria, harmony, well-being, ECSTASY, that is (3) ineffable, incommunicable, and (4) of supreme intensity; (5) a feeling of transcending time and reality, of becoming one with "eternity"; (6) a noetic feeling—something is known, disclosed, revealed, understood, incapable of being had in any other way, beyond all ordinary human knowledge and senses, and indefinable; (7) a feeling of surprise, awe, wonder mingled with fear, and sometimes dread; (8) a feeling of the objective presence of, or the nearness to, something that can only be called "divine" causing the experience (knowledge); (9) a passive feeling that one is being overwhelmed, "taken up," spiritually controlled and inspired to be in this state, and that this is not done of one's own choice; (10) an accepting feeling of the reasons why all common reality is the way it is, and (11) why that which transcends all common reality makes it what it is and will be.

mysticism (complete absorption). The experience of total union with all things or with a higher reality (God) in which there is no distinction between the self having the experience and that which is experienced; the "I" is completely absorbed into God, the All, and there is no subject-object separation.

In complete absorption (identification) with the One, all individuality is lost and there is total unity of the consciousness with "all that there is," that is, there is no separation of the ego from that One that is the object of its perception. In partial absorption (see also MYSTICISM [PARTIAL ABSORPTION]) with the One, the individuality of consciousness remains, but nothing is distinguishable from that One; all things are united as a whole within It and can be seen only as a completely integrated whole, not as interrelated parts. See also other entries on MYSTICISM.

mysticism, extrovertive. The experience **1.** in which the self views the panorama of events in the universe as a living, organic, interrelated unity or movement with all things merging together without distinction in a continuous, harmonious flow, and **2.** in which the self perceives all events with an intensity and awareness surpassing anything in ordinary experience. Sometimes relates the operations of the universe to God as a World Mind (World Soul, Cosmic Intelligence).

mysticism, introvertive. The experience **1.** in which the self loses its awareness of itself as a distinct, independent, separate existent and becomes merged with God the All; the subject-object distinction dissolves, and **2.** in which the self only then fully understands its true essence as identical with that of God, the One, or All.

mysticism, (partial absorption). The experience of oneness with all things or with a higher reality (God) in which there is an awareness at the time of the experience of a distinction between the self having the experience and that which is experienced; the individual stands as a distinct perceiver before God, the All; the "I" encounters (confronts, is in the presence of) God. See also MYSTICISM (COMPLETE ABSORPTION).

myth (Gk., μῦθος *[mythos]*, "myth," "tale," "fable"). A story used to explain some belief, practice, aspect of human nature, natural phenomenon, etc., and having some divine, religious, spiritual significance or connection. Myth goes contrary to naturalistic, humanistic (if humanistic, it then is regarded as a *legend)*, and historical explanations. Myth is derived from sources such as poetic imagery and cultural narrative.

mythology (Gk., μυθολογία *[mythologia]*, from μῦθος *[mythos]*, "myth," "tale," "fable," and λόγος *[logos]*, "the study of"). **1.** The study of myths, their origin, importance, insights, and significance. **2.** The group of myths believed in by a people. **3.** The use of imagery (poetry, metaphor, symbolism, analogy, parable) to present a sense of the otherworldly nature of existence. **4.** The use of imagery to present insights about this world, and about human existence, which cannot be expressed as satisfactorily or emotionally by means of literal, figurative language.

Theologically, myth has been considered by some as the only legitimate way of communicating or objectifying the nature of God and the supernatural. Used derogatively, it implies an outmoded and unrealistic view of the world, having been superseded by the more modern insights of our times.

N

Nativity of the Blessed Virgin Mary, the Feast of the. Celebrated September 8, the birth of MARY, the mother of Jesus.

Nativity, the (L., *nativitas,* "birth"). The birth of Christ. The scene is depicted, for example, at Luke 2:1–20. One of the most famous representations in Christian art done in a variety of ways, from the Holy Family alone, to the presence of angels and/or the MAGI, to the inclusion of two midwives, Zebel and Salome. (Christian legend has it that Salome doubted the divine, virgin birth of Jesus and as a consequence her hand withered.)

natural law. **1.** In Christian theology, natural law is that aspect of natural theology (see THEOLOGY, NATURAL) that attempts by means of a rational analysis of nature to obtain moral knowledge—knowledge of right and wrong, knowledge of what humans should and should not do. It is believed that just as nature exhibits universal physical laws that govern natural phenomena and cannot be violated, so nature exhibits universal ethical laws that govern moral conduct and should not be violated. (The knowledge of natural law is not to be regarded as a substitute to revealed ethical laws but as an adjunct and/or support. See also THEOLOGY, NATURAL.) Natural law presents a set of codes (rules, precepts) intended by nature, sanctioned by and grounded in the will of God. These codes prescribe for us what should or should not be done. They act as regulative principles for our conduct. They are universally binding upon all humans. An example of a natural law: It is immoral to have sexual intercourse with the intention of mechanically or chemically preventing the sperm from meeting an ovum. Such a union is natural, intended by nature, sanctified by God, and any deliberate interruption of this process during sexual intercourse goes against natural law and is a sin. (In Roman Catholicism where natural law plays an important role, sex and the pleasure of sex in marriage are not sinful. The primary and divine purpose of sex is procreation. Intentional obstruction of this purpose goes against natural law and the Divine Will.)

2. The universal moral rules of conduct—for example, the sense of fairness and justice—that humans by nature possess by the pure activity of their reason given by God (or that can be *seen* by the pure activity of their reason given by God) and that are obligatory independently, and in spite of, what other forms of law command. Example: It is a natural law that when a person is using his/her property resourcefully for the benefit of the community, that property should not be taken away from him/her.

Natural law is contrasted with laws such as civil law, secular law, positive law, common law, public law, and state law. Natural law supersedes these forms of law and is used to judge them.

necromancy (Gk., *νεκρομαντεία [nekromanteia],* from *νεκρός [nekros],* "corpse," and *μαντεία [manteia],* "divination"). DIVINATION or revealing the future, founded upon communication with the spirits of the dead. Related to SORCERY and MAGIC.

neophyte (Gk., *νεόφυτος [neopytos],* "property newly planted," from *νέος [neos],* "new," and *φύειν [phyein],* "to grow"). A newly baptized person or a person newly accepted into a church or faith.

Nestorianism. The belief about the Holy Trinity propounded by Nestorius, a Syrian bishop of the first half of the fifth century, patriarch of Constantinople, and follower of ANTIOCHENES, that the divine and human natures were not united (merged, cosubstantial) in Jesus Christ. Nestorius was condemned as a heretic for holding this position.

Nestorianism also holds that Mary is not a THEOTOKOS. God was not given birth. Mary bore a human who served as the temple or bearer of God's being.

new birth. Implies a sense of a new beginning—a beginning unaffected emotionally by the entanglements of one's past personality traits, frailties, and regrets; a regrouping of one's intentions, sense of direction and self-image. In Christian faith, this is produced by the HOLY SPIRIT. See also CONVERSION; REBORN.

New Covenant, the. See COVENANT, THE NEW.

New Testament, the (L., *testamentum,* from *testari,* "to be a witness," "to make one's will," a translation from the Greek, διαθήκη *[diathēkē],* "covenant," "last will"). According to Chrisianity, God's New and final Covenant with humans, which replaces the Old Covenant made with the Jews in the Old Testament, and which presents the coming of Jesus Christ, his teaching, and his redemptive powers. (See also entries under COVENANT.) The New Testament reveals God's Word through Christ—through Christ's incarnation, death, and resurrection. According to Christian tradition, the New Testament is the only means by which humans can share in the divine reality and nature, purpose and desires of God.

The contents (CANON) of the New Testament took many years to become established. An early canon (between A.D. 120 and 130) consisted of the synoptic Gospels, the ten Pauline letters, Hebrews, and Acts. The Fourth Gospel of John was accepted as canonical about the time of Tatian of Assyria (110–172), Theophilis of Antioch (125–181), and Irenaeus (ca. 135–199). About the same time or earlier, the Pastoral Epistles, 1 Peter, and Revelation were accepted into the canon. Later, Jude, 2 Peter, and the Johannine Epistles were also accepted. At present, twenty-seven books and epistles are commonly accepted as comprising the New Testament:

St. Matthew
St. Mark
St. Luke
St. John
The Acts of the Apostles
St. Paul to the Romans
1 Corinthians
1 Corinthians
Galatians
Ephesians
Philippians
Colossians
1 Thessalonians
2 Thessalonians
1 Timothy
2 Timothy
Titus
Philemon
To the Hebrews
The Epistle of St. James
1 St. Peter
2 St. Peter
1 St. John
2 St. John
3 St. John
St. Jude
Revelation (Apocalypse) of St. John the Apostle

Christian tradition regards the New Testament as the inspired, revealed, and infallible Word of God—authored by God himself. The entire New Testament was written originally in Greek, which was the prevalent and universal language of the times. The sayings of Jesus were probably spoken in Aramaic, the language Jesus spoke. No original manuscript of the New Testament written during the first 300 years of Christianity exists. In addition, copies of the New Testament as a single whole, in contrast to separate books, do not exist from that period.

New Year's Day. A holy day celebrated on January 1 as the Feast of Jesus' CIRCUMCISION.

Nicaea, the Second Council of. (Also found as *Nicea.)* Held September 24 to October 23, 787, under Pope Hadrian I, and regarded as the Seventh Ecumenical Council. This council accepted the value and correctness of the veneration of images and icons, and allotted degrees of VENERATION OR REVERENCE to things related to God, or to the SACRED.

Nicene Creed. Also *Nicaene Creed* (Gk., *Νικαια [Nikaia],* "Nice," or "Nicaea," an ancient city of Asia Minor). The name *Nicene* derives from the first Ecumenical Council of the Christian Church, held at Nicaea, in Bithynia, in 325, during the pontificate of Sylvester I and attended by 318 bishops.

The principal discussion at this council concerned the question whether Christ was to be described as HOMOIOS (of *like* substance with God) or HOMOOUSIOS (of the *same* substance as God). The Athanasians (see ATHANASIANISM) won out and Christ was regarded as *homoousios,* identical in substance with the First Person of the Trinity: "The very God of very God, begotten, not made, being of one substance with the Father." There are two versions of this creed: the Nicene Creed of 325 and the Niceno-Constantinopolitan Creed of 381, which was a revised and enlarged form of the Nicene Creed of 325 and adopted by the Council of Constantinople in 381. In popular usage, they both go by the name Nicene Creed. The Niceno-Constantinopolitan Creed was formally adopted at the Council of Chalcedon in 451, over the original Nicene Creed (which is still used by some schismatic groups of the Eastern Orthodox church), and is regarded as the ecumenical creed of the Eastern church. The Niceno-Constantinopolitan Creed was adopted by the Latin (Western) church but the Council of Toledo in 589 added the FILIOQUE reference to the Holy Spirit, which proclaims a procession of the HOLY SPIRIT from the Son through the Father (or from the Son as well as from the Father). This creed is similar to the APOSTLES' CREED.

The revised and enlarged Nicene Creed of 381: "We believe in one God, the Father Almighty, Maker of heaven and earth, and of all things visible and invisible. And in one Lord Jesus Christ, the only-begotten son of God, begotten of the Father before all worlds, Light of Light, very God of very God, begotten, not made, being of one substance with the Father; by whom all things were made; who for us men, and for our salvation, came down from heaven, and was incarnate by the Holy Ghost of the virgin Mary, and was made man; he was crucified for us under Pontius Pilate, and suffered, and was buried, and the third day he rose again, according to the Scriptures, and ascended into heaven, and sitteth on the right hand of the Father; from thence he cometh again, with glory, to judge the quick and the dead; whose kingdom shall have no end. And in the Holy Ghost, who is Lord and Giver of life, who proceedeth from the Father, who with the Father and the Son together is worshipped and glorified, who spake by the prophets—In one holy catholic and apostolic church; we acknowledge one baptism for the remission of sins; we look for the resurrection of the dead, and the life of the world to come. Amen."

The Nicene Creed is spoken, chanted, or sung as an act of faith, praise, and glory to God during the formal worship service. It proclaims God's way and his salvation for all believers. Controversy has existed in Christianity as to whether any of the existing Christian creeds, such as the Nicene, the Apostles', the Athanasian, can be substantiated or justified by use of the New Testament, especially the Four Gospels.

Niceno-Constantinopolitan Creed. Also *Constantinopolitan Creed.* Refers to the NICENE CREED established at the Council of Nicea (325) and to its elaboration and defense at the Council of Constantinople in 381. It was a response by the Church to the Arian heresy (see ARIANISM).

nimbus (L., *nimbus,* "cloud," "halo"). See HALO.

notitia. Latin, "understanding." In medieval theology and philosophy, an essential item in FAITH, together with ASSENSUS and FIDUCIA.

numbers, Christian. In Christian tradition, numbers are symbolic. The number *one* stands for God, the ultimate unity. *Two* symbolizes the intimate union of the Father and Son, the interconnection between the divine and the human. *Three* is the symbol of the spiritual realm in general, of the Holy Trinity, and in particular the HOLY SPIRIT. It also symbolizes the three aspects of the human being: spirit or soul, mind, and body. *Four* symbolizes the world of matter (earth, air, fire, water), or the seasons (winter, spring, summer, fall), or the directions of the world (north, south, east, west—or up, down, left, right). The Gospels are four; the Evangelists are listed as four and represent the earthly kingdom of God; Paradise has four rivers; etc. *Seven* is the combination of four (the world of matter) and three (the world of the spirit) and is regarded in Christian tradition as the perfect number. There are seven sacraments, seven sorrows of Mary, seven gifts of the Holy Spirit, seven churches of Christ, etc. *Eight* symbolizes the New Dispensation, the coming of Christ and his baptism. Baptismal fonts, for example, were made with eight sides. *Nine* symbolizes the realm of the holy angels (as in the nine orders of angels). *Ten* stands for the moral life (as in the Ten Commandments). *Twelve* stands for the zeal of mission (as in the Twelve Apostles). *Thirteen* is regarded as unlucky because there were thirteen present at the Lord's table at the Last Supper and one of them betrayed Jesus. *Forty* is symbolic of travail, discipline, and overcoming. (As in Jesus' forty days in the wilderness, his fasting and overcoming temptation; the forty days of Lent, which commemorate this. In the Old Testament there are the forty days of Noah's anguish at the flood, the forty years the Jews spent in wandering in the wilderness, the forty days Moses spent on Mt. Sinai.)

numinous, the. A sense or experience of the transcendent reality or presence of God that has qualities associated with it such as holiness, awe, the sublime, the terrifying, infinite power, grandeur. The experience is of a Total Other that is so utterly different from anything in our experience that it is impossible to grasp rationally and impossible to communicate. The numinous evokes an inescapable feeling of our finiteness, of our complete and total dependence upon this transcendent reality, and of our insufficiency as we stand in contrast to the glory and power of that reality. Also referred to as the *mysterium tremendum et fascinans:* the sense of tremendous mystery and fascination.

nun (L., *nonna,* "nun," feminine of *nonus,* "monk"). A female under religious vows, such as chastity, obedience, and poverty, attached to a CONVENT or NUNNERY.

nunnery. A CONVENT for nuns.

O

obedience (L., *obidere,* "to obey"). **1.** The act of obeying the will of God. **2.** The state of being obedient to the will of God. Obedience is the due and voluntary submission to the will of God, his control, and his authority and is the highest demand made by the Christian faith.

According to Christian faith, Christ's final act on the cross is one of REDEMPTION thought of as complete obedience. Humans are made righteous by Christ's complete obedience (Rom. 5:19); humans too become righteous by complete obedience. Christian obedience is not an unquestioning, purely human, slavish, automatic, mechanical obedience. Obedience must be creative, spiritual, all-enveloping, accepting, completely personal, and voluntarily committed. True obedience for the Christian is acquired by means of suffering, pain, sacrifice, and acceptance of all that comes in life (for example, see Heb. 2:10; 5:8, 9). See also COUNSELS OF PERFECTION.

oblation (L., *oblatio,* "offering," "dedication"). In general, the act of offering a sacrifice to God. For Christian faith, the highest oblation was God's offering of his only begotten Son as the Redeemer of humanity.

Christians give as an oblation the bread and wine offered for CONSECRATION in Holy Communion or the EUCHARIST. For traditional Christianity, the Eucharist is a true oblation. It is not merely a symbolic IMMOLATION, not merely a representation of Christ's death, but a transformation (see also TRANSUBSTANTIATION) and elevation into a divine reality, of the bread and wine into the Body and Blood of Jesus Christ.

obsession (L., *obsessus,* "being beseiged," from *ob,* "to," "upon," and *sedere,* "to sit"). In Christianity, the act of an evil demon (spirit, devil) motivating the behavior of an individual. Used synonymously with POSSESSION. Often demonic obsession is the state of being overcome (possessed) by the devil from without.

oecumenical. See ECUMINICAL.

offertory (L., *offertorium,* "the place to which offerings are brought"). **1.** The bread and wine offered by church members (or by the priest), to be consecrated (see also CONSECRATION) by the rite of the EUCHARIST or to be used for Holy Communion. (In the early Christian church, and presently in the Greek Orthodox tradition, there is a tradition of having the members bring the bread and wine to be consecrated for the Eucharist. The *offertory procession* referred to the line of people waiting before the altar to present their offerings of bread and/or wine.) **2.** The part of the church service during which the bread and wine are offered for the Eucharistic rite, or Holy Communion. **3.** The moment at which the bread and wine are presented for consecration by the priest or celebrant. **4.** The part of a service during which the collection is made. **5.** The antiphon or anthem sung or said during the collection or the offering for the Eucharist.

office (L., *officium,* "office"). **1.** Any form of formal worship of God. **2.** In the Roman Catholic church, **(a)** the daily service of the BREVIARY; **(b)** the introit; **(c)** the service of the MASS. **3.** In the Anglican churches, **(a)** Morning or Evening Prayer; **(b)** the introit; **(c)** the Holy Communion (see COMMUNION, HOLY) service. **4.** An ecclesiastical position, or place, from which, or at which the business or work of the church is done, such as in 'the office of a bishop."

oil, olive. Olive oil is used in the rituals of many Christian faiths. In the Roman Catholic church, there are principally three different kinds of holy oil: **1.** the oil of catechumens, used in the ceremonies before BAPTISM. **2.** the oil of the sick and dying, used in Extreme Unction and anointing of the sick, and **3.** CHRISM, a mixture of olive oil and balsam used in baptism, CONFIRMATION, etc.

Old Catholics. See CATHOLICS, OLD.

Old Testament. The Jewish BIBLE, excepting the NEW TESTAMENT, believed by Jews to be the COVENANT God has made with them as the chosen people. See also COVENANT, THE OLD. The Hebrews divided the Old Testament into three main divisions: **1.** The *Law,* which comprises what is believed to be the five books written by Moses. (Referred to as the Pentateuch by Christians.) The word "Law" is also used to refer to the Old Testament as whole. **2.** The *Prophets,* which comprises the basic historical account of the Jews in twenty-one books such as Joshua, Judges, Samuel, Kings, Isaiah, Jeremiah, Ezekiel. **3.** The *Scriptures,* which is divided into three parts: (a) Job, Psalms, and Proverbs, used extensively in the synagogue for worship services; (b) the *Five Rolls* (The Song of Solomon, Ruth, Lamentations, Ecclesiastes, Esther), used as the "Lessons" for Jewish services, and (c) The *Appendix,* Daniel, Ezra, Nehemiah and the Chronicles.

omnibenevolent (L., *omnis,* "all," and *benevolent,* from *bene,* "well," and *volens,* "willing"). Applied to God to indicate that he is all-good—a pure, moral Being capable only of love, mercy, compassion, and charity, and incapable in any way of acting against virtue, good, and reason.

omnipotence, paradox of God's. Some of the traditionally stated "paradoxes" that have to do with God's omnipotence: If God is All-Powerful: **1.** Can he create a squared circle? **2.** Can he undo the past? **3.** Can he create a rock so big that he cannot move it? **4.** Can he invent problems that he cannot solve? **5.** Can he annihilate himself and never come back to life? **6.** Can he deny his essence? **7.** Can he make himself more perfect? **8.** Can he lie?

omnipotent (L., *omnipotens,* "all powerful," from *omnis,* "all," and *potens,* "powerful"). Applied to God to indicate that he is all-powerful and/or of infinite power. (The former need only imply that he is the most powerful and nothing is more powerful than he.)

Some of the variety of meanings for omnipotent that can be found in theology: **1.** God can do anything. He is able to bring about anything he wills or wants. **2.** God can do anything provided that it is logically possible to do, that is, provided that it is not self-contradictory. For example, his power cannot create a squared circle no matter how intensely he wills or wants that to happen since self-contradictions cannot be brought into existence. **3.** God can do anything provided that it is worthwhile to do and (which amounts to the same thing) provided that it is an expression of his necessary essence as God.

The focal implication in these definitions is that God is the absolute controller (and in most cases also creator) of all things.

omnipresent (L., *omnis,* "all," and *praesens,* "that is before one," present participle of *praesse,* "to be before," from *prae,* "before," and *esse,* "to be"). Applied to God to indicate that **1.** he is wholly present in all things at any given moment in time or **2.** his influence is present and felt in all things. The main element in the concept of God's omnipresence is that he is intimately related to all things as an efficient cause is related to that on which it acts.

omniscience, paradox of God's. If God is all-knowing (and all-powerful), how is this compatible with **1.** human freedom of the will and **2.** God's own freedom of the will, since presumably such complete foreknowledge entails that an all-powerful God has created things to occur exactly in the way that he knows—and wants—them to occur?

omniscient (L., *omni,* "all," and *sciens,* present participle of *scire,* "to know"). Applied to God to indicate that he is all-knowing—that he has infinite knowledge. Some of the variety of interrelatable interpretations for omniscience: **1.** God perceives all things as they happen and hence knows of their occurrence. **2.** God knows everything that has happened, is happening, and will happen. **3.** In addition, God knows everything that is possible to know.

The three primary notions in these definitions are **(a)** all truths (knowledge) are eternal; **(b)** they are all known (eternally) by God; and **(c)** nothing can occur unless it accords with these eternal truths, with God's knowledge.

omnitemporal (L., *omnis,* "all," and *temporalis,* from *tempus, temporis,* "time"). Used to refer to God as something that exists (as itself) at all times through eternity.

opus operatum. Latin, "the thing done," "the power of affecting." The holy SACRAMENTS have their own operating power, or principle, in producing effects upon individuals, whose legitimacy comes directly from God and *not* from the recipient's attitudes and states of mind at the time of the Sacrament.

The recipient's subjective predispositions and dispositions are important and valuable. One must be ready for a sacrament, accepting God's forgiveness and sanctification, but the power of affecting one's life comes from God directly, not from engaging in the sacrament. This also applies to the atittudes and states of mind of the person who administers the sacrament, such as a priest, who may be a sinner in actual life or a saint. As long as the intention is present in him to administer the sacrament *and* the appropriate ritual is performed, this is enough to signify the objective, absolute, unconditional, valid promise of God's grace and salvation. This concept was formally approved by the COUNCIL OF TRENT.

ordain (L., *ordinare,* "to order"). To confer upon one the ecclesiastical (ministerial, sacerdotal, holy) powers and privileges of the Christian ministry. These powers enable one to do such things as perform marriages, baptize, confirm, bury, etc., under the sacred sanction of Jesus Christ and the HOLY SPIRIT.

Some Christian traditions, such as the Roman Catholic, affirm that a person validly ordained by the Church continues to possess the peculiar power and gift (see also LAYING ON OF HANDS) put into that person by the sacred, sacramental rite of *ordination.* It is generally thought that this power continues to operate regardless of the status, nature, and condition of the person ordained and performing the SACRAMENTS of the Church. See also OPUS OPERATUM; ORDERS, THE SACRAMENT OF HOLY.

order, holy. **1.** Any of the sacred levels or ranks of the church. **2.** Any of the organizations or institutions within the church that follow a common emphasis or theology and into which one enters in community with definite vows and practices, such as the Augustinian, Benedictine, Cistercian, Carthusian, Dominican, Franciscan, etc.

orders, contemplative. Orders such as the Carthusian and the Carmelite that dedicate themselves to prayer, contemplation, and the glorification of God. See also CONTEMPLATION.

orders, major holy. The rank of priesthood above the minor orders (see also ORDERS, MINOR HOLY). In the Roman Catholic tradition, there are four major orders or rank in a hierarchy of celebites: The *subdeacon,* who serves the priest at High Mass, sings the Epistle, recites the Divine Office, etc. Subdeacons are allowed to touch the sacred vessels that do not contain the Blessed Sacrament. The *deacon,* who serves the bishop and priest at the altar, sings the Gospel at High Mass, and is allowed to carry the Blessed Sacrament in the sacred vessels. Under some conditions a deacon may give Holy Communion, baptize, preach, etc. The *priest,* who is granted power to change the bread and wine into the Body and Blood of Christ, handles the Blessed Sacrament, administers the SACRAMENTS (except that of Holy Orders), preaches, counsels, blesses, etc. A priest is in loyalty and obligation subservient to his bishop. *Bishop,* who is in essence a higher priest than the priests—a second degree of priest. A bishop is consecrated by three other bishops. A bishop has not only all the powers of a priest, but the power to make a priest a priest—the power to grant priesthood. A bishop rules over many priests, over a diocese granted to him by other ecclesiastical groups, authorities, or the pope. See ORDERS, THE SACRAMENT OF HOLY.

orders, minor holy. The first ranks to the priesthood; those below the major orders (see also ORDERS, MAJOR HOLY). In the Roman Catholic tradition, there are four such orders or steps: *porter* or doorkeeper, who excludes unbelievers from church, rings the bells, acts as treasurer of the church; *lector* or reader, who instructs catechumens in the mysteries of the faith, reads Scripture to the people, is responsible for the sacred books, and acts as secretarial assistant to priests and bishops; *exorcist,* who exorcises those possessing evil demons, but only with the bishop's permission; and the *acolyte,* who carries lights at mass and presents to the deacon the offering of the sacrifice.

There is no ordination (see ORDAIN) for minor orders, although there is a benediction by a bishop and a symbol entrusted of the duties of the order. Frequently, minor orders are regarded as stages to the priesthood.

Orders, the Sacrament of Holy. One of the seven sacraments, by means of which individuals receive the power and grace to perform sacred tasks and rituals. All the other Sacraments (Matrimony, Baptism, Confirmation, the Eucharist, Penance, Anointing of the Sick) are based on this one for legitimate administration. This Sacrament is referred to as "Holy Orders" because it establishes spiritual orders, ranks, or rules in the Church, placing individuals into a hierarchy. See also ORDAIN; ORDERS, MAJOR HOLY; ORDERS, MINOR HOLY.

Holy Orders are transmitted by the LAYING ON OF HANDS and conferred by a bishop. The recipient receives a permanent CHARACTER, power, or gift (as in 1 Tim. 4:14 and 2 Tim. 1:6). Some Christians, for instance some Protestants, do not accept Holy Orders—or what they refer to as "ordination"—as producing an indelible, permanent character. For them, ordination gives authority, privileges, and rights but is not an imprint, sign, mark, or gift given by a supernatural power.

The Sacrament of Holy Orders is based on the belief that Jesus created a priestly class and gave them spiritual powers to go out into the world and preach his message. Some of the scriptural references cited for this belief: Luke 22:19; John 20:21–23; Matthew 28:19.

In the Roman Catholic church, the person receiving the Sacrament of Holy Orders must be male, baptized, confirmed, of good and sound intention, educated by the Church with acceptance of the faith, acting voluntarily, born of a lawful marriage, age 21 or older, etc.

ordo salutis. Latin, "orders, or stages, of SALVATION."

orthodox (Gk., *ὀρθόδοξος [orthodoxos],* from *ὄρθος [orthos],* "right," "straight," and *δόξα [doxa],* "opinion," "belief"). **1.** True (correct, sound, valid) belief (opinion, doctrine, creed, idea) as opposed to heretical (see HERESY) or HETERODOX belief. The doctrine decreed by an institution or group as the true one and the one to be followed. **2.** Approved belief. **3.** Conventional or traditional belief.

original sin. See SIN, ORIGINAL.

ox, winged. The ox is a traditional symbol of strength and sometimes represents an Apostle. In Christian art, a winged ox is the symbol associated with St. Luke, one of the four Evangelists. See also CREATURES, THE FOUR LIVING; EVANGELISTS, THE FOUR.

P

paedobaptism. Also *pedobaptism* (Gk., *παιδός [paidos],* "a boy," or *παῖς [pais],* "a child"). INFANT BAPTISM.

pagan (L., *paganus,* "countryman," "peasant," "pagan," "rustic," from *pagus,* "a village," "a rural area," "the country"). **1.** Heathen. Not a Christian. Hence anyone who does not worship the true God, and Jesus Christ. **2.** An idolater (see IDOLATRY). One who does not believe in and who does not worship the one true God. **3.** An irreligious or nonreligious person with reference to Christian customs and practices. **4.** One who worships many gods. **5.** Anyone not a Christian or Jew (and in some contexts, anyone not a Christian, Jew, or Moslem).

palingenesis (Gk., *πάλιν [palin],* "again," and *γένεσις [genesis],* "birth," "origin"). Being born again. A rebirth. A new birth. A regeneration. Palingenesis usually refers **1.** to the actual physical rebirth of an individual such as in the continued rebirths found in the doctrines of METEMPSYCHOSIS, REINCARNATION, AND TRANSMIGRATION. It may also refer **2.** to the psychological and spiritual rebirth of the spirit of an individual such as in conversion experiences.

palm leaf, the (Gk., *παλάμη [palamē],* "the palm of the hand"). The palm leaf or branch was an ancient Roman symbol of triumph, victory, or conquest, of rejoicing and celebration. On Jesus' entry into Jerusalem, the people took fronds from palm trees to wave with them and to lay on the ground before Jesus' procession (see also PALM SUNDAY).

In Christian art, the palm has been a symbol of victory and of martyrdom—the martyrs being victorious over death by means of their faith. The palm was a general symbol of triumph over adversity. The palm tree, always green, was also a symbol of immortality.

Palm Sunday. The Sunday before EASTER, the first day of Holy Week (PASSIONTIDE) commemorating Jesus' triumphal entrance into Jerusalem, which consummated his work of redemption and salvation. It receives its name from the palm branches people spread under the feet of Jesus' procession as he rode into Jerusalem on a donkey (see also PALM LEAF, THE). On Palm Sunday, palms are blessed and given to the members of the faith. (Some Christian church services at Palm Sunday have a procession with each carrying a blessed palm. Some of these processions commemorate not only Jesus' entry into Jerusalem but also the deliverance of the Jews from their slavery in Egypt and their entrance into the Promised Land.)

Pancake Tuesday. See SHROVE TUESDAY.

panentheism (Gk., *πᾶν [pan],* and *ἔν [en],* "in," and *θεός [theos],* "God"). All things are imbued with God's being in the sense that all things are *in* God. God is more than all that there is. He is a consciousness and the highest unity possible. To be distinguished from: PANTHEISM (God *is* identical with *all* that there is), PANPSYCHISM (God is the spirit pervading all things but in no way supernatural), THEISM (God is immanent in the universe but also transcendent), and DEISM (God is wholly transcendent to the universe).

panhenic feeling (Gk., *πᾶν [pan],* "all," *ἔν [en],* "in," and *ἕν [hen],* "one"). The feeling of oneness with all things. See also entries under MYSTICISM.

panpsychism (Gk., πᾶν *[pan]*, "all," and ψυχή *[psychē]*, "soul," "spirit," "mind"). God is completely immanent *in* the universe and is the psychic force (mind, spirit) embodied in every particle of matter.

pantheism (Gk., πᾶν *[pan]*, "all," and θεός *[theos]*, "God"). God is All; All is God. God and the universe are identical. *God* and *nature* (universe, the totality of all that there is) are synonymous, or two words for the same thing.

pantocratōr. Greek, παντοκράτωρ from πᾶν *[pan]*, "all," and κράτος *[kratos]*, "strength," "might," "power." **1.** The name given in Christianity to God and translated as Almighty, Absolute Power, Absolute Master, Absolute Controller, Absolute Governor. **2.** In Christian art, the image of Christ as the Absolute Ruler of the Universe, for example, as found in the domes of Byzantine churches representing Christ as God the Father, combined with qualities of the Son Jesus, who will be judging all humanity at the Last Judgment, or Second Coming (see PAROUSIA).

Papacy, the (Gk, πάπας *[papas]*, πάππας *[pappas]*, "father"). **1.** The POPE—the bishop of Rome. **2.** The pope's area of jurisdiction and authority. **3.** The hierarchy of the governing body of the Roman Catholic church as found in the Vatican and headed by the pope. **4.** The popes of the Roman Catholic church thought of collectively.

papal infallibility. See INFALLIBILITY OF THE POPE.

papal supremacy. Based on the superiority or privilege of St. Peter over the other Apostles. Four main references are cited in defense of papal supremacy (superiority, privilege): **1.** Peter's confession and Jesus' promise to build his church upon "this rock" (πέτρας *[petras]*, is translated as Peter) at Matthew 16:18; **2.** the gift to St. Peter of the keys at Matthew 16:19 (see KEYS, THE POWER OF THE); **3.** Peter's restoration at Luke 22:31; and **4.** the admonition to St. Peter at John 21:15.

parable (Gk., παραβολή *[parabolē]*, "a comparing," "a parable," from παρά *[para]*, "beside," and βάλλειν *[ballein]*, "to cast," "to throw," "to place"). A short narrative or story that embodies a message or moral by means of comparison. Jesus (and others in philosophic and religious traditions) uses parables as illustrative stories embodying essential truths about humans and their condition. Parabolic teachings make use of ordinary, down-to-earth happenings in order to present their message, and they are usually simple, uncomplicated, concrete, insightful, and appeal to the familiar. There are over two dozen parables told by Jesus. Some of the more famous: the Parable of the Prodigal Son (Luke 15:11–32), signifying repentence, compassion, and forgiveness; the Parable of the Good Samaritan (Luke 10:25–37), signifying an obligation of love to our neighbor; the Parable of the Unmerciful Servant (Matt. 18:23–35), indicating that we must forgive if we are to be forgiven; the Parable of the

Mote and Beam in the Eye (Luke 6:41–42), signifying that we should judge ourselves rather than others. For other parables, refer to: Matthew 7:24–27 (and Luke 6:47–49); 13:3–9, 18–23; 13:24–30, 37–43; 13:31–32 (and Luke 13:18–19; Mark 4:30–32); 13:33 (and Luke 13:20–21); 13:44; 13:45–46; 13:47–50; 18:12–14; 20:1–16; 21:28–32; 21:33–44 (and Mark 12:1–12; Luke 20:9–19); 22:2–14; 24:32–33; 24:42–51; 25:1–13; 25:14–30 (and Luke 8:18); 25:31–46. Mark 4:3–9, 14–20; 4:26–29; 13:34–37. Luke 7:40–50; 8:5–8, 11–15; 10:30–37; 11:5–13; 11:24–26; 12:15–21; 12:35–40; 12:42–48; 13:24–30; 13:69 (and Matt. 21:19–20; 24:32–33); 14:8–11; 14:16–24; 14:26–30; 14:31–33; 15:4–7; 15:8–10; 15:11–32; 16:1–13; 16:19–31; 17:7–10; 18:2–8; 18:10–14; 19:12–27. John 10:1–5, 7–18.

paraclete (Gk., *παράκλητος [paraklētos],* "one called to someone's aid," from *παρά [para],* "beside," and *καλεῖν [kalein],* "to call"). **1.** The Comforter, the Intercessor, referring to Jesus Christ and the HOLY SPIRIT (as in John 14:16, 26; 15:26; 16:7). Also helper, sustainer, strengthener, consoler of the spirit. Jesus and the Holy Spirit, who assist us in our distress and give support and a spiritual uplift. **2.** One who "bears witness" to Jesus as the Christ and to the power of the Holy Spirit.

paradise (Gk., *παράδεισος [paradeisos],* "paradise," "park," "garden"). **1.** Originally referred to the Garden of Eden. **2.** The resting place of sanctified souls after death awaiting the Final Judgment before entering HEAVEN. Early Christians believed that the souls of the faithful rested in tranquility, peace, joy, happiness in paradise. These souls would live there until the Last Day of Judgment or Jesus' Second Coming, when they would be reunited with their spiritualized bodies and then proceed to a higher blessed life in heaven. **3.** Heaven itself, or a level of the heavens, such as the third heaven. (Refer to New Testament references such as Luke 23:43; 2 Cor. 12:4; Rev. 2:7.) **4.** Infrequently, the place of the righteous dead (or "saints") who lived before Jesus' resurrection.

pardon (L., *perdonare,* "to remit a debt," "to pardon," from *per,* "through," and "thoroughly," and *donare,* "to give"). **1.** Forgiveness. **2.** To free from punishment, penalty, fault, or guilt. **3.** To remit or excuse an offense. **4.** An INDULGENCE.

Christians interpret the Gospels as declaring that there is unconditional, free pardon for all human sin and complete acceptance by God of all humans, purely by God's Grace working through Jesus Christ and the HOLY SPIRIT.

parousia. Greek, *παρουσία* translated as "a being present," "presence." In Greek philosophy, *parousia* referred to the presence of an essence, or idea, in a thing that made the thing what it was, usually because it imitated a perfect model. In Christianity, *parousia* **1.** as a general term refers to the presence of Christ in man's spirit and **2.** as a specific term refers to the presence of Christ at the Second Coming, or the Second Advent. For New Testament references, see 1 John 3:2, ". . . we shall see him as he is"; Revelation 1:7, "Behold, he cometh with clouds; and every eye shall see him"; 1 Corinthians 13:12; 1 Peter 1:12; 2 Peter 1:16; Matthew 10:23; 16:27ff.; 19:28ff.; 24:36; 25:31ff.; Acts 1:11; 1 Thessalonians 5:2; Revelation 1:4, 7; 20:11ff.; 22:17, 20.

Parthenos. Greek, *παρθένος* "virgin." Name given to the Blessed Virgin Mary, mother of God.

Pascha. Greek, Πάσχα "EASTER," from Hebrew, *pesach* (or *pesakh*), "a passing over," "the Passover," the annual celebration on the fourteenth of the first month, of Israel's Exodus from Egypt (Exod. 12:11). The principal part of the celebration was the sacrifice of a lamb at the Temple and a sacrificial meal in the household, with rites filled with symbolism depicting a hasty departure, unleavened bread, bitter herbs, a drink passed around four times, a reference to the Exodus, hymns of praise, etc. The *pesach* is a memory of God's covenant with the Jews to free them from slavery in Egypt. See PASSOVER, THE CHRISTIAN; PENTECOST.

In Christianity, CHRIST himself is seen as the sacrificial, paschal meal, for example, at 1 Corinthians 5:6–8; Mark 8:15; Galatians 5:9. Christians believe that JESUS initiated the New Covenant at the LAST SUPPER in anticipation of his death as a sacrifice. Jesus acted as the father at the table, distributing bread and passing the chalice to those at his table.

Paschal Week. See HOLY WEEK.

Passion, Instruments of the. Also *Emblems of the Passion*. The tools or implements used in Christ's CRUCIFIXION or related to his suffering during the PASSION OF CHRIST. In Christian art, the list includes: the CROSS, nails (or spikes), a spear or lance, a sponge, vinegar, a column, a CROWN OF THORNS, a cup (see CUP OF WINE) or chalice (see CHALICE, THE EUCHARISTIC), a washbasin, a lantern, a torch, rope, a sword, a club, a staff, a moneybag, thirty pieces of silver, a flagellating tool such as the cat-o'-nine-tails, a rooster, a ladder, a hammer, pincers, garments, a seamless coat, dice. (The five wounds of Christ are often specifically included in medieval art. See also WOUNDS OF CHRIST, THE FIVE.)

Passion of Christ, the (Gk., *πάσχα [pascha]*, "Passover," "EASTER," or *πάθος [pathos]*, "a suffering," or Latin, *passio*, "suffering"). Jesus Christ's suffering to redeem humans, in particular Jesus' last days starting at the Lord's LAST SUPPER and ending in his humiliating CRUCIFIXION. See also MASS.

Passion Sunday. Commemorates the PASSION OF CHRIST, traditionally celebrated on the fifth Sunday in LENT, two weeks before Jesus' CRUCIFIXION.

Passiontide. **1.** Jesus' suffering or the PASSION OF CHRIST at the CRUCIFIXION. **2.** The two weeks preceding EASTER.

Passion Week. Also *Holy Week, Paschal Week*. **1.** The week before EASTER. Commemorates the PASSION OF CHRIST and traditionally begins on the sixth Sunday in LENT—PALM SUNDAY—and lasts until HOLY SATURDAY or EASTER EVE. **2.** The second week before Easter that begins with PASSION SUNDAY.

Passover, the Christian. Celebrated as EASTER. The Jewish Passover, or *Pasch,* commemorates the Exodus of the Jews from Egypt. Analogously, Easter has been referred to as the Christian Passover, or *Pasch,* commemorating the exodus of humans out of darkness into a new and promised life of redemption and eternal life. See also PASCHA.

pastor (L., *passere,* "to pasture," "to feed"). Literally, a shepherd of a flock. The spiritual overseer of a faith or church body such as a MINISTER or PRIEST. (Usually does not apply to officials above the level of a parish or specific church locale.)

pastoral. **1.** The caring for souls in the faith. **2.** The duties of a PASTOR of a church. **3.** The things that pertain to the affairs of the pastor.

pastoral epistles. Specifically, the EPISTLES (letters) to Timothy and Titus in the New Testament that deal with pastoral affairs.

pastoral letter. A letter written by the bishop to all members of his diocese and/or to the clergy.

pastoral staff. A staff, similar to a shepherd's crook, used as a formal emblem by an official or prelate. Usually the insignia of the office of a bishop or abbot. See also CROSIER.

Paternoster. The LORD'S PRAYER, from the first two Latin words of the prayer: *pater,* "father," and *noster,* "our."

patriarch (Gk., *πατριάρχης [patriarchēs],* "forefather," "chief of a race or tribe," from *πατρία [patria],* "lineage," "a race," and *ἄρχος [archos],* "leader," "ruler"). **1.** In the early Christian church, any high official such as a BISHOP, or higher. **2.** The head bishop of any of the Eastern Orthodox sees (see also SEES, THE FOUR ANCIENT). **3.** The bishop of the highest status in the Eatsern church, ranking above all the other patriarchs and metropolitans (also referred to as the Ecumenical patriarch), and stationed in Constantinople (see also METROPOLITAN; PATRIARCHATES, THE FIVE ANCIENT). **4.** In early Christian times, the official name given to the bishops of such metropolitan sees as Rome, Constantinople, Antioch, Alexandria, Jerusalem. In the Roman Catholic church, the word is no longer in use except as a purely honorary title (for example, Pope Pius X was patriarch of Venice). **5.** The name given to the great men of the Old Testament such as Abraham and Moses. These patriarchs are believed to be precursors of the Christian faith, previsioning and preparing the way for Jesus Christ as the final divine event of history (see Matt. 17:3ff.; Rom. 4:1; 1 Cor. 10:1–12; Heb. 11; etc.).

patriarchates, the five ancient. The five ancient jurisdictions of the early Christian patriarchs were Rome (the only one in the West), Antioch, Alexandria, Jerusalem, and Constantinople. At the time of the Council of Nicaea (325), only the first three were patriarchates or had patriarchs. By the second general Council of Nicaea (381), Constantinople was added. Jerusalem was added later.

patripassianism. Regarded as a Trinitarian HERESY that stresses the notion that since Christ is God and Christ suffered, so too God the father suffered. See also MODALISM.

patristics (Gk., *πατήρ [patēr]*, "a father"). A branch of theology that studies the writings of the Church Fathers. The *patristic age* is usually considered to be the period from the New Testament writings to the end of the eighth century. During the patristic period of Christianity, ASCETICISM, martyrdom, and celibacy were regarded as highlights of the Christian way of life. These it was felt were the essentials in the Imitation of Christ (see CHRIST, IMITATION OF). See also PATROLOGY.

patrology (Gk., *πατήρ [patēr]*, "a father," and **λόγος** *[logos]*, "the study of"). The study of the writings, lives, and times of the early CHURCH FATHERS. In the Western (Latin) church, this period is generally regarded as ending with St. Isidore of Seville (560–636) and in the Eastern church with St. John Damascus (about 749). See also PATRISTICS.

peacock, the. A Christian symbol of immortality because it was believed that its flesh never decayed.

pectoral cross. See CROSS, PECTORAL.

pedilavium. See FOOT WASHING.

Pelagianism. The system of belief that stems from Pelagius (360–420), a British monk who went to Rome about 400 and preached doctrines such as: BAPTISM does not regenerate; there is no original sin; pain, suffering, and death are not consequences of original sin; humans have complete freedom of the will granted by God, but it is obligated to, and directed toward, by predisposition, acceptance and the following of God's commands; a life of complete sinlessness is possible; God's GRACE is not necessary for salvation, although it can be of aid. AUGUSTINIANISM and Pelagianism were in direct conflict. Pelagianism has been condemned as a heresy many times, for example, at the Synod of Carthage in 412 by Pope Innocent I, at the Council of Ephesus in 431, at the Council of Trent (1545–1563).

Pelican, the. A Christian symbol or emblem for Jesus' sacrifice to redeem humanity. In Christian art, the pelican is often depicted piercing its breast with its beak and feeding its young with its blood. This was a symbol of Jesus' loving self-sacrifice in redeeming and saving humanity.

penance (L., *paenitentia*, "penitence"). **1.** The activity of showing penitence, or sorrow, for sins. **2.** The satisfactions (fines, punishments, penalties) imposed for having sinned (see also SATISFACTION). **3.** In the Roman Catholic church, penance is one of the seven SACRAMENTS and is the prescribed method for the remission (see also FORGIVENESS) of one's mortal sins committed after baptism. This ability to forgive sins is the exclusive right of the priesthood. Not all sins are forgivable by a priest. The essential features of penance as a sacrament: asking of repentance for having sinned (CONTRITION); confession to a priest; satisfaction, such as some task or observance to be performed; and ABSOLUTION by the priest. The absolution is uttered by the priest while the penitent is present and usually has the form: "I absolve thee from all censures and sins in the name of the Father, and of the Son, and of the Holy Ghost. Amen." Unlike the other sacraments, penance (and BAPTISM) does not presuppose that one is in a state of God's Grace. It does presuppose (as baptism also does) a state of FAITH. (See also GRACE, SANCTIFY.) This sacrament is necessary as a means of SALVATION. It readmits a human to the other sacraments (especially the EUCHARIST) since a sinner is estranged from the Church after committing mortal sins. Damnation is prevented and the power of the devil is lessened by the administration of the sacrament of penance. Scriptural support of penance is found in Matthew 6:12; 18:15; 1 John 5:16; 1 Timothy 1:19, 20; 5:5, 10–25; John 20:19–23; 1 Corinthians 5:4ff.; 2 Corinthians 2:5–11; 5:18ff.

PROTESTANTISM does not regard penance as a sacrament (although CONFESSION and ABSOLUTION, which are essential aspects of it, have been practiced in Protestantism in some form or other). Yet Christian thought in general regards penance as a theological virtue. The following are some of the beliefs and attitudes associated with the concept. Penance signifies the correct personal, moral, and religious attitude of humans toward their own sin and toward sin in general. The essence of true penance is contrition, METANOIA. Penance involves, among other things, a respect for the power and presence of God, a fear of God, the courage to accept God and face up to the truth about one's existence, sin, limitations, and helplessness, the sincere desire to make amends for one's sins and life in general. There are consequences of sin that remain even after the sin has been forgiven. Those in the true spirit of penance must willingly humble themselves to accept and endure the consequences of that remaining sin. Penance involves the awareness and acceptance of the responsibility for the sin, distress, and suffering of humanity in general.

Penance as a human action, in distinction from its being a gift of God, is an active turning away from our past, which past is producing guilt, pain, and alienation from God. This past is abhorred. Penance is based on a hope that God's presence in us will work toward our conversion and redemption.

Penance must be seen in connection with works, charity, love, faith, satisfaction, justification, resolve, conversion, and dedication to oneself into the future in a Christian way. Forms of penance: penitential works, fasting, charity, almsgiving, vigils, indulgences, etc.

penitence (L., *poenitere,* "to repent"). **1.** Sorrow or REPENTANCE for one's sins. **2.** CONTRITION. See also PENANCE.

Pentecost. Also *Whitsunday* (Gk., *πεντηκοστή [pentēkostē]*, with *ἡμέρα [ēmera]*, "day," "the fiftieth day," from *πεντηκοστός [pentēkostos]*, "fiftieth"). The Christian festival celebrating the descent of the HOLY SPIRIT in the form of the power of tongues (see GLOSSOLALIA) upon Jesus' Apostles, fifty days after Jesus' Resurrection, the seventh Sunday after Easter, ten days after Jesus' Ascension. (Acts 2:2–4: "And suddenly there came a sound from heaven as of a rushing mighty wind, and it filled all the house where they were sitting. And there appeared unto them cloven tongues like as of fire, and it sat upon each of them. And they were all filled with the Holy Ghost, and began to speak with other tongues, as the Spirit gave them utterance.")

Pentecost ceremonies are based on the sermon given by Peter that produced the baptism of 3,000. Regarded as the birthday of the Catholic church. (Pentecost coincides with the Jewish festival of Pentecost celebrated the fiftieth day [seven weeks] after the second day of the Passover, and Easter is the Christian version of the Jewish Passover.)

Pentecostal. Also CHARISMATIC. The experience of spiritual conversion to Christianity by the entrance of the HOLY SPIRIT, similar to that experienced by the Apostles at the first PENTECOST. Pentecostal churches (often referred to as Revivalist or Charismatic) stress the literal interpretation of the Bible (see also FUNDAMENTALISM) and the working of the Holy Spirit upon an individual, which produces the gifts of the Holy Spirit, such as "speaking in tongues" (see also GLOSSOLALIA), faith, power of healing, recognition of spirits. See also REVIVALISM; SPIRITUAL GIFTS.

Perfection, Counsels of. See COUNSELS OF PERFECTION.

perichōrēsis. Greek, *περιχώρησις*, "penetration." Also *circumincessio*. **1.** The reciprocal relationship and interaction of Jesus' two natures, the human and divine. **2.** The being-in-one-another, totally without residue, of the Holy Trinity. Scriptural references can be found at: John 10:38; 14:10ff.; 17:21; 1 Corinthians 2:10ff. **3.** The love relationship in the Holy Trinity between God the Father and Jesus the Son. See also VINCULUM AMORIS.

perseverance (L., *perseverare*, "to persevere," "to persist in a thing," from *per*, "through," "by means of," "by," and *severus*, "strict," "severe"). The state of continued GRACE (as opposed to a momentary, present grace, or one that is temporary).

perseverance, final. Also *the perseverance of the saints*. **1.** The state of continued GRACE succeeded by a state of glory. **2.** Having grace while alive and dying in that continued state of grace.

Regarded as a gift from God; derived purely from the Providence of God and assured and known only by him. A view held in Roman Catholicism, Calvinism, and by a variety of Reformed churches.

personalism, theological. **1.** Reality has two fundamental levels: **(a)** The level of God as Supreme Personality from which all persons (personalities) derive their being. God is supernatural and a completely spiritual consciousness. **(b)** The level of nature, created by the Supreme Person but which is nonpersonal (nonspiritual, nonmental). **2.** Reality is God as the person who maintains all activities in the universe by his creative personal consciousness and will. **3.** God is the *final* cause or final form toward which the universe is striving, as opposed to a FIRST CAUSE.

Pietism. **1.** The faith and practice of the Pietists, a German seventeenth- and eighteenth-century movement primarily within German Lutheranism. They objected to the formalism and intellectualism of the church and stressed religious feelings, emotions, devotion, and the sense of duty to God's commands. They sought the experience of personal CONVERSION and emphasized personal and social discipline. They stressed a stern, practical Christianity of active love, pragmatic goals, spiritual inwardness, individuality, the Bible as the only true inspiration for humans, personal conversion, personal devotion to Jesus Christ as the only means of SALVATION, as opposed to the dogmas of the church. **2.** Often used in a derogatory sense to refer to excessive stress upon, or demonstration of, religious devotion, as opposed to reason, and/or the affectation of devotion.

pistology (Gk., *πίστις [pistis],* "trust in others," "faith," "belief in," "confidence," "assurance," and **λόγος** *[logos],* "an account of," "the study of"). **1.** The study of a theological belief or faith. **2.** The study of the nature, source, ground, and value of faith (belief) in contrast to the status of reason or revelation.

plenitude, principle of. The universe acquires its highest actualization and perfection whenever God allows (or we allow) his nature to enter into things.

plērōma. Greek, *πλήρωμα,* meaning a "full measure," "the sum total," "fullness," "a full and perfect nature of being," "fulfillment." The filling up of matter with the rationality of true reality (the light of God). Used, for example, by St. Paul to mean that Jesus Christ is the "all-in-all," the only and total divine reality and not one of a number of spiritual realities or powers; that Jesus Christ expresses the completeness, the fullness of the only true divine reality functioning in the world (see Col. 1:19; 2:9; Eph. 1:23; John 1:16).

pneuma. Greek, *πνεῦμα,* "a blowing," "a wind," "breath," "spirit." The Greek *πνεύμον (pneumon),* meant "the lungs." *Pneuma* was used with a variety of meanings in the history of Greek philosophy but in general it meant "soul," "the spiritual cause of life." It is conceptually related to words such as *ψυχή (psychē), νοῦς (nous),* and *λόγος (logos).* In Christianity, *pneuma* was translated as "spirit," or "ghost" as in *τό Ἅγιο πνεῦμα (to Hagio Pneuma),* the HOLY SPIRIT (the Holy Ghost). It is also used specifically to refer to the vital energy or principle uniting, directing, revitalizing the Church, its life, spirit, work, and world. Scriptural references can be found at Luke 1:47; 23:46; Acts 7:59; John 11:33; Galatians 6:18; Romans 8:10ff.; 1 Thessalonians 5:23; 1 Corinthians 2:10–16; 3:16; 12:13; 2 Corinthians 3:17.

pneumatology (Gk., πνεῦμα *[pneuma]*, πνεύματος *[pneumatos]*, "wind," "air," "spirit," "soul," and λόγος *[logos]*, "the study of"). **1.** The study of spiritual beings intermediate between God and humans. **2.** The study of spiritual phenomena. **3.** The study of souls. **4.** The area of theology that studies the doctrines of and beliefs about the HOLY SPIRIT.

poena damni. Latin. A Scholastic phrase for "the pains of hell." At present, often interpreted figuratively as a feeling of separation or ESTRANGEMENT from God.

poena sensus. Latin. A Scholastic phrase for "the pains of sensation," referring to the means by which humans would be tortured in HELL.

Polydaemonism. See SPIRITISM.

Pontiff, the Holy. Another name for the pope of the Roman Catholic church. In Latin he is referred to as *Pontifex Summus,* the Supreme Pontiff.

pope, the (L., *papa,* "father," "bishop," from Gk., πάπας *[papas]*, "father"). The official title given to the bishop of Rome in his power as the supreme leader on earth of the universal Church founded by Jesus Christ himself. According to the Roman Catholic church, Jesus Christ founded his Church under the authority of his disciples, the Apostles (see also APOSTOLIC COLLEGE). He appointed Peter as the head—the rock, the foundation—of his Church. Peter, as the vizier, steward, leader of this Church, would hold the keys and powers, such as of binding and loosing, baptizing, applying the sacraments, etc. Scriptural references for this have been seen in places such as: Matthew 10:2; 16:16–18; John 21:15ff.; Luke 22:32.

According to Roman Catholic faith, St. Peter was the first pope, the first bishop of Rome, in the year 42. He held that position for twenty-five years. Peter was bishop of Rome when he died. The bishop of Rome succeeded Peter in authority, power, and privileges—they were transferred and are continuously transferred to each succeeding bishop of Rome. Just as St. Peter was endowed with primacy and supremacy, so too the pope is endowed with primacy and supremacy. See also KEYS, THE POWERS OF THE.

The Reformation challenged the Roman Catholic church's contention that the keys to the Church were given only to St. Peter. The Reformers believed that the keys were given to all those in the Christian faith and all members of the Christian community.

pope, the primacy of the. A Roman Catholic belief in the pope as the supreme and infallible source of authority, power, and inspiration. St.

Augustine (354–430) devoutly proclaimed the SEE at Rome as the guarantor of Christian unity that signified by the presence there of St. Peter, the true successor of Jesus Christ.

Pope Leo the Great (440–461) formalized this belief in several ways: **1.** Jesus passed on his authority and powers to the disciple Peter; **2.** Peter was the first bishop of Rome; **3.** Peter passed on his authority, status, and powers upon his successor who was to continue this until the Second Coming; **4.** St. Peter is spiritually present, as is Jesus, in the SEE at Rome; **5.** The authority and power of the bishop of Rome (the pope) is obtained directly, supernaturally, spirtually, and by tradition from Jesus Christ. All other bishops obtain their authority and power through St. Peter and the bishop (the pope) who has replaced St. Peter; **6.** The influence, powers, and authority of each bishop are restricted to his diocese, but the bishop of Rome (the pope) has power, authority, and influence over all other dioceses as the spiritual and administrative head of the entire Church body. The first Vatican Council of 1870 formally established papal supremacy, proclaiming by divine institution the pope's full, final, and supreme infallible authority over the Church (see also APOSTOLIC SUCCESSION).

The concept of the primacy of the pope and the Church's papal hierarchy were challenged even before the Reformation as having no grounds in the Gospels, by such theologians as John Wyclif (1328–1384) and John Huss (1369–1415).

positive theology. See THEOLOGY, POSITIVE.

possession (L., *possessio,* from *possidere,* "to possess"). The state of being dominated, motivated, driven by a demon or evil spirit. Used synonymously with OBSESSION. See also DEMON; EVIL POWERS; EXORCISM.

poverty (L., *pauper,* "poor"). **1.** The state of being in need, destitute, or poor. Regarded favorably as one of the many qualities Christians should respect (see also VIRTUES, THE THEOLOGICAL). At Luke 6:24 ("But woe unto you that are rich! for ye have received your consolation"), Jesus denounces the rich. At Matthew 5:3 ("Blessed are the poor in spirit: for theirs is the kingdom of heaven"), Jesus blesses the poor in spirit. Also refer to Matthew 8:20; 26:11. **2.** One of the expressions of asceticism and monasticism. **3.** Infrequently, regarded as a symbol, or sign, that the last days of history have begun. See also COUNSELS OF PERFECTION.

powers, evil. See EVIL POWERS.

prayer (L., *precarius,* "got by prayer," from *precari,* "to pray," "to supplicate"). The act of supplication (or adoration, thanksgiving, confession, meditation) to God as the Supreme Being. In Christianity, all prayers are made in Christ's name. Many have the common form of "Lord, have mercy on us." Prayer is seen as an expression of the need for salvation and assistance from God. At Matthew 7:7–11 and John 16:23ff.; 15:7, 16, prayer is a form of petition. There are liturgical and public prayers, and private prayers. There are prayers to have sins forgiven, to receive personal salvation, to help the dead receive forgiveness and salvation, to the saints as intercessors, to Jesus Christ himself, to praise God, etc. The EUCHARIST in essence is a prayer of thanksgiving.

prayers for the dead. A common, perennial Roman Catholic and Eastern Orthodox custom. Related to the Communion of Saints (see COMMUNIO SANCTORUM). Those in purgatory can, by means of prayers, be helped to reach heaven, the final state of blessedness.

Prayer, the Lord's. See LORD'S PRAYER.

precious blood. See BLOOD, PRECIOUS.

predestination, divine. (L., *pre,* "before," and *destinare,* "to destine"). Also referred to as *preordination; foreordination.* The belief that God has foreordained every event that has happened, is happening, and will happen in the universe, in accordance with his divine purpose and OMNISCIENT nature. No deviation in the slightest is possible. For example, in Calvinism, God has preordained humans to eternal misery or happiness and nothing can be done about this (except by God—but if God does cause a change in the predetermined plans for things, then this too was predetermined by God, which is in effect "double predestination" or "double predetermination"). See also PROVIDENCE.

predetermination, divine. See PREDESTINATION, DIVINE.

premundane fall. See FALL, THE PREMUNDANE.

presbyter (Gk., *πρεσβύτερος [presbyteros],* "elder," "older," comparative form of *πρέσβυς [presbys],* "an old man"). **1.** An elder in the early Christian church. **2.** A priest. **3.** A minister. **4.** In Presbyterianism, a member of the presbytery or church, whether lay or clerical.

At Luke 22:66 and at Acts 22:5, the Greek *πρεσβυτέριον (presbyterion)* is used to refer to the Jewish elders and at 1 Timothy 4:14 to the elders of a Christian congregation.

presbyterianism. A form of church government that puts spiritual authority and power into the hands of its presbyters, or elders, without clergy, bishops, or prelates above them, and that is TRINITARIAN and Calvinistic in faith (see CALVINISM).

presbytery. **1.** In Presbyterianism, the church itself, which includes ministers and laypersons. **2.** The jurisdiction of a presbyter. **3.** That part of a church reserved for those priests, or clergy, who are officiating.

Presentation of the Blessed Virgin Mary, the Feast of the. Celebrated on November 21 in commemoration of Mary's presentation in the Temple of Jerusalem by her parents St. Joachim and St. Anne.

Presentation of Jesus in the Temple, the Feast of the. Celebrated on February 2 in commemoration of Jesus' presentation to God in the Temple of Jerusalem by Mary and Joseph (Luke 2:22–39), forty days after his birth, according to Jewish tradition (as in Lev. 12:2–8; Exod. 13:2). St. Anna the prophetess was present and hailed Jesus as the Redeemer. St. Simeon, who had been told "by the Holy Ghost, that he should not see death, before he had seen the Lord's Christ," was also present and took Jesus "up in his arms, and blessed God." At this presentation Mary, in accordance with the "law of the Lord," offered as a sacrifice "a pair of turtledoves, or two young pigeons."

This feast is also called CANDLEMAS from the custom of blessing and handing out of candles to be lighted as a symbol of Jesus' light in the world, in accordance with St. Simeon's hailing Jesus as "a light to lighten the Gentiles, and the glory of thy people Israel." Also celebrated as the Feast of the Purification of the Blessed Virgin Mary, commemorating the purification of the Blessed Virgin Mary, which occurred as she presented Jesus at the Temple (see PRESENTATION OF JESUS IN THE TEMPLE, THE FEAST OF THE.)

pride. **1.** Putting human desires (drives, wishes) ahead of God's. **2.** Being anthropocentric as opposed to theocentric. Having humans dominate and be the center of life rather than God. **3.** Self-esteem that overwhelms any esteem for God. Lack of humbleness and humility in reference to God. In Christian faith, pride is regarded as one of the highest sins (see also SIN).

priest (Gk., *πρεσβύτερος [presbyteros],* "older," "elder," the comparative form of *πρέσβυς [presbys],* "an old man"; implies wisdom, experience, authority, and credibility). **1.** An ordained person, set apart from the LAITY, who is authorized to perform religious rites, sacred activities, or functions of the faith; one ordained to perform the ministerial, pastoral, sacerdotal, and administrative tasks of a church. **2.** Specifically, an ordained person below a bishop (and where deacons are found, above a DEACON/DEACONNESS). See also CLERGY; MINISTER; PRESBYTER; PRIESTHOOD, THE HOLY.

priest, Christ as. Christ as priest fulfills the highest function of a priest: to allow himself to be a sacrifice in order to remove the sins of humanity and allow a new covenant to be made with God (Mark 14:58ff.; Matt. 26:62–68; Heb. 13:20). See also JESUS AS PROPHET.

priesthood, the holy. Regarded, for example, by the Roman Catholic church as the spiritual state highest in sacredness, power, dignity, and privileges. Priests are disciples of Christ active in the present on his divine behalf and legitimately represent Christ among the faithful. The priesthood is Christ acting in the world. At 1 Corinthians 4:1–2: "Let a man so account of us, as of the ministers of Christ, and stewards of the mysteries of God. Moreover it is required in stewards, that a man be found faithful." At John 20:21: "Then said Jesus to them again, Peace be unto you: as my Father hath sent me, even so I send you. And when he had said this, he breathed on them, and saith unto them, 'Receive ye the Holy Ghost.' "

The authority to say mass, receive the Body and Blood of the Savior, perform the sacraments, etc., is conferred upon a priest by Christ at ordination or consecration, not by the congregation, not directly by the

Church, but through the powers of apostolic succession, going back to Christ's transfer of power to St. Peter and the Apostles.

Primate. See METROPOLITAN.

Prince of Peace. Also *Prince of Light, Prince of Heaven, Prince of the Kingdom,* etc. Refers to Jesus Christ.

Prince of the Power. See EVIL POWERS.

prior (L., *prior,* "former," "previous," "preceding in order of authority, rank, knowledge"). **1.** The superior, head, or ruler of a PRIORY. **2.** The head of an ABBEY ranking next to the ABBOT in authority and dignity.

prioress. A female superior, or head of a PRIORY of nuns, ranking next to the ABBESS in authority and dignity.

priory. **1.** A religious house or habitat usually regarded as a rank below (or as part of) an ABBEY (or MONASTERY). **2.** A monastery or NUNNERY headed by a PRIOR or PRIORESS.

process theology. See THEOLOGY, PROCESS.

profane (L., *profanus,* from *pro,* "before," and *fanum,* "temple"). **1.** Not SACRED or HOLY, but SECULAR. **2.** Ungodly, unholy, or unsanctified. **3.** Temporal; of this world. **4.** Sometimes, irreverent, disrespectful, blasphemous; treating sacred things with contempt or ridicule. Compare with CONSECRATION.

profession (L., *professus,* from *profiteri,* "to profess," from *pro,* "before," and *fateri,* "to confess," "to own"). **1.** That which one professes to believe; a religious faith openly proclaimed or avowed. **2.** A religious calling or vocation. Compare with CONFESSION.

prophecy (Gk., *προφητεία [prophēteia],* from *προφήτης [prophētēs],* "one who speaks for God"). The foretelling of things to come. The NEW TESTAMENT is regarded by Christians as the ultimate and final prophecy; and the OLD TESTAMENT is itself a prophecy of the coming of Jesus Christ. Prophecy has usually been associated with ECSTASY, inspiration, an intense emotional and spiritual experience, a being overcome by the HOLY SPRIRIT, etc.

prophet, Jesus as. See JESUS AS PROPHET.

prophets, the. Early Christianity regarded John the Baptist and Jesus as prophets—inspired by God, able to speak in his name and foretell future events. There is reference in the New Testament to prophets at Acts 2:14–36; 11:27; 21:10ff.; and 1 Corinthians 14:3, 24, 29, 31. Prophets were recognized as a lesser rank than the Apostles, as chief-priests, and had considerable authority over Christian communities.

propitiation (L., *propitius,* "favorable"). The WRATH OF GOD, must be *propitiated* (pacified, appeased, conciliated). Christ's obedient sacrifice of his life in love is a propitiation of our sins. Christ bore our sins, absorbed the earth's sins into himself. He was condemned as a sinner and died a hostile, horrible death. He faced the consequences of sin for a sinner. Yet he was pure, free of sin, innocent. He did not deserve the wrath of anyone. (At Isa. 53:10, where Christ is thought to be previsioned: "Yet it pleased the Lord to bruise Him.") Christ, as a human, may have thought God had forsaken him: "And about the ninth hour Jesus cried with a loud voice, saying 'Eli, Eli, lama sabachthani?' that is to say, 'My God, my God, why hast thou forsaken me?' " (Matt. 27:46. Refer also to Mark 15:34). According to Christianity, Christ was the propitiation: God had to allow Christ to suffer and die, to become fully human and serve us as the perfect ideal. At John 10:17, 18, Jesus says: "Therefore doth my Father love me, because I lay down my life, that I might take it again. No man taketh it from me, but I lay it down of myself. I have power to lay it down, and I have power to take it again. This commandment have I received of my Father."

proskynēsis. Greek *προσκύνησις*, "adoration," "obeisance." The VENERATION given to icons and sacred objects. Also used in the Greek Orthodox church to refer specifically to the making of the SIGN OF THE CROSS.

prosopon. Greek, *πρόσοπον* "person," "presence." Used to refer to the members of the Trinity. See also HYPOSTASIS.

prosyletism (Gk., *προσήλυτος [prosēlytos],* "one who has come to a place," "a stranger," "a convert"). The activity of converting others to a particular faith or sect.

Protestant (L., *protestans,* from *protestari,* "to protest," from *pro,* "before," "in," and *testari,* "to be a witness"; may be derived from the "Protestation" of the Lutherans at the Second Imperial Diet of Speyer in 1529; "Protestant" implied one who protested against a belief and declared for a belief). **1.** Any Christian who adheres to any of the churches that separated from the Roman Catholic church at the REFORMATION or any of the sects descended from them. **2.** Historically, one of those Lutheran princes who signed a protest at the Diet of Speyer (also Spires), on April 19, 1529 (against an edict whose purpose was to destroy the Reformation), requesting Emperor Charles V to summon a general council to discuss church matters.

Protestant Episcopal church. The Christian church representing the Anglican Communion in the United States, organized in 1789 as separate from the Church of England.

Protestantism. The Christian faith of Protestants, the religious sects that sprang from the Reformation of the sixteenth century (see also PROTESTANT) and united mainly in that they were all a protest against the Roman Catholic church. Some basic tenets: **1.** Toleration. **2.** Separation of church and state powers. **3.** Individualism. **4.** A return to the Bible as a source of inspiration, belief, and direction.

providence (L., *providere,* "to provide," from *pro,* "before," and *videre,* "to see"). **1.** The foresight, love, concern, and care God has for all his creatures. Timely care. **2.** God. **3.** Fate decreed by God; an event divinely ordained or preordained. **4.** The belief that the universe is governed by God so as ultimately to produce the good (Rom. 8:28: "All things work together for good to them that love God, to them who are called according to his purpose"). See also PREDESTINATION, DIVINE.

psalm (Gk., ψαλμός *[psalmos]*, from ψάλλειν *[psallein]*, "to play on a stringed instrument," "to sing to the harp," "to sing," "to chant"). A sacred song or poem. A HYMN.

psilanthropism (Gk., ψιλάνθρωπος *[psilanthrōpos]*, "merely human," from ψιλός *[psilos]*, "mere," "bare," and ἄνθρωπος *[anthrōpos]*, "man"). The belief that Jesus Christ was merely a human being and not divine.

punishment, eternal. Punishment that cannot be remitted or absolved here on earth or in PURGATORY. Everlasting punishment in HELL has been described in terms of physical pain caused by fire (refer to 1 Cor. 3:12–15; 1 Pet. 1:6–9).

punishment, temporal. Punishment on earth or in PURGATORY, which is given by God and received by means for the remission of their sin.

purgatory (L., *pugare,* "to purge," from *purus,* "pure," and *agere,* "to make," "to do"). The place after death where human souls have the opportunity of being cleansed (purged) of their sins.

The doctrine of purgatory was officially declared at the Council of Florence in 1439. (Eastern Orthodoxy has no official doctrine of purgatory.) St. Augustine (354–430) is sympathetic to the notion of a purgatory where the spirits of the dead will be purgated (purified) by fire somewhere between their death and their judgment. The Council of Trent accepts the notion of purgatory: "that there is a purgatory and that souls there detained are helped by the intercessions of the faithful, but most of all by the acceptable sacrifice of the altar."

Some of the beliefs related to purgatory: **1.** It is a period of discipline and punishment after death to purge sin that was committed in life. **2.** The unbaptized are not allowed entrance (see also LIMBO). **3.** Not all the baptized are admitted, since some go directly to HELL. **4.** The time spent in purgatory is relative to the sins committed and the penance and indulgences given in life for the absolution of sin. **5.** Purgatory will cease to exist at the Last Judgment or the Second Coming of Christ. **6.** Those faithful alive can by means of prayers, intercessions, works of charity, the mass, influence the condition and status of those in purgatory.

Scriptural references used in defense of purgatory: Matthew 5:25, 26; 12:32. The Reformers rejected purgatory as not in accordance with Scripture.

Puritan. **1.** In general, a *puritan* is one who is austere, rigid, or strict in religious observances and/or in conduct. Often used in a derogatory sense. **2.** Specifically in ecclesiastical history, *Puritan* referred to an English Protestant sect at the time of Queen Elizabeth and the first two Stuarts, that opposed the traditional and formal religious observances and advocated a simpler style of worship than that which was established by law. In its original use, *Puritan* was a term of reproach. See also PURITAN ETHIC, THE.

Puritan ethic, the. Some of the views associated with the Puritan ethic: **1.** The highest human values to be gotten out of life are through hard physical work that has definite practical results for oneself and the community in which one lives. **2.** Living is a dedication to work that produces and is pervaded by moral values such as industriousness, discipline, honesty, moderation, temperance, devotion, humility before God, frugality, thrift, simplicity, acceptance of toil, hardship and pain, self-sufficiency, dedication to family life and to others in developing a sense of community, and awareness of the purpose and presence of God from whom these values stem and for whom these values are expressed.

Puritanism. Refers specifically to the doctrines or beliefs of the PURITANS. They adopted many of the general principles of John Calvin (1509–1564). Some of their basic views: **1.** God is the absolute authority and sovereign over all the universe and all humanity. (Puritans tend to be theocratic.) **2.** Humans are totally dependent upon God for all their endowments, fortune, fate, and very existence. **3.** Humans are tainted with original sin that can never be eradicated except by God. God's Grace secures us salvation and is the only source of salvation. **4.** Salvation cannot be earned through good works, although the merit earned by good works prepares a human being to receive God's Grace. **5.** God has preordained who is selected to go to heaven or elected into the "Company of Saints." **6.** The authority of the church is not primary and is generally rejected. Puritans stressed the immediate and private relationship of each individual with God. (However, the Puritans did not tolerate deviation from their general principles and authority.)

Q

Quakers. The name given to the Society of Friends (or Religious Society of Friends), probably by Justice Bennet in 1650, who is supposed to have said that the founder of the Society, George Fox (1624–1691), had preached at him to "tremble" at the Word of God. Another possible derivation: Members of the Society would sometimes tremble (quake) when ovecome by religious ecstasy or experience (probably originally used in derision or scorn).

The name "Friends" is taken from John 14:14: "Ye are my friends, if ye do whatsoever I command you." Early Quakers also called themselves "Children of the Light," "Friends in the Truth," "Seekers," "Finders." Their principal tenets: **1.** Rejection of all formalism, ritualism, and liturgy in worship and belief. **2.** Rejection of any ecclesiastical hierarchy or priesthood. **3.** Rejection of the sacraments as necessary to salvation. **4.** Belief in Jesus as the living Savior. **5.** Rejection of all creeds. **6.** Belief in an inner divine light (an inner voice), implanted by God, that may be used to guide humans to truth and righteousness. **7.** The essence of worhsip is silence, during which God reveals his direction and goodness. One is then moved to speak and to act. **8.** Pacifism. The refusal to take up arms. **9.** The attempt to live as simply, honestly, truthfully, and deeply committed as possible.

quod ubique, quod semper et quod ad omnibus. Latin, referring to the care that should be taken that people hold that faith "which has been believed everywhere, always, and by all." Sometimes referred to as the Vincentian Canon after Vincent, a monk of Lerins who presented it in his *Commonitorium* written in 434.

R

reborn. Being "reborn"implies accepting without question Jesus Christ as one's personal Savior, Lord, and Master in virtue of his suffering, death, and resurrection. See also CONVERSION; NEW BIRTH.

rector (L., *regere,* "to rule," "to lead [oneself and others] straight"). In the Protestant Episcopal and Anglican tradition, a cleric (clergyman or clergywoman) in charge of a parish.

rectory. **1.** In general, any of the benefices of a parish including its rights, privileges, compensation, etc. **2.** Specifically, one of the BENEFICES held by a RECTOR, namely, the parsonage.

Redeemer, the. Christ. See entries under JESUS.

redemption (L., *redemptio,* from *redimere,* "to redeem," "to buy back again," from *re,* "again," and *emere,* "to buy"). **1.** The deliverance from sin and its punishment and attainment of SALVATION through Jesus Christ and the HOLY SPIRIT. **2.** The ATONEMENT or ransom of Christ in order to liberate humans from sin and fulfill God's love and promise to humankind. **3.** Jesus' making amends for God's dissatisfaction and returning us back to God's ways and light.

According to Christian tradition, redemption requires a payment (or a gift, or a ransom) as a prerequisite for setting humans free from the bondage of sin. God's sole purpose is to redeem all humanity. God's love, goodness, righteousness are so intense and part of his nature as to necessitate him to redeem humanity and give them his kingdom. The cost of redemption was great: God had to lose his only begotten Son, Jesus. This event reveals God's immeasurable love for humanity. The redemptive act that is the foundation of SALVATION involves Jesus' INCARNATION, CRUCIFIXION, RESURRECTION, AND ASCENSION. See also ALIENATION; ATONEMENT; METANOIA; OBEDIENCE; RECONCILIATION.

Redemptorist. A member of a Roman Catholic holy order, the Congregation of the Most Holy Redeemer, founded in 1732 and devoted to service and preaching to the poor and neglected.

Redemptrix. Latin, *redemptor,* "redeemer," from *redimere,* "to redeem," from *re,* "again," and *emere,* "to buy." Applied to the Virgin MARY as the redeemer of the world. See also CO-REDEMPTRIX.

Reformation, the. Also the *Protestant Reformation* (L., *reformare,* "to reform," from *re,* "again," and *forma,* "form"). The religious movement in the Western church that began in the early sixteenth century and resulted in the formation of a multitude of Protestant churches. In general, the Reformation can be grouped into three major categories: **1.** Lutheran (in Germany), **2.** Reformed (Zwingli and Calvin in Switzerland), and **3.** Anglican (the reformed movements in England.)

Believed that what was not strictly expressed (expounded, shown, illustrated) in the Bible was to be rejected or forbidden. Emphasized the individual's response in a state of FAITH to the BIBLE, or the Word of God, as opposed to the proclamations, accretions, and traditions of the Roman Catholic church. The Bible was to be recognized as the sole authority for all of life. The Reformation rejected the Roman Catholic view of the SACRAMENTS, GRACE, PENANCE, indulgences, PURGATORY, and accepted the notion of justification by faith alone (although true faith led to good works, good works did not obtain God's salvation, which was unmerited and freely given). The Reformation objected to the hierarchy of the priesthood of the Roman Catholic church, its ultimate authority and jurisdiction, and its serving as a mediator between humans and God.

reincarnation (L., *re,* "again," and *incarnare,* "to incarnate," from *in* "in," and *caro,* "flesh"). The rebirth of the soul in another body after death. St. Origen (185–254) held to reincarnation. Christian tradition in the main has not believed in successive rebirths as accepted in reincarnation (or sometimes referred to as METEMPSYCHOSIS OR TRANSMIGRATION), but rather holds to a belief in one REBIRTH (by means of baptism into the new life of Jesus Christ) and one RESURRECTION.

relic. **1.** In general, anything venerated or held in high esteem as a reminder of some spiritual or holy presence, or as possessing powers of healing or religious conversion. **2.** Specifically, the remains of a sacred person or object that is revered. This may include pieces of the bones, hair, skin, clothing, etc., of a dead person such as a SAINT.

The Roman Catholic church has veneration for any object related to any saint of the Church. The highest relics are those of Jesus' true CROSS and the Instruments of the Passion (see also PASSION, INSTRUMENTS OF THE). Any part of the body of a saint is regarded as a *first-class relic.* A *second-class relic* is any piece of a saint's clothing or any object used by a saint. Any object that a saint has touched or been in contact with is classified as a *third-class relic.* Relics are often housed in a vessel called a *reliquary.*

religion, natural. Religion based on the belief that humanity has the ability to create a system of thought about God and the universe by the use of reason alone. Contrasted with RELIGION, REVEALED.

religion, revealed. Religion based on the belief that humans do not have the ability to construct with unaided reason a system of thought about God and the universe but must rely upon Revelation (see REVELATION, DIVINE) **1.** for its fundamental starting principles, **2.** for the correction of reason gone astray, **3.** for supplementing the incomplete knowledge provided by reason, and **4.** for adding knowledge that cannot be obtained by reason. Contrasted with RELIGION, NATURAL.

religious experience. The characterization of the religious experience takes a variety of forms, from the view **1.** that the experience is of an object, that one directly confronts a divine being, to **2.** that the religious experience refers to a *quality* of experience rather than to an object; to a consummatory or peak experience in which one feels actualized or in which one becomes ecstatically aware of his/her highest spiritual ideals and aspirations. See also entries on MYSTICISM; NUMINOUS, THE.

Religious Society of Friends. See QUAKERS.

renunciation (L., *renuntiar,* "to bring back word," "to announce," "to renounce"). The act of renouncing, abandoning, recanting, disavowing, disclaiming, rejecting, abjuring. In Christian tradition, renunciation takes the form of sacrificing and suffering for purposes such as accomplishment, control, order, dedication, revitalization, simplicity of action and life, achievement of spirituality and the contemplative life. At Matthew 11:7–19; Luke 7:31–34; Mark 7:15ff., Jesus alerts others to the signs of the kingdom of God and asks them to be ready to respond to them. This will require painful renunciation.

reparation (L., *reparatio,* from *re,* "again," and *parare,* "to prepare"). Any compensation for a wrong or sin. In Christian tradition, life consists in making amends for the original sin committed by Adam and for the fundamental wickedness inherent in human nature and a society alienated from God's ways.

repentance (L., *re,* "again," and *poenitere,* "to make repent"). **1.** CONTRITION. **2.** PENITANCE. The feeling of regret for what one has done. **3.** The change in one's state of spirit and conduct from regret, remorse, despair to satisfaction, accord, and serenity. In Christian tradition, awareness of the need for repentance, as well as the expression of repentance, are of paramount importance to one's spiritual development.

reprobation (L., *reprobare,* "to disapprove," from *re,* "again," and *probare,* "to prove," "to test"). The state of being condemned, rejected, abandoned, or rebuked by God.

requiem. Latin, "rest." The first word of the Roman Catholic MASS. **1.** A mass, or service, for the repose of the dead. **2.** A musical piece in honor of the dead.

respect (L., *rescipere,* "to look back," "to respect," from *re,* "again," and *specere,* "to look"). The emotion of high regard for sacred or significant persons or objects in one's faith, which are worthy of honor and confidence (or even worship and HOMAGE).

resurrection, human (L., *resurrectio,* from *resurgere,* "to rise again," from *re,* "again," and *sugere,* "to rise"). The rising from the dead. Christian faiths hold several views about the resurrection of humans: **1.** Humans are resurrected in body and soul. (For example, St. Augustine [325–430] held to the actual physical, material resurrection of the body.) **2.** Human bodies become ethereal, or bodies of light. (In Rev. 6:11, there is reference to the "white robes." Also Rev. 3:4.) **3.** Paul talks of a "spiritual body" in 1 Corinthians 15:44 in contrast to our material body of flesh. **4.** During the Reformation, there was a common belief that there would be a general resurrection at the ultimate end or consummation of history at which all the corpses of the dead would be raised from their graves and their spirits would again enter them. See also CREMATION.

Resurrection, the. The rising of Christ from the dead. According to the Gospels, after his Resurrection on EASTER morning until his Ascension into heaven forty days later, Jesus appeared several times (see Mark 16:9–10; John 20:11–29; Luke 24:13–35). Jesus' appearance is depicted as spiritual in the sense of being independent of the laws of ordinary physical nature (his body appeared and suddenly disappeared, passed through closed doors, etc.) and as material or physical: " 'Behold my hands and my feet, that it is I myself: handle me and see; for a spirit hath not flesh and bones, as ye see me have.' And when he had thus spoken, he shewed them his hands and his feet" (Luke 24:39–40). Also refer to John 20:17, 20, 25; Matthew 28:9. Jesus' resurrected body could be touched and sensed just as any other physical body; Jesus ate fish in the presence of his disciples; his body showed the marks of his crucifixion. For further scriptural references, see Matthew 27:61–66; 28:1–20; Mark 16:1–20; Luke 24:1–53; John 20:10–31. See also ASCENSION OF JESUS, THE.

revelation, divine (L., *revelare,* "to unveil," "to reveal," from *re,* "again," and *vela,' "veil").* The supernatural communication directly by God to humans of knowledge of God's nature and/or of his will by means other than the use of ordinary human powers for knowing or experiencing (see also FAITH, AUTOPISTIC). Prophetic visions such as at Isaiah 6:1–8 and Revelation 1:1–20 have been considered one of the major means for receiving divine revelation. According to Christian tradition, the Bible is the divinely revealed Word of God, unalterable, unerring, and complete. According to Roman Catholic faith, revelation of the New Testament writings was closed with the first generation of Christians with the death of the last of Jesus' Apostles. No new revelation can be received, although the church can declare what has been revealed and inspired by God and what has not.

Revelation of Saint John the Divine, the. Also the *Apocalypse*. The last of the canonical books of the New Testament. It is also a revelation in the sense that it reveals or prophesies events that will soon take place, such as the Final Judgment by God. John believed this revelation he was writing was revealed by God to Christ. Christ communicated to John by means of an angel. John addressed his revelation from the island of Patmos to the SEVEN CHURCHES OF ASIA: Ephesus, Smyrna, Pergamum, Thyatria, Sardis, Philadelphia, Laodicea.

reverence (L., *reverentia,* "reverence," from *re,* "again," and *vereri,* "to fear"). Synonymous with words such as *deference, veneration, obedience, awe, adoration, worship, respect, esteem*. Reverence is often mingled with fear and affection, awe and devotion, profound respect and commitment.

reverend (L., *reverendus,* "reverence"). **1.** One worthy of reverence or who is revered. **2.** The title of respect and reverence given to the CLERGY in Protestant denominations. ("Father" is the title given to PRIESTS in the Roman Catholic church and Eastern Orthodox churches.)

revivalism. A form of EVANGELISM. The spirited preaching of the Bible in order to "revive," revitalize the Christian faith. See also PENTECOST.

righteousness, original. The state of perfection and goodness humans were in when they were created, which they retained until the FALL.

ritual (L., *ritualis,* "ritual," from *ritus,* "a rite"). A stylized, formal, and established way of conducting worship or ceremonies.

Roman Catholic church, the. Recognizes the bishop of Rome as the pope, the vicar of Christ on earth and as the supreme authority of the Church, who derives this authority from St. Peter, who was assigned the keys of the kingdom by Jesus himself and who was the first bishop of Rome. See also KEYS, THE POWER OF THE.

Rosary, Mysteries of the. While reciting the ROSARY, or using the Rosary, one prays meditating on the Mysteries of the Christian religion. These Mysteries have been divided into those that are **1.** *joyful:* Annunciation, Visitation of the Angel to Mary, Divine Birth of the Christ, Jesus' Baptism, Jesus' Presentation at the Temple; **2.** *sorrowful:* Jesus' Agony in the Garden, Jesus' Scourging and Crowning with Thorns, Jesus' Carrying of the Cross, Jesus' Crucifixion; **3.** *glorious:* Jesus'

Resurrection, Ascension, the Descent of the Holy Ghost upon the Apostles, Jesus' Assumption, the Coronation of Mary as Queen of Heaven.

Rosary, the (L., *rosarium,* "a string of beads," "a rose garden"). **1.** In the Roman Catholic church, a series of prayers recited in a specific order. The form of the prayers is usually in honor of the Blessed Virgin Mary and contains "Hail Marys" (also referred to as "decades," since there are ten of them). The prayers usually begin with "Our Father," end with "Glory be to the Father," and contain reference to the Apostles' Creed. There are many rosaries and they have a variety of specific forms and references. **2.** A string of beads for counting prayers and for assisting in concentration upon the prayers. (Usually the greater rosary consists of 165 beads and the lesser rosary of 55.)

Rose without Thorns, the. Refers to the Blessed Virgin Mary, the Mother of God. In Christian art, roses symbolize Mary's love, compassion, and charity. (The rose was also the flower of Venus, the goddess of love.)

S

Sabbatarian. One who practices observance of strict religious rules with reference to what may and may not be done on the SABBATH, the Holy Day. Sabbatarians abstain from all secular activities on the Sabbath, which is regarded as the Lord's Day—a day devoted to the praise and glory of God.

Sabbath (Gk., *σάββατον [sabbaton],* from Hebrew, *shabbath,* "to rest from labor"). **1.** In the Jewish calendar, the seventh or last day of the week (corresponding to our present Saturday) observed by Jews as a holy day of worship and rest as demanded in Exodus 20:8–11. **2.** Regarded by Christians as the last (or the first) day of the week, called Sunday, and devoted to rest and worship of God.

Sabellianism. The doctrine of the Holy Trinity advocated by Sabellius (ca. 200) that held that the Father, Son, and HOLY SPIRIT were an inextricable unity and expressions of three primary manifestations of one divine being, none having a distinct subsistence in their own right. This divine being has manifested itself as a Creator and Ruler (the Father), as a Redeemer (the Son), and as a Giver of Life-Spirit (the Holy Spirit). Sabellianism is considered a Christian heresy. Sabellius was a bishop and was excommunicated by Pope Calistus in 217.

sacerdotalism (L., *sacerdos,* "a priest"). **1.** Devotion to the priesthood or priestly class. **2.** The structure, system, methodology, spirit, and character of the priesthood or priestly class.

sacraments (L., *sacramentum,* "oath," "a soldier's oath," "sacred object," "a mystery," "initiation," "sacrament"). The solemn and sacred acts and oaths, such as BAPTISM and the EUCHARIST, which serve as an outward, visible sign of an inward, spiritual, divine GRACE and CHARACTER. The celebration or ceremony of a sacrament is enjoined by God, Christ, and the HOLY SPIRIT. By means of the grace given by the sacraments, fallen humans can again receive those gifts lost at the FALL or strengthen those that were still retained. See also SACRAMENTS, THE SEVEN.

The attitude toward the character associated with the sacraments has varied. In some cases, the moral integrity of the priest administering the sacrament affected the supernatural quality being imprinted upon the recipient. In other cases, it was believed that the character of the sacraments, their spiritual value and efficacy were obtained directly from God. The clergy were merely means through which God worked; God administered the character of the sacraments through the personage of the priest. See OPUS OPERATUM.

sacramental confession. See CONFESSION.

sacramentals. The objects, rites, or actions used by the Roman Catholic church and the Eastern Orthodox churches to secure favorable spiritual and secular treatment from God and Jesus Christ for their adherents. The SACRAMENTS were initiated by Christ himself, but sacramentals have been instituted by these churches, on the basis of Christ's teachings and effects. Sacraments bestow grace directly from God. Sacramentals bestow benefits indirectly by means of the efficacy of human prayers and actions and the inner spiritual changes that may occur. Some of the benefits obtained by the use of sacramentals: the receiving of grace from God; the forgiveness of venial sins; the remission of earthly punishment for sin committed; improved physical health; material goods; protection from evil spirits. Examples of sacramentals: objects that have been blessed for devotion; rites to exorcise demons; blessings given by the priestly class. See also AGNUS DEI.

sacraments, dominical. (L., *dominicalis, dominicus,* "of a master or lord," from *dominus,* "master," "lord," "governor of"—as in our English word *dominate).* Those sacraments in which Jesus Christ himself participated: BAPTISM and the LORD'S SUPPER.

sacraments, justifying. BAPTISM and PENANCE are regarded as the justifying sacraments. See also JUSTIFICATION.

sacraments, the seven. The Roman Catholic church and the Eastern Orthodox churches accept seven sacraments as instituted by Christ, as holy, and as providing salvation: **1.** BAPTISM, **2.** CONFIRMATION, **3.** the EUCHARIST of Holy Communion, **4.** PENANCE, **5.** Extreme

Unction (see UNCTION, EXTREME) and Anointing of the Sick, **6.** Holy Orders (see ORDERS, THE SACRAMENT OF HOLY and entries under ORDERS), or ordination (see ORDAIN), **7.** Matrimony.

The Roman Catholic church affirms that REDEMPTION, SALVATION are attainable only through the sacraments. Those who died before Christ were not saved, but the hope is that they are not lost (see also LIMBO).

Most Protestant churches accept only Baptism and Holy Communion as true sacraments since they were initiated directly by Christ. Some, such as the QUAKERS, believe in no sacred observances of the sacraments, since all of life is regarded as a sacrament to God.

The seven sacraments have been divided into a number of categories: Individual (Baptism, Confirmation, Penance, Eucharist, Extreme Unction) and Social (Holy Orders and Matrimony). Conferring of Grace (Baptism, Penance), and increasing grace (the remaining five). Ultimately necessary for the cleansing of the soul of original sin (Baptism) and necessary for the forgiveness of sins committed after baptism (Penance). Sacraments of the dead (Baptism and Penance) give a renewal of life, and sacraments of the living (the remaining five, which enhance the life of grace). Sacraments received only once (Baptism, Confirmation, Holy Orders, imprint an unerasable character on the soul), and sacraments that may be received more than once (the remaining four). The highest in dignity (the Eucharist, since it is the very body and blood of Christ) and the second highest (Holy Orders, since this is the highest form of the imitation of Christ). Those that must be administered by a priestly class (Holy Orders, Confirmation, Eucharist, Penance, Extreme Unction) and those that under extreme emergencies need not be administered by a priestly class, provided the correct matter and form are followed (Baptism and Matrimony). Administration of any of the other six sacraments depends on Baptism.

Sacrament, the Blessed. Another name for the sacrament of the EUCHARIST, at which the bread and wine become Jesus Christ.

sacred (L., *sacer,* "holy"). To designate as sacred is to single out as divine or for divine, spiritual, or religious use and as requiring veneration, respect, reverence. See also HOLY. Compare with PROFANE; SECULAR.

sacred history. History as written down in the Scriptures. A common assumption: Those who existed in earlier ages such as the Prophets were closer to the truth of God, since they were nearer to his creation; those who existed as Apostles to Christ were closer to the source of divine truth than later periods—therefore their writings must be venerated, trusted, and correctly preserved and presented. This has been used to support the position that the true Christian faith was given to, can be found in, the Apostles and Saints since they stood nearer in time to Christ.

sacred, the. **1.** To make sacred is to specify a particular site, place, time, object, act as HOLY, or as being able to produce the NUMINOUS, or as having the powers to produce miraculous events or healings, or as being the place at which miracles have occurred. **2.** The point at which the transcendent or the SUPERNATURAL affects the natural world. **3.** The attitude taken toward and emotions felt about an object or site that is believed to be extraordinary, otherworldly, and mysterious. Sometimes this encompasses fear, dread, wonderousness, a sense of the sublime, majesty, grandeur.

sacrifice (L., *sacer,* "sacred," and *facere,* "to make"). In general, an offering to God of something of high or supreme value. In making such an offering, one atones for sin, or procures a favor, or expresses gratitude or thanks. The main purpose of sacrifices among the Jews was as sin offerings—to expiate one's sin. Two themes predominated: **1.** to gain God's attention and favor, and **2.** to retain God's attention, favor, and special privileges. God demanded sacrifices.

Christians believe that the Old Testament sacrifices are anticipatory and in crude form what the perfect sacrifice was of Christ (Heb. 9:3ff.; 5:3–10). See also INCARNATION, THE. In Christianity, sacrifices are works toward SALVATION.

saint (L., *sanctus,* "sacred," from *sancire,* "to understand"). **1.** In general, a holy, pious, or godlike person. **2.** Specifically, a holy or godly person who has been canonized by a church. **3.** Sometimes used to refer to one who has entered heaven (the assumption usually being that this was due to a person's piety or holiness.) See also CANONIZATION; RELIC; SANCTIFICATION.

Saint Gabriel, the Archangel. Gabriel means "God is my strength." Regarded as one of the three highest angels, together with Michael and Raphael. He rules over PARADISE, is the prince of the First Heaven and sits on the lefthand side of God, who resides in the Seventh Heaven. Gabriel is the angel of mercy, death, vengeance, inspiration, revelation, resurrection, annunciation, hope, truth. Gabriel destroyed cities of sin such as Sodom and Gommorah. Gabriel, with 140 pairs of wings, revealed the Koran to Mohammed. He inspired Joan of Arc to fight for the King of France. Gabriel brought the good news to the Virgin Mary that she would give birth to the Son of God. See also ARCHANGEL.

Saint James the Great. One of the Twelve Apostles of Christ. The brother of St. John the Evangelist. In the Gospels, the Apostles James, John, and Peter are often singled out by Jesus as of special significance. (For example, they were chosen by Jesus to be at the TRANSFIGURATION OF CHRIST and to be with Jesus during his agony at Gethsemane.) James carried the message of Jesus throughout the Mediterranean world. During his life he was revered in Spain as a saint. He was beheaded in Judea by Herod Agrippa, thus becoming the first Apostle to be martyred. His body rests in Compostela, Spain.

Saint John the Baptist. Christian tradition regards John as the last of the Old Testament Prophets and the first saint of the New Testament—the first Christian saint; the first martyr; the herald of Jesus Christ. John was the first to proclaim to the world that Jesus was the true Messiah. John was conceived six months before Jesus. His mother was Elizabeth, the wife of the priest Zacharias. They were old and childless but continued to pray for a child. God sent the Archangel Gabriel to Zacharias to announce that his wife had conceived: "But the angel said unto him, 'Fear not, Zacharias: for thy prayer is heard; and thy wife Elizabeth shall bear thee a son, and thou shalt call his name John . . . For he shall be great in the sight of the Lord . . . and he shall be filled with the Holy Ghost, even from his mother's womb. And many of the children of Israel shall he turn to the Lord their God . . . to make ready a people prepared for the Lord' " (Luke 1:13–17). Zacharias doubted Gabriel and was struck dumb until after John's birth.

Elizabeth was the Blessed Virgin Mary's cousin. Mary visited the house of Zacharias and "when Elizabeth heard the salutation of Mary, the babe leaped in her womb; and Elizabeth was filled with the Holy Ghost" (Luke 1:41). According to Christian tradition, John was thus sanctified by the Holy Ghost and was born without original sin.

John became a prophet, preaching redemption, penance, baptism, and ways to prepare for the coming of the Messiah. He lived as an ascetic in the wilderness of Judea: "And the same John had his raiment of camel's hair, and a leathern girdle about his loins; and his meat was locusts and wild honey" (Matt. 3:4). John recognized Jesus as the Messiah: "John seeth Jesus coming unto him, and saith, 'Behold the Lamb of God, which taketh away the sin of the world' " (John 1:29). He baptized Jesus in the Jordan River. John is recognized as the precursor of Christianity.

John opposed Herod's living in sin with Herod's brother's wife, Herodias. Herodias' daughter Salome danced for Herod and pleased him so much that he offered her whatever she wished. Salome's mother persuaded her to ask for John's head. John became a martyr.

In Christian art, St. John is depicted with the highest reverence and respect. He is frequently pictured at the side of Jesus and the Blessed Virgin Mary, as an intercessor for humans. His feast day is June 24, which celebrates his birth rather than his death as is usually the case with other saints, and many regard this as the oldest feast for a saint.

Saint John the Evangelist. One of the four evangelists and author of the Gospel according to John. His brother was SAINT JAMES THE GREAT. They were fishermen of Galilee and among the first disciples of Christ. John was the youngest of the disciples and the last to die. He was a follower of John the Baptist. John is referred to as the "Beloved Disciple." At John 13:23, he is seen "leaning on Jesus' bosom . . . whom Jesus loved" at the Last Supper. John was present at the first miracle Jesus performed in Cana of Galilee. Jesus from the CROSS gave the care of his mother to John.

John preached in Judea with St. Peter, in Ephesus and throughout Asia Minor, and in Rome. He is said to have survived the persecutions under Emperor Domitian. One attempt was to kill him with poisoned wine (he is sometimes depicted holding a cup with a SERPENT in it); another was to burn him in oil. John was exiled to the island of Patmos where he wrote what is regarded as the last book of the New Testament, the Revelation of St. John the Divine, or the Apocalypse. He is also thought to be the author of the three Epistles of John. John lived to be over a hundred years old and is the only disciple of Jesus to die a natural death. The EAGLE is the emblem for John in Christian tradition and art, signifying his spiritual flight in contemplating the WORD OF GOD and Jesus' divinity (see also CREATURES, THE FOUR LIVING). The feast day for St. John is December 27.

Saint Joseph. The husband of the Blessed Virgin Mary. Christian tradition holds that God entrusted Joseph with the care and protection of Jesus, God's divine offspring, and of Mary, Jesus' mother. He is depicted as a carpenter and is referred to as the saint of the working class. St. Joseph is considered by the Roman Catholic church to be the patron and protector of Christ's Church. He has been honored on a variety of dates: March 19, May 1, July 20.

Saint Luke the Evangelist. One of the four evangelists and author of the Gospel according to Luke. A physician in Antioch who became a disciple of St. Paul and went with him to Rome to preach the message of Jesus. (Luke's Gospel is sometimes referred to as "St. Paul's Gospel".) He spent a great deal of time in Greece as a missionary, where according to one tradition he was crucified and according to another he died a natural death. He is reputed to be the author of the Acts of the Apostles, which covers a period from Jesus' Ascension to the first captivity of St. Paul by the Romans.

A winged OX is the emblem for St. Luke, signifying the emphasis Luke placed on Jesus' sacrifice for humanity and on the priesthood of Christ (see also CREATURES, THE FOUR LIVING). The ox was regarded in ancient times as an example of one of the highest forms of sacrifice offered to God by the priesthood. St. Luke is regarded as the patron saint of painters. He converted people by exhibiting pictures he painted of Jesus and Mary.

Saint Mark the Evangelist. One of the four evangelists and author of the Gospel according to Mark. He was a disciple of St. Paul and St. Peter and was with them on some of their missionary journeys. (Mark's Gospel is sometimes referred to as "St. Peter's Gospel," since it contains personal reminiscences of St. Peter, who converted Mark to Jesus. At 1 Pet. 5:13, Peter calls Mark his son.)

Mark is regarded as the first bishop of Alexandria. He was martyred by being dragged through the streets of Alexandria with a rope tied around his neck. The winged lion is the emblem for St. Mark, signifying the emphasis Mark placed in his Gospel on Jesus' royalty, dignity, and uniqueness (see also CREATURES, THE FOUR LIVING).

Saint Matthew the Evangelist. One of the Twelve Apostles of Jesus. He was a tax collector named Levi at Capernaum where Jesus approached him: "And as he passed by, he saw Levi the son of Alphaeus sitting at the receipt of custom, and said unto him, 'Follow me.' And he arose and followed him" (Mark 2:14). (Also refer to Matt. 9:9 and Luke 5:27. These accounts are followed by a feast Matthew had prepared for Jesus.) *Matthew* means "the gift of God" in Hebrew.

Matthew preached to the Jews, Egyptians, and Ethiopians. It is believed that he received his martyrdom by being stabbed in the back while praying at his Ethiopian church. In Christian art he is depicted with a sword. His emblem is a winged man (or angel), symbolizing his emphasis upon the humanity of Christ as illustrated in the long beginning reference to Jesus' ancestry in Matthew's Gospel (see also CREATURES, THE FOUR LIVING).

Saint Michael the Archangel. Considered the greatest of all the angels. The name *Michael* means "similar to God" and he serves as the head of the heavenly angels whom he lead against Satan's angels, who rebelled against God during the war in heaven between God and Satan. Revelation 12:7–9: "And there was war in heaven: Michael and his angels fought against the dragon; and the dragon fought and his angels, and prevailed not; neither was their place found any more in heaven. And the great dragon was cast out, that old serpent, called the Devil, and Satan, which deceiveth the whole world: he was cast out in the earth, and his angels were cast out with him."

In Christian tradition, St. Michael is regarded as the governor of dead souls, as holding the keys of the kingdom of heaven, as the patron saint of the military and of policepersons, as the leader of all other angels in the hierarchy of angels, and as superior even to the archangels Gabriel and Raphael. St. Michael is connected with the HOLY SPIRIT, the LOGOS, salvation, immortality and the inspiration, as the Prince of Light leading us into a life of eternal light.

In Christian art, St. Michael is often depicted in scenes of the Last Judgment in full armor, usually holding the scales of justice. He is usually represented as winged, eternally youthful, and of utmost beauty.

In the Old Testament, for example, in Daniel 12:1, Michael is the great prince who is the protector of God's Chosen People. He is the head of the archangels, the angel of repentance, mercy, righteousness, sanctification, conqueror of Satan, ruler of the Fourth Heaven (or in the Muslim tradition, ruler of the Seventh Heaven). It was Michael who prevented Abraham from sacrificing his son Isaac and it was Michael who appeared to Moses as the fire in the burning bush. See also ARCHANGEL.

Saint Paul. Born a Jew at Tarsus and named Saul. He was a devout Jew who studied in Jerusalem and a persecutor of Christians. At Acts 7:55–60, Paul is present at the stoning of St. Stephen. Paul was heading for Damascus, continuing to persecute Christians, when "suddenly there shined round about him a light from heaven: And he fell to the earth, and heard a voice saying unto him, 'Saul, Saul, why persecutest thou me?' And he said, 'Who art thou, Lord?' And the Lord said, 'I am Jesus who thou persecutest: *it is* hard for thee to kick against the pricks.' And he trembling and astonished said, 'Lord, what wilt thou have me to do? And the Lord *said* unto him, 'Arise, and go into the city, and it shall be told that what thou must do. And the men which journeyed with him stood speechless, hearing a voice, but seeing no man." (Act 9:1–7.) This was a conversion experience for Paul. He dedicated the rest of his life to writing and preaching the message of the Christ.

Both Peter and Paul are regarded as the founders of the Roman Catholic church. Each is referred to as a Prince of the Apostles. Their saint day is June 29. Paul was martyred in Rome under Emperor Nero. His emblem is a sword.

Saint Peter. One of the Twelve Apostles of Jesus. Also referred to as Simon and as Cephas. The Greek for Peter is **Πέτρος** *(petros),* a derivative of **Πέτρα** *(petra),* "rock." At Matthew 16:18, Jesus says, "And I say also unto thee, That thou art Peter, and upon this rock I will build my church; and the gates of hell shall not prevail against it." Since Peter is regarded as the first bishop of Rome, the Roman Catholic church bases its belief in being the true Church of Jesus upon this passage (see also APOSTOLIC SUCCESSION). Jesus continues at Matthew 16:19: "And I will give unto thee the keys of the kingdom of heaven: and whatsoever thou shall bind on earth shall be bound in heaven: and whatsoever thou shalt loose on earth shall be loosed in heaven." See also KEYS, POWER OF THE.

Peter accepted Jesus as the Christ: "And Simon Peter answered and said, 'Thou art the Christ the Son of the living God' " (Matt. 16:16). At Luke 22:23 Peter says, "Lord, I am ready to go with thee, both into prison, and to death." The soldiers came to arrest Jesus. Peter swung a sword and cut off the right ear of Malchus, a servant of the high priest (John 18:10). Afterwards Peter three times denied that he knew Jesus (Mark 14:66–72).

Peter preached in Asia Minor. He was martyred on a cross. Christian tradition believes that he asked that his cross be turned upside down and he be nailed upside down since he felt unworthy of being crucified as Jesus was crucified. It is believed that Peter's burial place is beneath the altar of the Basilica of St. Peter's in Rome. Peter (and Paul) are honored by the Roman Catholic church as the Princes of the Apostles and their saint day is June 29. Peter's emblem is a key, or keys.

Saint Raphael the Archangel. In Jewish tradition, regarded as one of God's seven holy angels, the guide into SHEOL, the healer of humans and of the earth *(Raphael* means "God heals"), the angel of the sun, the Prince of the Second Heaven, the guardian of the Tree of Life in the Garden of Eden, the angel of prayer, joy, love, light, repentance, the bearer to Solomon of a magic ring with a five-pointed star that had the power to control evil demons (King Solomon used the labor of demons to build the Temple).

In Christian art, St. Raphael is variously depicted as an earthly beast, a winged saint eating with Adam and Eve, a six-winged angel holding a pilgrim's staff. In Christian tradition, he is the patron of science, medicine, knowledge. See also ARCHANGEL.

Saints, Communion of. All Christians united in the spirit of Jesus Christ and thereby united with each other as members of the BODY OF CHRIST, or of his mystical body. See also COMMUNION SANCTORUM.

saints, invocation of the. See INVOCATION.

saints, the intercession of the. See INTERCESSION OF THE SAINTS.

Saint Thomas. One of the Twelve Apostles of Jesus. He refused to believe in Jesus' Resurrection and has been called the "Doubting Thomas." He believed after Jesus appeared to him and he was allowed to touch Jesus' wounds. St. Thomas is regarded as the Apostle to India, where he was martyred. He is regarded as the patron saint of builders, architects, construction.

Saint Uriel the Archangel. *Uriel* means "the fire or flame of God." Ranked as one of the highest of the holy angels in God's realm. Uriel rules the sun, thunder, and HELL (Hades, Tartarus, SHEOL); is the archangel of deliverance, repentance, and salvation; stands with a sword at the closed gates of the lost Eden. He helped bury Adam and Adam's son Abel in Paradise. He was the angel sent by God to warn Noah of the flood. In Christian art, he is often depicted holding a flame. See also ARCHANGEL.

salvation (L., *salvatio,* from *salvare,* "to save"). **1.** The deliverance by God from sin, its penalties, and punishments. REDEMPTION. **2.** Eternal life granted by accepting Jesus Christ as Lord and Master. (See also ATONEMENT).

Early Christian faith—as early as the fourth century Church Fathers—held, as it does today, that salvation was impossible outside the Church. Christian theology following the temper of the Gospels has for the most part held that only some souls are predestined to be saved eternally and some are predestined to be eternally lost. The universalist (see UNIVERSALISM) strain in Christian theology, which has been in the minority, has held that eventually all human souls will be saved.

A common version of salvation: No one can be saved from sinning by his/her own free will and powers. Human volition and natural faculties lead humans to damnation. Only God's GRACE and the complete subjection of the human will to God's will enables one to avoid sin. All things humans do without God's grace are evil. Nothing good can exist by the use of human capacities. All human actions that are good are caused by God and they are accompanied by or occasioned by FAITH.

sanctify (L., *sanctificare,* from *sanctus,* "holy," and *ficare,* "to make"). **1.** To purify or free of sin. **2.** To make or be SACRED, HOLY. **3.** To single out for holy and sacred use. **4.** To imbue with divine respect, dignity, veneration, grace. **5.** To renew life by means of the INFUSION of the HOLY SPIRIT. See also CONSECRATION; GRACE; HALLOW.

sanctity (L., *sanctus,* "holy"). **1.** Holiness, godliness, having divine qualities. **2.** Sacredness.

sanctuary (L., *sanctuarium,* from *sanctus,* "sacred," "holy"). **1.** A holy, sacred, or consecrated place of worship such as a church. **2.** That area of a Christian church at which the altar is put. **3.** The church building itself as a place of refuge, asylum, or protection for those persecuted or in need.

Sanctus. Latin. The angelic hymn "Holy, holy, holy . . . " part of the prayer in the *anaphora.*

Satan (Heb., *satan,* "an adversary"). The prince of darkness; the god of this world who has all humankind in his power; the deceiver; the liar. Christ is victor over Satan. Satan is the archetype or highest form of evil and powers hostile to Christ's message. (Refer to John 12:31; Col. 2:15; Eph. 6:12; Heb. 2:14; 1 John 3:8; Matt. 4:10; Luke 4:1–12.)

St. Origen (185–254) believed that even Satan, the DEVIL, would in the end be converted by God. Origen had faith in the total, universal love and mercy of God and God's eventual victory over all the universe. Compare with ELECT, THE.

satisfaction (L., *satio,* "enough," and *ficare,* "to make"). Making of a reparation or compensation for sinning against, for insulting God.

The belief in satisfaction presupposes that in all fairness sinners must be punished for their sins here on earth or in PURGATORY—they must do recompense for their sins. Satisfaction may be made by the sinners themselves or by others on their behalf. Amends can be made for sinners already here on earth or in purgatory and can be done by individual prayer (and/or the purchase of INDULGENCES) or by special expiatory processes of the church or faith.

Savior, the. Also *Saviour* (L., *salvare,* "to save"). Jesus Christ, the Redeemer, who brings eternal SALVATION to humans.

schism. (Gk., *σχίσμα [schisma],* from *σχίζειν [schizein],* "to split"). **1.** A formal separation from a church in order to create a new church or sect. **2.** In early Christianity, the dissension, factions, conflict, difference of opinions within the organization of the church (refer to, for example, 1 Cor. 1:10,; 11:18; 12:25).

Schism, the Great. **1.** The SCHISM in 1054 that separated the Christian church into East and West—Eastern or Greek Orthodox and the Roman Catholic. **2.** Also refers to the schism of 1378–1429, when Pope Urban VI and his successors lived in Rome and Pope Clement VII and his successors ruled from Avignon.

scholasticism (Gk., σχολάζειν *[scholazein],* "to have leisure," "to educate"). The education, beliefs, methods, and faith of the Christian thinkers (often referred to as medieval schoolmen) of the Middle Ages. Their main task was to reconcile Christian faith with the conclusions of reason. They taught that humans are saved or justified by means of faith supplied by love; both faith and love are supernaturally infused into the soul by divine grace, and all sin is removed and humans are then acceptable to God.

Scripture (L., *scriptura,* from *scribere,* "to write"). The Holy Bible (see BIBLE, THE HOLY). The books of the Old and New Testaments.

seal (Old Fr., *seel,* from L., *sigillum,* "a little image, seal"; related to *signum,* "mark," "sign"). **1.** Identification mark (compare with Eph. 1:-13). **2.** To grant authenticity; to confirm; to signify (a member, an action, a relationship).

Second Advent, the. See ADVENTISM; PAROUSIA.

Second Coming, the. See PAROUSIA.

Second Council of Nicea (787). See NICAEA, THE SECOND COUNCIL OF.

sect (L., *secta,* from *sequi,* "to follow"). **1.** A group believing in a specific creed and practice with its own leadership. **2.** A group that disavows itself from an established church. **3.** A denomination within the Christian community.

sectarian. Being devoted, usually in a prejudiced, narrow, and bigoted way, to a sect or specific religious point of view.

secular (L., *saecularis,* from *saeculum,* "a race," "the world," "an age"). **1.** Worldly. Earthly. Temporal. **2.** PROFANE. Not religious, spiritual, HOLY, or SACRED. **3.** Sometimes: not bound by monastic or religious rules, doctrines, vows, or church authority. Compare with ECCLESIASTIC.

see (L., *sedere,* "to sit"). **1.** The seat or center of a bishop's, or archbishop's, or pope's authority. **2.** The authoriy (office, status, rank) of a bishop or cleric of higher rank.

Sees, the Four Ancient. Constantinopole, Alexandria, Antioch, and Jersualem of the Eastern Orthodox church. Each has its own PATRIARCH.

See, the Holy. **1.** The POPE of the Roman Catholic church. **2.** Also has been used to include the Papal Court or the immediate area of the pope's jurisdiction.

sermon (L., *sermo,* "discourse"). A public address (lecture, discourse, speech) given by a member of the clergy for the purpose of instruction, spiritual inspiration, and exegesis of the Bible or Gospels. See also HOMILY.

Sermon on the Mount, Jesus'. The sermon given by Christ as recorded, for example, in Matthew 6:9–13 and Luke 11:1–4. See also LORD'S PRAYER.

serpent (L., *serpere,* "to creep"). A snake or snakelike figure representing SATAN or the DEVIL in Christian art. It implies temptation, evil, the obscene. (The serpent was also an ancient symbol of death and destruction.)

seven churches of Asia, the. At Revelation 1:11, St. John addresses his prophecies and comments to the seven churches of Asia: Ephesus, Smyrna, Pergamos, Thyatira, Sardis, Philadelphia, Laodicea. See also REVELATION OF SAINT JOHN THE DIVINE, THE.

seven corporeal acts. See CORPOREAL ACTS, THE SEVEN.

seven sacraments, the. See SACRAMENTS, THE SEVEN.

Seven Sorrows of Mary, the. See SORROWS OF MARY, THE SEVEN.

Sheol. Hebrew, "the underworld which is the abode of the dead," "the grave." See also HELL.

shepherd. **1.** A herder of sheep. Used as a metaphor to refer to a priest or pastor or minister of Jesus' "flock." **2.** Used to depict the personal, caring relationship between Jesus and humanity: Jesus is the provider, director, savior of humans. For example, at 1 Peter 5:4, Christ is referred to as the shepherd of his church. Those who held office, such as bishops, were also referred to as shepherds. (Also see John 21:15; Acts 20:28.) The phrase *pastoral offices* applied to those in authority in the Roman Catholic church implies the use of the metaphor of a shepherd governing (having jurisdiction over) his flock.

Shepherd, the Good. Jesus is depicted in early Christian art as the Good Shepherd with reference to scriptural texts such as Luke 15:3–7 and John 10:1–18.

ship. Used as an emblem by early Christians. The yard arm and mast formed a cross above the ship. The ship represented the Church of Christ sailing in the troubled seas of life, carrying the faithful to salvation. In the Roman Catholic tradition, St. Peter is often at the helm.

The main body of a Christian church is called the "nave" from the Latin for "ship." The World Council of Churches uses a ship afloat as its emblem, with the Greek word **οἰκουμένη** *oikoymenē,* symbolizing the ministry of the Christian faith to all the world.

ship flying before the wind. One of the allusive symbols used by early Christians. Clement of Alexandria in the second century recommended its use, together with symbols such as the marine anchor (see ANCHOR, MARINE), the FISH, the DOVE.

Shrove Tuesday. The holy day before ASH WEDNESDAY that designates the end of the carnival season. Also known as Mardi Gras (Fat Tuesday), and in England as Pancake Tuesday. Fats, which were not allowed to be eaten during Lent, were used up.

Sign of the Cross. See CROSS, SIGN OF THE.

similitudo Dei. Latin, "likeness of God."

Simon. See SAINT PETER.

sin (Anglo-Saxon, *syn).* **1.** Disobeying or neglecting God's laws. **2.** The rebellion against the will of God. Violating God's decrees. **3.** Lawlessness (see also AMARTIA) and lack of conformity to God's commands, purposes, and plans.

According to Christian faith, humans by their very nature are not righteous (just, moral, fair, saintly). They are sinful. This means that humans are not in a correct relationship with God. They were, but lost this at Adam's Fall. Humans cannot of their own get back into harmony with God. They can do this by seeking PARDON, seeking JUSTIFICATION, sanctification, acceptance of God by means of God's GRACE. See also FREEDOM FROM BONDAGE.

The Christian concept of sin is based on the notion that humans must believe that what God forbid is evil per se and what God demands is good. The Christian is not to believe that God demands what is good because it is good, but good because God demands it. The core ingredients of sin are self-righteousness, self-centeredness, and an anthropomorphic (as opposed to a theocentric) view of the universe.

Reformers such as Martin Luther and Calvin considered sin in terms of PRIDE and nonbelief (or unbelief)—a state whereby humans live alienated from Christ and the HOLY SPIRIT. PENANCE, or other methods, cannot forgive sins. Only God's loving grace through Jesus Christ can eliminate one's sins.

sin, mortal. In the Roman Catholic church, a grave sin that estranges a person from God. A most serious deliberate transgression of God's wishes (commands, laws). If one dies without being forgiven for a mortal sin, the consequence is eternal damnation. The grace afforded by the sacraments may sometimes forgive mortal sins, but in general, mortal sin prevents the work of grace. See also SINS, THE DEADLY; SIN, VENIAL.

sin, original. The innate tendency to sin with which all humans are born, inherited from our parents, originally caused by the FALL of ADAM and EVE, the first humans. It is a state of inward spiritual alienation from God. In Christian tradition, original sin accounts for all human suffering, personal conflict, and death. Original sin is a deprivation of original innocence and righteousness. Original sin produces an inherited sense of inferiority, guilt, shame, and an inherited predisposition toward a life of continued sin. (Refer to Gen. 2:7–8; 3:24; 1 Cor. 15:21ff.; Rom. 5:12–21, where St. Paul establishes a parallel between Adam and Christ). See also ADAM, THE NEW; DEPRAVITY. Contrasted with RIGHTEOUSNESS, ORIGINAL.

sins, the seven deadly. Pride, covetousness, lust, envy, gluttony (greed), anger, and sloth.

sin, unforgivable. Jesus at Matthew 12:32 speaks of an unforgivable sin: "And whosoever speaketh a word against the Son of Man, it shall be forgiven him: but whosoever speaketh against the Holy Ghost, it shall not be forgiven him, neither in this world, neither in the world to come."

sin, venial. In the Roman Catholic church, a sin less serious than a mortal sin, usually regarded as a sin done in ignorance, passion, temper, instinct. Usually thought of as a sin that does not lessen God's love towards the sinner and that does not cause the soul spiritual death. Venial sin disposes the soul to spiritual death but does not deprive it of sanctifying grace. Venial sins may be atoned for by PENANCE or in PURGATORY. See also SIN, MORTAL.

Society of Friends. See QUAKERS.

sola fide. Latin, "faith alone." Used to refer to Luther's JUSTIFICATION BY FAITH ALONE.

Son of God, Jesus as the. The sonship of Jesus to God stresses the most intimate relationship that one can have with God. For Christianity, no other word than *Son* can convey that intimacy of Jesus with God. John 1:18: "the only begotten Son, which is in the bosom of the Father, he hath declared him." According to Christianity, something of God's nature, of God's own person and very being, is in Jesus the Son. For Christian faith, Jesus is a deity, a divine being. (Refer also to John 5:18; Phil. 2:6.)

This phrase proclaims the unique connection and relationship between Jesus and God but also indicates the effect of God upon Jesus, and the action of God through Jesus upon humans. See also SON OF MAN, JESUS AS THE.

Son of Man, Jesus as the. In the Old Testament, this phrase denotes reference to a human with the implication of the dependency upon God, of the inferiority and lowliness of humans in comparison to God. (Ps. 8:4; Ezek. 2:1; etc.) At Mark 14:61, the High Priest asks Jesus, "Art thou the Christ, the Son of the Blessed?" And Jesus answers, "I am: and ye shall see the Son of Man sitting on the right hand of power, and coming in the clouds of heaven." See also MESSIAH, CHRIST AS THE.

Mention is made at Matthew 8:20; Mark 8:31; 9:31; 10:33, of Jesus' poverty, humiliation, suffering and death as the Son of Man.

sorcery (Old Fr., *sorcerie,* "casting of lots," "magic," from L. *sors,* "lot"). The use of power obtained from evil spirits for purposes such as divination, NECROMANCY, MAGIC, witchcraft.

Sorrows of Mary, the Seven. Also *the Seven Dolours of Mary.* **1.** The sorrows (grief, distress, anguish) endured by the Blessed Virgin Mary for her suffering son: **a.** Simeon's prophecy at Jesus' Presentation in the Temple (Luke 2:34, 35: "And Simeon blessed them, and said unto Mary his mother, 'Behold, this *child* is set for the fall and rising again of many in Israel; and for a sign which shall be spoken against; [Yeah, a sword shall pierce through my own soul also,] that the thoughts of many hearts may be revealed.' "); **b.** the flight from King Herod into Egypt with Joseph and the infant Jesus (Matt. 2:13–15; "And they were departed, behold, the angel of the Lord appeareth to Joseph in a dream, saying, 'Arise, and take the young child and his mother, and flee into Egypt, and be thou there until I bring thee word: for Herod will seek the young child to destroy him.' When he arose, he took the young child and his mother by night, and departed into Egypt."); **c.** the loss of Jesus by Mary in the Temple at Jerusalem (Luke 2:41–51: "Now his parents went to Jerusalem every year at the feast of the passover. And when he was twelve years old, they went up to Jerusalem after the custom of the feast. And when they had fulfilled the days, as they returned, the child Jesus tarried behind in Jerusalem; and Joseph and his mother knew not *of it.* But they, supposing him to have been in the company, went a day's journey; and they sought him among *their* kinsfolk and acquaintance. And when they found him not, they turned back again to Jerusalem, seeking him. And it came to pass, that after three days they found him in the temple, sitting in the midst of the doctors, both hearing them and asking them questions."); **d.** Jesus' taking leave of his mother on his way to the CROSS, and his bearing of the cross; **e.** Jesus' CRUCIFIXION and dying; **f.** Jesus' removal from the cross into his mother's arms; and **g.** the burial of Jesus. **2.** Has also been used to refer to the sorrows Mary, the Mother of Jesus, felt at the stations of the cross (see also CROSS, THE STATIONS OF THE) during Jesus' CRUCIFIXION.

soteriology (Gk., σωτηρία *[sōtēria],* "safety," "salvation," and λόγος *[logos],* "the study of," "the rational inquiry into"). The branch of theology that deals with the SALVATION of humans through Jesus Christ. It includes topics such as the FALL, the concepts of SIN, God's revelation, God's REDEMPTION of humans by means of Christ's CRUCIFIXION, the ATONEMENT, GRACE, PAROUSIA.

soul (Anglo-Saxon, *sāwl).* The spiritual, immaterial entity or agent that gives life to a body and causes all its bodily, mental, and emotional activities and experiences. Usually regarded as separable from its body and immortal.

Debate has long existed as to *when* the soul of a human enters its body (and as to *how* this occurs). Some Christians believe that the soul is created by God and implanted at conception when the sperm and ovum meet (see also CREATIONISM). Some hold that the soul is ingested at the first moment of the child's breath. (Other points in the development of the embryo have also been given.)

Some early Christians held to the Platonic and Neo-Platonic view of the soul: The soul existed prior to its entrance into the body. Other early Christians believed that the soul was one of the emanations from God's being in his creative activity. Some early Christians believed the doctrine of TRADUCIANISM: The soul is of human, material substance that comes into existence by means of the sexual, procreative union of male and female.

spirit (L., *spirare,* "to breathe," "to blow," connoting the breath of air or life). **1.** Any supernatural being. **2.** The essential, immaterial characteristic of God. **3.** In Christianity, a part of the divine nature, namely, the HOLY SPIRIT.

spiritism. The belief **1.** in the existence of spirits affecting the real world and/or humanity and **2.** that human beings can by specific means such as propitiation, ritual, initiations, etc., come into contact with spirits in order to **3.** receive their powers, alter their activity, or communicate with them. The acts, services, or works produced by a spirit are called *spiriting*. The belief in and worship of many spirits is often called *polydaemonism*. These spirits may take a variety of forms, from disembodied nature spirits, to Manes, to deities. Spiritism is often used interchangeably with SPIRITUALISM.

Spirit, the fruit of the. According to St. Paul at Galatians 5:22, 23: "The fruit of the Spirit is love, joy, peace, longsuffering (patience), gentleness (kindness), goodness, faith, meekness (gentleness), temperance (self-control): against such there is no law."

Spirit, the Holy. See HOLY SPIRIT.

Spirit, the seven gifts of the Holy. Wisdom. Understanding. Counsel (good judgment, prudence). Fortitude. Knowledge. Fear of God. Piety. (Refer to Isa. 11:2.) In Christian art, the seven gifts or endowments are each represented by a dove and also by seven flowers or seven petals on a flower. See also SPIRITUAL GIFTS.

spiritual. **1.** God-minded. Mindful of heaven. Pure in thought and deed. Holy. **2.** Those things that pertain to the sacred objects, places, and teachings of a church. **3.** The state of the soul as influenced by a church and/or by the Holy Spirit. **4.** Nonmaterial religious feelings, emotions, ideals, and values.

spiritual gifts. A concept found especially in St. Paul (see also CHARISMA). He believed that the HOLY SPIRIT instills in Christians the required "gifts" (talents, powers, capacities) required of them to individually serve the needs of the church (1 Cor. 12:8–10). There are nine of these *charismata* (plural of *charisma,* "gifts of grace"): **1.** wisdom, **2.** knowledge, **3.** faith, **4.** gifts of healing, **5.** working of miracles, **6.** prophecy, **7.** discerning of spirits, **8.** speaking in diverse kinds of tongues, **9.** interpretation of tongues. These are also referred to as the *Nine Gifts of the Holy Spirit*. See also FALL, THE; PENTECOSTAL; SPIRIT, THE SEVEN GIFTS OF THE HOLY.

spiritualism. **1.** The belief that all that exists is spirit. **2.** The belief that departed spirits can communicate with the living, especially through one regarded as a medium.

sponge. One of the several instruments of Christ's Passion (see PASSION, INSTRUMENTS OF THE), usually shown in Christian art attached to the end of a staff or reed and placed at Christ's mouth while he was dying on the CROSS. Matthew 27:48: "And straightway one of them ran, and took a sponge, and filled it with vinegar, and put it on a reed, and gave him to drink." This act has been interpreted as an act of mercy shown to Christ, but it has also been regarded as the final humiliation of Christ.

station (L., *statio,* from *stare,* "to stand"). In the MASS, the significant point or phase of Jesus' life that is being reproduced, or imitated, for recognition, reappraisal, and veneration.

Stations of the Cross. See CROSS, THE STATIONS OF THE.

stigmata (Gk., *στίγματα [stigmata],* "the pricks of a pointed instrument"). The formation of visible marks, usually accompanied by areas of pain, on the human body at the same places at which Christ was pierced during his Passion—on the hands, feet, side, and sometimes on the head and back. St. Francis of Assisi (1182–1226) is an example of someone showing stigmata. He received them while fasting alone on Mount Alverna. There are hundreds of others who have displayed such markings, some permanently, some only during the Easter period.

sublapsarianism (L., *sub,* "under," "beneath," and *lapsus,* "a falling," "fall"). Held by CALVINISM: The Fall of humans was foreseen by God, allowed, but not decreed. See also INFRALAPSARIANISM.

subordinationism (L., *sub,* "under," and *ordinare,* "to arrange"). The hierarchical placing of Jesus below God in versions of the Holy Trinity.

supernaturalism. **1.** The belief in a realm of existence over and above the material realm of existence. **2.** The belief that there are powers (forces, agencies, energies) beyond the universe that affect the course of events in the universe. **3.** The belief in a transcendent God: a God who exists in another realm and as a totally different existent from the universe.

supernatural, the (L., *super,* "over," "above," "beyond," and *naturalis, natura,* "nature"). A realm of being, God, that **1.** is superior in power and reality to the universe, **2.** exists beyond the universe, **3.** transcends the powers and laws of the universe, **4.** is in some manner and to some degree in control of the unvierse, **5.** (usually) is able to suspend the laws of the universe in order to produce MIRACLES, **6.** (usually) creates the universe.

superstition (L., *superstitio,* "a standing still over or by a thing," "an excessive fear or dread of the gods," "unreasonable religious belief"; used in contrast to *religio,* which referred to a proper, correct, reasonable awe of the gods). **1.** An excessive fear of or reverence for the mysterious. **2.** An irrational and false belief or practice.

Supper, the Last. See LAST SUPPER, THE.

supralapsarianism (L., *supra,* "before," and *lapsus,* "a falling," "a fall"). The belief originating in CALVINISM that God's decree of election predetermined that ADAM should fall (see also FALL, THE). All humans subsequently fall in order that there be an opportunity for their REDEMPTION, which would show God's power to save humanity and his goodness in so doing. All this was eternally conceived by God *before* and not after the Fall of Adam. Opposed to INFRALAPSARIANISM.

synapheia. Greek, *συναφεία,* "combination." Refers to the combination of the two natures, the human and the divine, found in Jesus Christ. Compare with HĒNOSIS. See also ANTIOCHENES.

synod (Gk., *σύνοδος [synodos],* "a meeting," from *σύν [syn],* "with," and *ὁδος [hodos],* "a way," "road"). **1.** A formal meeting or assembly to consider church matters, usually at the council, governing, advisory, or policy-making level. **2.** The governing body in some churches. See also COUNCIL.

synoptic Gospels. See GOSPELS, THE SYNOPTIC.

T

temptation (L., *temptare,* "to test," "to urge," "to prove"). **1.** The enticement to evil and **2.** the allurement to stray from the path proclaimed and necessitated by God. In Christian belief, humans are constantly being tempted. Life is a battle against temptation. The concept implies that humans must resist or overcome temptation in some fashion before they can become HOLY OR SACRED. See also FALL, THE.

testimonium internum. Latin used to refer to the act of HOLY SPIRIT inspiring the believer to a testimony (witnessing) of the truths of the Bible.

thanatology (Gk., *θάνατος [thanatos],* "death," and *λόγος [logos],* "the study of"). The study of death and dying in all its aspects.

thanatopsis. (Gk., *θάνατος [thanatos],* "death," and *ὄψις [opsis],* "sight". In Greek mythology, Thanatos was the personification of Death. His twin brother was Hypnos (Ὕπνος) meaning Sleep. Nyx (Νύξ) the goddess of Night was his mother. Thanatos lived in the lower world.) **1.** A view of or belief about death. **2.** A meditation or work on death.

theism (Gk., *θεός [theos],* "divine," "God). **1.** Belief in divine things, gods, or a God. **2.** Belief in one God transcending but yet in important ways immanent in the universe.

theistic naturalism. The belief that God is a process or tendency within the natural order of things striving toward the expression of creative values and the emergence of more integrated complex wholes. See also THEOLOGY, PROCESS.

theocentric (Gk., *θεός [theos],* "God," and *κέντρον [kentron],* "center"). A view is theocentric if it attempts to view everything from the perspective of God and/or with reference to God as the source and focal point of all things.

theocracy (Gk., *ϑεοκρατία*, from *θεός [theos],* "God," and *κρατεῖν [kratein],* "to rule," "to govern," "to hold in power."). A state ruled according to God's will as interpreted by those regarded as representing him.

theocracy (Gk., *θεός [theos],* "God," and *κράσις [krasis],* "a mixing," "a blending," "a combining"). **1.** The blending of the beliefs in and/or worship of different gods. **2.** In Christianity, the state of an ecstatic and intimate contemplative unity with the Godhead.

theodicy (Gk., *θεός [theos],* "God," and *δίκη [dikē],* "justice," "right"). The discipline that attempts to justify the ways of God to man, especially the attempt to make compatible God's omnipotence and omnibenevolence with the existence of evil. See also EVIL, THE THEOLOGICAL PROBLEM OF.

theologia crucis. Latin, "THEOLOGY OF THE CROSS." Contrasted with THEOLOGIA GLORIAE. The Reformers, especially Luther, advocated a Christianity stressing not a theology of glory, but a theology of the cross and crucifixion, in which Christ is thought of as a suffering, sacrificing, and loving being and power. As Luther put it, Christ must be seen as a "worm on the cross, fly-ridden, derelict, broken and rejected." Christ paid the ultimate cost, humiliation, and agony for his obedience, yet accepted it, trusting God, and loved all in spite of it.

theologia gloriae. Latin, "THEOLOGY OF GLORY." Contrasted with THEOLOGIA CRUCIS.

theological dualism. See DUALISM, THEOLOGICAL.

theology (Gk., *θεολογία [theologia],* from *θεός [theos],* "God," and *λέγειν [legein],* "to speak," or from *λόγος [logos],* "the study of", "the rational analysis of"). **1.** The study of the relation of the divine world to the physical world. **2.** The study of the nature, being, and will of God. **3.** The doctrines or beliefs about God held by individuals and/or a religion. **4.** Any coherently organized body of dogma (faith, creeds, confessions, doctrines, beliefs) concerning the nature of God and his relationship with humans and the universe propounded by a religious institution. **5.** The systematic attempt to present, interpret, and justify in a consistent, rational, and meaningful way the belief in God (and the doctrine surrounding him—the faith).

theology, apophatic (Gk., ἀπόφασις *[apophasis],* "denial," from ἀποφάναι *[apophanai],* "to speak out," "to deny"). Theology that asserts that God's characteristics (see also DIVINE NAMES) far exceed our ability to describe or even predicate.

theology, ascetical (Gk., ἀσκητικός *[askētikos],* "ascetic," from ἀσκεῖν *[askein],* "to exercise"). Theology that asserts that God's being can only be known by means of austerity, discipline, the solitary, contemplative life, rigorous self-denial. Only these means allow the spirit to transcend the present, mundane realm of existence into the true divine reality underlying and pervading all things.

theology, biblical. The attempt to understand the Bible as a whole in all contexts—historical, anthropological, philological, philosophical, theological, sacred, profane, revealed, etc.—in all its connections with writings that have been accepted and those not authenticated as biblical, and to find a unity among its diversity of thought patterns and mores.

theology, cataphatic. Theology that assigns DIVINE NAMES to God.

theology, Christian. See CHRISTOLOGY.

theology, conservative. See FUNDAMENTALISM.

theology, dialectical. Also *via dialectica.* The dialectical method in theology using thesis/antithesis, yes/no, statement/response. It presents the polar opposites, the paradoxical and contradictory character of human thought about God: his Goodness, yet his wrath; his infiniteness, yet his finiteness in Jesus; his timelessness, yet his timely existence and effect upon time (history); his grace, yet his freely exercised mercy and love; his predestination of all things, yet his allowance for human freedom and deviation from his path; his omnipresence, yet his ineffectiveness at eliminating or avoiding human misery and suffering.

Dialectical theology stresses dialogue, debate, pushing of a point of view to any conclusion it can be pushed to without defensiveness or subjectivity. It supports the position that divine truth cannot be set down systematically and consistently in dogma or doctrine or creed. It is nevertheless based on an *apologia* of Christian faith that itself must be seen as divine truth surpassing and transcending all human rationality. Compare with VIA AFFIRMATIVA; VIA EMINENTIAE; VIA NEGATIVA.

theology, doctrinal (L., *doctrina,* from *docere,* "to teach"). Theology that teaches the tenets (principles of faith, divine truths, doctrines) held by Christian faith. See also DOCTRINE.

theology, dogmatic. Theology that affirms and teaches the doctrines laid down by church authority as part of its CONFESSION of Christian faith. See also DOGMA; DOGMATICS.

theology, liberal (L., *liberalis,* from *liber,* "free"). Theology that regards itself to be free from doctrinal restraint in its EXEGESIS of the Bible and doctrines, and thus broad-minded, independent in its opinions and of established traditions, tolerant of opposing views but attempting to keep up with modern, scientific, historical, theological, and philosophical changes in thought, perspective, and research.

theology, mystical. **1.** Theology that attempts to describe, analyze, systematize, and defend the MYSTICAL EXPERIENCE as *a* way—or *the* way—of knowing God. **2.** Theology that asserts that God's being can never be known by means of intellectual or rational analysis. God's nature far surpasses all human understanding. God can only be known as a nonrational ECSTASY, an ineffable state of love, during which a person becomes one with God—becomes deified.

theology, natural. **1.** Theology based on the belief that God can be known through the rational study of natural phenomena without the assistance of revelation or GRACE. **2.** Theology that holds that humans can obtain knowledge of God and his will by means of the natural capacity of human reason without the assistance of divine revelation.

theology, negative. **1.** Theology based on the belief that God's being so vastly exceeds man's finite being that none of his characteristics can be known in any real or full sense. None of the attributes of God reveals his true nature. We can know *that* God is but not *what* he is in himself. **2.** Theology that holds that we can only know what God is by knowing what he is not. See also APOPHATIC WAY, THE; AGNOSTICISM, RELIGIOUS.

theology of glory. Latin; *theologia gloriae.* Luther's pejorative phrase referring to humans' speculative and futile attempts at understanding the glory, majesty, and mystery of God. Luther contrasts this with the THEOLOGY OF THE CROSS.

theology of grace. See GRACE.

theology of the Cross. Latin, *theologia crucis.* Luther's phrase referring to the attempt to understand God in terms of his humanness as expressed in Jesus Christ; the attempt to encounter God in the life of Jesus Christ and his teaching; the attempt to benefit and receive gifts from God in our everyday life through acceptance of Jesus Christ. Knowledge of God could only be found in the INCARNATION, not through a study of nature. The complete and true essence (being, nature, substance) of God was hidden to humans (see also DEUS ABSCONDITUS; DEUS INCOGNITUS).

Luther emphasized the suffering, the humanness of Christ, his powerlessness, weakness, sacrifice, humiliation and exaltation, death, pain and defeat. Luther deemphasized the majesty, glory, grandeur, power, and deification of Jesus. Luther believed that humans could more easily identify and involve themselves with this aspect of the incarnation.

theology, pastoral. Sometimes *pastoralia* (L., *pastoralis,* from *pascere,* "to pasture," "to feed"). The branch of theology that trains clergy for work in their church. It deals with a variety of subjects such as: doctrine, devotion, the religious life, conducting of holy services, church administration, giving of the sacraments, homiletics (the art of preaching and teaching), service to the sick and poor, counseling the bereaved, spiritual counseling, ministry to those of the community.

theology, positive. Some of the central themes in positive theology: **1.** The affirmation of the divine characteristics of God: The divine characteristics of God can be known by human thought and language and are an adequate representation of God. Men and women have been created in the image of God. The highest aspects of a human being can be used as signs that reveal God's highest characteristics and perfections. **2.** The acceptance of the letter and the spirit of the Scriptures as revealing the will and purposes of a Creator and Personal God. **3.** Dependence upon revelation as a source of justification of our knowledge of the Spirit of God and as a source of personal illumination (inspiration) and salvation. **4.** An investigation into the historical facts of the Bible and its revelation; the customs, doctrines, and practices of the Christian Church and its faiths.

theology, process (L., *processus,* from *procedere,* "to proceed," from *pro,* "forward," and *cedere,* "to move"). Theology that stresses God as a process, an activity in the universe (or *of* the universe) as opposed to being a substance or entity that has location in space and fully realized characteristics that have eternally endured; God is a series of progressive processes that makes for integration, increase in value, complexity, and perfection. See also THEISTIC NATURALISM.

theology, revealed (L., *revelare,* "to unveil," "to reveal"). **1.** Theology that asserts that knowledge of God's being and his will is and can be obtained only by the means of divine revelation and attempts to understand why and how this revelation comes about. Some knowledge that human reason cannot of its own acquire but that must be disclosed through revelation: the Virgin Birth; the Holy Trinity; the INCARNATION; the RESURRECTION; the ATONEMENT. **2.** Theology based on the belief that the nature of God cannot be ascertained by reason (or by reason alone) but must be obtained from a revelation (or founded upon revealed knowledge). God illuminates the soul. There is a divinely illuminated faculty (or intellect) in all humans filled with content that can be stimulated under proper conditions and made to actualize. All humans have the ability to see by and be guided by the divine light. This ability is a natural, human ability originally placed in all humans. All have access to the Divine Light. Truth cannot be discovered without the aid of this divine light or illumination. See also REVELATION, DIVINE.

theomachy (Gk., ϑεομαχία *[theomachia],* from θεός *[theos],* "God," and μάχη *[machē],* "a battle"). **1.** Battle (strife, arguments) among the gods. **2.** Refers to the god of light (good, beauty, justice) fighting against the god of darkness (evil, ugliness, injustice). **3.** The battle between God and Satan. **4.** Any opposition to the will of God.

theomorphic (Gk., θεός *[theos]*, "God," and μορφή *[morphe]*, "form"). Possessing a divine form, aspect, or quality.

theopathy (Gk., θεός *[theos]*, "God," and πάθος *[pathos]*, "feeling"). **1.** The direct experience of God or of a divine illumination or communication. **2.** The capacity for **1.** **3.** Intense absorption in or concentration upon theological devotion, religious experiences, or objects.

theophany (Gk., θεός *[theos]*, "God," and φαίνεσθαι *[phainesthai]*, "to appear"). The physical appearance, usually in human form, of God, or of a god, to a human being or beings. See also EPIPHANY.

Theotokos. Greek, "who gave birth to God." The name given to the Virgin MARY.

Thomism. The doctrines based on the writings and beliefs of St. Thomas Aquinas (1225–1274). The theology, more than any other, that has influenced the Roman Catholic church. Some if its tenets: **1.** Philosophy (including natural science) deals with the realm of nature and human nature created by God; theology (including religion) deals with the realm of the supernatural and the nature of the divine. Philosophy is supreme in the area of reason; theology is supreme in the area of faith. (But philosophy is the handmaiden of theology; faith and revelation supersede reason. Reason must be made to support the dogmas of the faith.) Truths of the supernatural: revelation, predestination, grace, merit, the Trinity, the Incarnation, the Virgin Birth, the Resurrection. Truths of the natural that reason can demonstrate: the existence of the soul, the immortality of the soul, providence. **2.** The existence and nature of God can be proven by means of reason (as well as revelation): God is the Prime Mover, the First Cause, the Necessary Being, the Supreme Being in a Hierarchy of Beings and Value, the Governor of the Universe. **3.** God is the only self-subsistent, pure, and fully actualized Being, possessing no limitation, changeless and unchangeable. **4.** Humans possess free will given by God. (What good humans do is due to God's Grace; what sin humans commit is due to humans themselves.) **5.** The Roman Catholic church is the Mystical Body of Christ and the Church is the sole purveyor of the true faith and revelation of Jesus Christ. **6.** The Sacraments are causes of divine grace and Jesus Christ is the force for their operation. **7.** God can be seen in an ecstatic vision that is the aim of all life.

Those of the Way. See DISCIPLES, JESUS' TWELVE.

Thnetopsychism (Gk., θνητός *[thnētos]*, "liable to death," "mortal," and ψυχή *[psychē]* "soul," "spirit"). The belief that the soul dies with the death of the body but that at resurrection (see also RESURRECTION, HUMAN) it again comes to life.

Thursday, Holy. Commemorates the LAST SUPPER and the sacrament of Holy Communion.

tiara (Gk., τιάρα *[tiara]*, "a form of headdress," used by Herodotus and other Greek writers to refer to the headdress worn by Persian kings). The headdress worn by the POPE as a symbol of his temporal sovereignty. The papal tiara is encircled with three crowns. In purely spiritual functions, the pope wears the MITRE and not the tiara. See also CROWN OF THORNS.

tithe (Anglo-Saxon, *teoda,* "tenth"). The voluntary giving of a tenth or a small part of one's earnings as a contribution to one's church.

traducianism. A belief propounded primarily by Tertullian (155–222) that held that the soul is of human, material substance that comes into existence at the moment of procreation; human souls are propagated by generation just as are human bodies. Original sin was interpreted as an act of sexual and biological connection and transmission through the parents who continued to pass this sin on from Adam. St. Augustine (354–430) taught a form of this belief. Opposed to CREATIONISM; see also SOUL.

transcendency. The doctrine that **1.** God exists in a realm beyond or apart from the universe; **2.** God is not dependent for his essential nature upon the universe; the universe is dependent upon him for its existence; **3.** God is prior to and perfect in value and in existence to the universe; **4.** God is in major respects different in characteristics from the universe; **5.** God operates upon the universe as an external force as opposed to an immanent force.

Transcendentalism. The belief in the superiority of the intuitive or spiritual over the empirical and scientific. Holds that there is an ideal, spiritual reality beyond the space-time world of our experience that can be grasped and with which all things are infused. Associated especially with Ralph Waldo Emerson and his followers, who have been called TRANSCENDENTALISTS.

Transcendentalists. The name given to the followers of an American New England intellectual movement of the 1800s (TRANSCENDENTALISM) centered around Boston. Some of the advocates: William Ellery Channing (1780–1842), Ralph Waldo Emerson (1803–1882), Theodore Parker (1810–1860), Henry David Thoreau (1817–1862), Walt Whitman (1819–1892). The movement was a liberal and optimistic Unitarian response against the stringencies and pessimism of Calvinism, Puritanism, Deism, Trinitarianism and against the total otherness or transcendence of God from the processes of nature. It opposed materialism, strict varieties of empiricism, extreme rationalism. The Transcendentalists were poetically, mystically, and religiously inclinded; they held that there was more to the universe than that which reason and empirical knowledge (science) gave us. Transcendentalists believed that truth about that more to the universe could be attained through subjective intuition. The Transcendentalists believed God is living, just, and good, (There is no HELL because God is too good to create such a world and humans are too good to be sent there.) God is immanent in all existence and can be grasped as the ideal form attempting to manifest itself in all things. The universe contains two realms; **1.** the nonreal, or less real, world of sensations and phenomena (appearances), which is what science deals with, and **2.** the ultimate, true, transcendent reality of spirit, of over-soul, cosmic mind, which realm can be discovered and is expressed by philosophy, poetry, music, the arts, the religious experience. Humans can, and must, attain moral virtue (salvation) only by their own efforts. The Transcendentalists stressed the worth and dignity of the person and the importance of strong individualism free from the shackles of custom and the established order. One must have individual liberty to rely on one's own developed conscience and personal values; slavery of any kind is anathema. See also UNITARIANISM.

Transfiguration of Christ. Celebrated August 6. An event that happened on Mount Thabor before Jesus' CRUCIFIXION and RESURRECTION that is believed to show Jesus' divinity. Jesus is seen in the form of a spiritual, mysterious brilliance, praying, speaking with Moses and Elias (Elijah) about the fate he is to undergo. A voice is heard from a cloud: "And after six days Jesus taketh Peter, James, and John his brother, and bringeth them up into an high mountain apart, And was transfigured before them: and his face did shine as the sun, and his raiment was white as the light. And behold, there appeared unto them Moses and Elias talking with him" (Matt. 17:1–3). "Who (Moses and Elias) appeared in glory, and spake of his decease which he should accomplish at Jerusalem" (Luke 9:31). At Mark 9:7, "And there was a cloud that overshadowed them: and a voice came out of the cloud, saying, 'This is my beloved Son: hear him.' " (Also refer to 2 Pet. 1:16–18.)

transmigration (L., *transmigrare,* from *trans,* "across," and *migrare,* "to migrate"). See REINCARNATION.

transubstantiation (L., *transubstantiatus,* present participle of *transubstantiare,,* "to transubstantiate," from *trans,* "across," "over," "beyond," "through," and *substantia,* "substance"). The transformation at the CONSECRATION OF THE EUCHARIST of the bread and wine into the actual body and blood of Jesus Christ. The Fourth Lateran Council (1215) and the COUNCIL OF TRENT (1545–1563) both formally presented, defined, and defended transubstantiation. Distinguished from CONSUBSTANTIATION and IMPANATION. See also CONCOMITANCE; HOMOOUSIS; LORD'S SUPPER.

A basic and traditional theological interpretation of transubstantiation is found in St. Thomas Aquinas' (1225–1274) *Summa Theologica,* 3.75–77. The substance of the bread and wine is not present in transubstantiation but their accidents continue to operate as spatial qualities. The bread and wine are not thereby (physically) annihilated or altered but retain their spatial dimensions in our empirical perception, or its appearance to us. (The substance or essence of Christ's body and blood replaces the substance of the bread and wine, but the perceptual qualities—the "accidents"—of the bread and wine remain.)

Trent, Council of. See COUNCIL OF TRENT (1545–1563).

triangle, the. Used as a symbol of the Holy Trinity. Sometimes the HALO above the depiction of God is in the shape of a triangle.

Trinitarian. One who believes in the Holy Trinity—that the Father, Son, and HOLY SPIRIT are united in one divine being. See entries under TRINITY.

trinity, Immanent. Also referred to as *essential Trinity*. The belief that God is one God in so far as he is not associated with his creation. But God manifests (reveals) himself in three ways, in a TRINITARIAN manner, as a TRIUNE nature. This triune nature of God is immanent in God's nature, God's essence, and is essential to his being what he is—God.

Trinity Sunday. The Sunday after WHITSUNDAY, celebrated as a feast in honor of the Holy Trinity.

Trinity, the Holy. The inseparable unit or union of three persons in one God: the Father, the Son, and the HOLY SPIRIT. The unity is such as to stress, usually, that they are one God as to substance (see also CONSUBSTANTIATION) and three persons as to individuality and expression. The conservative Christian attitude toward the Trinity has been one of rejecting the concept of the Son and the Holy Spirit as being subordinate to the Father. This would lead to a form of TRITHEISM. The Roman Catholic church holds to the notion of the Trinity as propounded in the NICENE CREED: The three members of the Trinity are all present eternally in the divine Essence; the Son is the generation of the LOGOS of that Divine Essence; the Holy Spirit is the spirited expression proceeding from both the Father and the Son. In the Greek orthodox tradition, the Son proceeds from the Father and the Holy Spirit also proceeds from the Father —God is present and active in the Holy Spirit as God is present and active in Jesus Christ. See also entries under HOLY SPIRIT.

According to Christian tradition, the true "mystery" of the Holy Trinity is that the relationship of the Father, Son, and Holy Spirit cannot be put into words, analogies, or pictures since it goes against all rational analysis: It wants to assert that God is identical in substance and essence with each of the three members of the Trinity (and each of the three members is identical with God). This it is believed would affirm the pure divinity of Christ—Christ *is* God and God is Christ; Christ is consubstantial with God, the very same identical being (see also HOMOOUSIOS).

In the history of Christianity, a number of what are now regarded as heretical relationships of Christ with God have been expressed. Some of them: Christ was *unlike* (ἀνόμοιος, *anomoios)* God (ANHOMOEANS); Christ was *like* or similar (ὅμοιος) to God (homoeans); Christ was of like substance (ὁμοιούσιος, *homoiousios)* with God (homoiousians).

Some of the New Testament references upon which interpretations of the Trinity have been formed: 2 Corinthians 5:19: "God was *in* Christ reconciling the world unto himself." Philippians 2:6: "who, being in the form of God, thought it not robbery to be equal with God." John 10:30: "I and my Father are one." (Also refer to John 1:1, 14, 18; 5:18).

In Christian art, God the Father is depicted as a Creator, as a hand, as an old man; God the Son as a shepherd, as a young man holding a cross, or on the cross (or as the cross above); God the Holy Spirit as a DOVE. See also ANHYPOSTASIA; APPROPRIATION; AUTOTHEISM; ENHYPOSTASIA; PERICHŌRĒSIS.

triplex munus. Latin, "three-service," "three-gift." The states of prophet, priest, and king. Jesus christ was regarded as possessing all these qualities. As prophet, Jesus is the revealer of God. As priest, he mediates (intercedes) between a Perfect God and imperfect humans. As king, Jesus reigns in the kingdom of God (kingdom of heaven).

tritheism (Gk., *τρία [tria],* "three," and *θεός [theos],* "God"). **1.** Belief in three gods. **2.** In Christianity, any belief that holds that the three members of the Trinity, the Father, the Son, and the HOLY SPIRIT, are three distinct Gods. See entries under TRINITY.

triune (L., *tri,* "three," and *unus,* "one"). **1.** Being three in one. **2.** Being three yet one. Applied to the unity of the Trinity in the Godhead. See entries under TRINITY.

Twelfthide. The twelfth day after Christmas. Also referred to as the EPIPHANY. Also called *Twelfthday* and its evening *Twelfthnight.*

Twelve Apostles, the. See APOSTLES, THE TWELVE.

typology (Gk., *τύπος [typos],* "model," "type," and *λόγος [logos],* "the study of," "the rational principles for"). A form of EXEGESIS whereby an event in the past is compared with an event in the present or future. Examples of typology may be found especially in the New Testament, for example, where events referring to Adam and to Moses are compared with events related to Christ (1 Cor. 15:45–49; 2 Cor. 3:12–17; Rom. 5:12–21; Heb. 3:1–6) or where the first Passover is compared with Christ's death (1 Cor. 5:6–8), or where the travails of Israel in the wilderness are compared to the happenings of Christians (1 Cor. 10:1–11). See also ALLEGORY.

U

ubiquity (L., *ubique,* "everywhere," from *ubi,* "where"). **1.** God's (or Christ's) presence in more than one place at the same time. **2.** God's presence in an indefinite number of places at the same time. **3.** God's presence everywhere—even infinitely—at the same time (see also OMNIPRESENT). **4.** The Lutheran doctrine of the Lord's Supper, or EUCHARIST, that holds to the transference of the attribute (property, quality) of actual presence (ubiquity) from the divine nature to the human nature of Jesus Christ—from the supernatural to the natural (the bread and wine).

ultramontanism (L., *ultra,* "over," and *montanus,* "mountain"; the mountains refer to beyond the Alps south to Rome). The Roman Catholic attitude that supports papal supremacy over the powers of regional and national churches.

una sancta. Latin, "one holy," referring to the Church as one, holy, indivisible, and true.

Unction, Extreme. Also *Anointing of the Sick.* Regarded as a sacrament by the Roman Catholic Church (see also ANOINTING). Given by priests to those who are gravely or terminally ill (or in danger of dying from accident or old age); it may not be given as second time during the same illness, except when death again becomes imminent. The oil used in Extreme Unction is blessed by a bishop on MAUNDY THURSDAY. The priest anoints the five senses with Holy Oil: the closed eyes, the ears, the nostrils, the closed mouth, the hands, and the feet. (The right parts of the body are anointed before the left and, where possible, the holy oil is applied with a piece of tow [flax, hemp]). The formula pronounced is of this form: "By this holy unction and His most gracious mercy may God forgive thee whatsoever thou hast done wrong by thy senses, namely, thy sight, hearing, taste, smelling, and touch."

The sacrament of Extreme Unction removes mortal sins (provided there has been ATTRITION). Humans can prepare themselves for this sacrament by a thorough CONFESSION, faith, hope, charity, and by acceptance of the will of God. It is better to receive Extreme Unction while still conscious. Extreme Unction is not necessary for SALVATION but can be a contributing factor when a proper attitude and preparation are taken toward it.

The purposes of Extreme Unction are **1.** to give the soul courage in the agony of death; **2.** to remove remaining sin; **3.** to remove all punishments still incurred; **4.** to restore, where possible, life and health. The sacrament of Extreme Unction has principally James 5:14, 15 as its scriptural basis: "Is any sick among you? Let him call for the elders of the church; and let them pray over him, anointing him with oil in the name of the Lord: And the prayer of faith shall save the sick, and the Lord shall raise him up; and if he have committed sins, they shall be forgiven him." (Anointing is used here in the expectation of a cure.)

Unction, Holy (L., *unctio,* from *ungere,* "to anoint"). **1.** The anointing with holy oil of five crosses on an altar stone by a bishop at the CONSECRATION of an altar. **2.** The anointing of one who has been confirmed, by use of the sign of the cross, usually by a bishop. **3.** The anointing of a priest at ordination. **4.** The anointing of the sick, dying, or dead (see also UNCTION, EXTREME). **5.** The anointing of sovereigns at their coronation as a sign of their sacredness.

uniat. Also *uniate* (Polish and Russian, *uniat,* from Russian *uniya,* Polish *unija,* "union"). A sect of a Greek or Eastern church that acknowledged the pope's supremacy but retain its own rites, litany, liturgies, etc.

unio mystica. Latin, "mystical union," referring to the merging of consciousness with God, the supreme cosmic consciousness.

Unitarianism. **1.** The denial of the doctrine of the Holy Trinity and the affirmation that God exists as only one being. **2.** The community of seekers stemming in modern times from reformers such as Michael Servetus (1509–1553) who was burned at the stake in 1553 in Geneva for the unitarian heresy of denying the concept of God as Three in One and affirming the oneness of God. Unitarianism as a denomination spread from England to America in the 1700s, where it had a strong influence on the religious movements in New England. Early Unitarianism regarded Christ not as God but as a perfect human or perfect model to be followed in life. (The American Unitarian Association merged with the Universalist Church of America to form the Unitarian-Universalist Association in May 1961. See also UNIVERSALISM.)

In theistically inclined Unitarian-Universalism, it is quipped that the difference between a Unitarian and a Universalist is that a Universalist believes God is too good to send humans to HELL, whereas the Unitarian believes that humans are too good to be sent to hell.

Universalism. **1.** The belief that all humans will eventually be saved by God and restored to heaven and a state of bliss similar to the condition of humans before the Fall. This universalist belief was held by Origen (185–254), St. Clement of Alexandria (150–220), Christian Gnostics, and others in the third century. Universalism was declared a heresy at the Council of Constantinople in 543. **2.** The community of believers whose origin was in the German Reformation of the seventeenth and eighteenth centuries. As a denomination, Universalism influenced areas in early America such as New England and Pennsylvania. Universalism denied the traditional concept of the Holy Trinity and affirmed a form of subordination of Christ to God. See also UNITARIANISM.

unorthodox (Anglo-Saxon, *un,* "not," "undoing," "contrary," and ὀρϑόδοξος *[orthodoxos],* "orthodox," from ὄρϑος *[orthos],* "right," "straight," and δόξα *[doxa],* "opinion," "belief," "faith"). Not of sound (correct, true, legitimate) doctrine (faith, creed, opinion), hence not holding the approved Christian faith as propounded by the sect. Used synonymously with HETERODOX and heretical. See also HERESY. Opposite of ORTHODOX.

V

Vatican City. A sovereign territory within Rome, containing the VATICAN.

Vatican Council I. Held at St. Peter's Basilica in the Vatican from December 8, 1869 to September 1, 1870 and attended by over 800 ecclesiastics of the Roman Catholic church. The most important issue was the formulation of the doctrine of the supremacy and infallibility of the pope (see also INFALLIBILITY OF THE POPE). Pope Pius IX suspended the Council, which was to resume a century later as VATICAN COUNCIL II.

Vatican Council II. Called by Pope John XXIII. Held in four separate sessions at St. Peter's Basilica in the Vatican from October 11, 1962 to December 8, 1965 and attended by over 2,500 Roman Catholic ecclesiastics. It was an ecumenical council in the sense that observers were invited from all the major Christian churches. Pope John XXIII died on June 3, 1963 after the first session, and Pope Paul VI continued the Council in session. Some of the issues discussed at Vatican Council II: revision of canon law; the Church's attitude toward non-Catholic and non-Christian churches; reemphasis upon divine revelation; the education of priests; the missionary role of the Church; Mary as the Blessed mediatrix of all graces; Mary as the Mother of the Church.

Vatican, the. The area on the right bank of the Tiber in Rome that includes the pope's palace, the Church of St. Peter, the Sistine Chapel, museums, libraries, archives, art galleries, etc. This area is regarded as sacred and the burial place of SAINT PETER and SAINT PAUL. (The Basilica of St. Peter's is the specific site of Peter's burial, together with subsequent saints and popes.)

veneration (L., *venerari,* "to venerate," "to regard with respect"). **1.** Respect mingled with awe, wonder, mystery (and sometimes fear or dread). **2.** Worship; the act of expressing reverent feelings, adoration, reverential respect. **3.** A deep or exalted REVERENCE.

At the Second Council of Nicea (787) a hierarchy of veneration was established: LATREIA was to be given to God and God alone; HYPERDOULEIA was to be expressed upon the Virgin Mary; DOULEIA to the saints; PROSKYNESIS to icons and sacred objects. Saints, images, relics may be venerated but ADORATION is due only to God. See also NICAEA, THE SECOND COUNCIL OF.

veneration of the Cross. See CROSS, ADORATION OF THE.

venial sin. See SIN, VENIAL.

verissime et maxime esse. Latin, translated as existing "in the truest and most ultimate (maximum, greatest) way." Applied to God as the highest (the most supreme) good in the hierarchy of values and to God as the completely perfect Being.

vestigium Dei. Latin, "vestige of God." Refers to all creatures and creations (except humans) who show reflections of a trace of God as in Romans 1. Contrasted with IMAGO DEI.

Vespers (L., *vesper,* "evening"). The daily hour of devotion, music, and prayer held in the evening, usually at 6 P.M. (often referred to as the evening prayer or evensong in Anglican tradition).

vestment (L., *vestementum,* from *vestis,* "garment"). The garment worn by the clergy, or others such as the choristers, in the performance of worship services.

vestry (L., *vestire,* "to clothe"). **1.** The small chamber in a church where vestments, sacred utensils, objects, and books are kept. **2.** A room or an attached building used, for example, as a Sunday school area, chapel, or for other specific religious purposes. **3.** In the Church of England tradition, the body of persons who govern the secular affairs of a parish.

via affirmativa. Also *via positiva.* Latin, "the positive, affirming way" of arriving at God's existence and characteristics: For example, God can be known as the infinite and perfected extension of all that is perfect in humans, and more that is not human; God can be known as a FIRST CAUSE; FIRST MOVER; Grand Designer; the Highest Good. See also THEOLOGY, POSITIVE.

via crucis. Latin, "the way of the cross," referring to the road to Calvary over which Christ carried his cross to his crucifixion. See also CROSS, THE STATIONS OF THE. See also VIA DOLOROSA.

via dialectica. Latin, "the dialectic way" of arriving at God's existence and presence. See also THEOLOGY, DIALECTICAL.

Via Dolorosa. Latin, "the way of sorrows." The road or route in Jerusalem that Jesus took bearing his cross to his crucifixion (see also CROSS, THE STATIONS OF THE). This route is followed by pilgrims—laypeople and priesthood—in a procession on Good Friday. See also VIA CRUCIS.

via eminentiae. Latin, "the highest, loftiest way" of arriving at God's existence and characteristics: Every quality of the finite human being is possessed by God but to a perfect degree. God's characteristics have a relationship to our characteristics. Contrasted with VIA NEGATIVA.

via illuminativa. Latin, "the way of enlightenment or illumination." The way to God through illumination (enlightenment, inspiration, revelation, mystical apprehension or experience)—seeing the light, a unique light of truth, and thereby recognizing God's nature.

Via Matris. Latin, referring to the seven sorrows Mary the Mother of God felt on the way to Jesus' CRUCIFIXION. See CROSS THE STATIONS OF THE; SORROWS OF MARY, THE SEVEN.

via negativa. Also *via negationis.* Latin, "the negative way" of knowing God (by knowing what God is *not).* God can only be characterized in negative terms: incorporeal, immutable, infinite, invisible, etc. God cannot be known as goodness, as love, as being, as infinite, as power, as knowledge—none of the DIVINE NAMES are ultimately intelligible. None can ever be descriptive or serve as properties of God. God transcends all affirmative statements about him. God transcends all negations of him as well. See also THEOLOGY, NEGATIVE.

via purgativa. Latin, "the way of purgation." The way of arriving at knowledge of God through purgation (purification, katharsis) and, in general, through asceticism.

via unitiva. Latin, "the unifying way," "the way of unity." The way of arriving at knowledge of God through a perfect unity of one's being, through perfection.

vicar (L., *vicarius,* "a place, status, or authority belonging to one person but assumed by another"). **1.** In general, someone ordained who is representing Jesus' authority. **2.** In Protestant Episcopalianism, a clergyman who is the head of a chapel or (sometimes) a parish. **3.** Sometimes refers to an incumbent of a parish who is not a RECTOR. **4.** In Roman Catholicism, an ecclesiastic who represents, as a deputy, the pope or a bishop (often referred to as a VICAR-GENERAL).

vicarage. Chiefly of British usage. The residence, office, status, privileges, function, and the BENEFICES accorded to a VICAR.

vicar apostolic. **1.** A titular Roman Catholic bishop assigned to a country or region where there is an episcopal SEE, or where, due to some event such as illness or death, the succession and charge has been interrupted. **2.** In past Roman Catholic tradition, a bishop or archbishop to whom the pope delegated part of his jurisdiction.

vicar-general. **1.** An ecclesiastical representative of the pope or of a bishop. **2.** In the Church of England, it refers to a lay legal officer who acts as a deputy of the archbishop of Canterbury (or York).

Vicar of Jesus Christ. Refers to the pope of the Roman Catholic church.

vicarship. The office, status, position, privileges, rights of a VICAR.

vice (L., *vitium,* "a fault," "corruption"). **1.** A moral defect or fault. **2.** A failure of conduct. **3.** Depravity. **4.** Evil. **5.** Sin. See also entries under SIN.

vices, the seven. See SINS, THE SEVEN DEADLY.

vinculum amoris. Latin, "binding or uniting love." Used to refer as in St. Augustine (354–430) to the HOLY SPIRIT of the Holy Trinity being the bond of love binding the Father to the Son, and the Son to the Father. See also PERICHŌRĒSIS.

virgin birth, the. The belief that Jesus was born of a virgin, Mary, and was fathered by God. See also IMMACULATE CONCEPTION OF THE BLESSED VIRGIN MARY, THE MOTHER OF GOD.

virtue (L., *virtus,* "strength," "courage," "virtue," from *vir,* "man"). Ethical excellence—in thought, practice, and action. Virtues have been classified in a number of ways. One is a division into three categories:

intellectual virtues (such as intelligence, wisdom, knowledge, aesthetic or artistic sensitivity, natural prudence); moral virtues (such as temperance, self-discipline, courage, prudence); theological virtues (faith, hope, compassion, charity, love). See also subsequent entries on VIRTUE.

virtues, cardinal (L., *virtus,* "strength," "courage," from *vir,* "man"; *cardinalis,* from *cardo,* "hinge," "that upon which a thing depends or turns"). Also sometimes referred to as the *natural virtues.* The highest ideals or forms of conduct sought after by a culture. All others are regarded as of secondary importance and are derived from them or depend upon them for their existence. Greek culture, for example, stressed the four basic (cardinal) virtues: wisdom (prudence), courage (fortitude), justice (righteousness), moderation (temperance). Christian teaching added the theological virtues (see also VIRTUES, THE THEOLOGICAL) of faith, hope, and love (charity): 1 Corinthians 13:13. Together with the four cardinal virtues, they constitute the seven virtues.

virtues, Christian. See VIRTUES, THE THEOLOGICAL.

virtues, the four cardinal. See VIRTUES, CARDINAL.

virtues, the seven. See VIRTUES, CARDINAL.

virtues, the theological. Also *Christian virtues.* The three cardinal ones: hope (see HOPE, CHRISTIAN), FAITH and LOVE (CHARIS: charity; see also AGAPE). Theological virtues are known by means of revelation or the INFUSION by the HOLY SPIRIT and can be truly performed only by those who have received redeeming grace. They are contrasted to the natural virtues (see also VIRTUES, CARDINAL) that are known by means of natural law.

There is a long list of other theological virtues: goodness, purity, wisdom, humbleness, humility, discipline, obedience, chastity, celibacy, loyalty, virginity, poverty, martyrdom, saintliness, suffering. At Philippians 4:8: "Finally, brethren, whatsoever things are true, whatsoever things are honest, whatsoever things are just, whatsoever things are pure, whatsoever things are lovely, whatsoever things are of good report; if there be any virtue, and if there be any praise, think on these things." See also CORPOREAL ACTS, THE SEVEN; GRACES, CHRISTIAN; PENANCE.

vision, beatific. See BEATIFIC VISION.

vision of God. See BEATIFIC VISION.

Visitation of the Blessed Virgin Mary. Mary's visit to her cousin Elizabeth, who was six months pregnant with SAINT JOHN THE BAPTIST. According to Christian tradition, Elizabeth was filled with the HOLY SPIRIT, realized that Mary was to be the mother of God, and was the first human to show ADORATION to God made flesh. (Refer to Luke 1:36, 41, 42.) The Feast of the Visitation of the Blessed Virgin Mary was fixed at July 2 by the Council of Basil in 1441.

vocation (L., "a bidding," "an invitation," "a calling," from *vocare,* "to call"). God's calling (summons) to the Christian way of life and to special spiritual service in the name of Jesus Christ and the HOLY SPIRIT. The Christian vocation is to love God and fulfill his will.

vow (L., *vovere,* "to vow"). A sacred, solemn promise made to God, or Christ, that commits (devotes, binds) oneself to his service and will. Usually a vow to God includes obedience, love, reverence, devotion, fidelity. Vows for holy orders also include poverty, chastity, discipline, acceptance of or submission to authority.

vulgate. See BIBLE, THE VULGATE.

W

wafer (Old Fr., *waufre).* A thin, unleavened cake (or piece of bread) made of wheat flour and water and used in the EUCHARIST of the Roman Catholic church as the Body of Christ. See HOST, THE SACRED. (In the Eastern Orthodox churches, round, leavened loaves of BREAD, often contributed by a different parishioner on each occasion, are cut into small sections such as in the form of a cube and used for the Eucharist.)

washing of feet. See also FOOT WASHING (PEDILAVIUM).

water, holy. See HOLY WATER.

Whitsunday (Anglo-Saxon, *hwita sunnandaeg,* "white Sunday," probably referring to the white robes worn by those being baptized on Pentecost Day). Also *pentecost day.* The seventh Sunday and fiftieth day after EASTER, celebrated as a festival commemorating the descent of the HOLY SPIRIT at PENTECOST upon the Apostles. This is also celebrated as the birthday of the Roman Catholic church.

Whitsuntide. Also *Whitsun Tide.* The week beginning with WHITSUNDAY, especially Whitsunday, Whitmonday and Whit-Tuesday.

Word of God, the. (1) Expressed through preaching, seen by means of miracles, felt in contemplation, meditation, prayer, visions, dreams, understood in reading the Bible. Christian tradition holds that the twelve Apostles were closest to the Word of God since they directly and intimately witnessed Jesus Christ (the New Testament Word of God) in the flesh (see FLESH, JESUS AS) and in his reappearance at the Resurrection as the Lord and Master risen from the dead. (2) Also another name for the Bible (see BIBLE, THE HOLY).

Word, the. See LOGOS.

works, good. Also *good deeds.* Acts of Christian duty and piety that stem from faith in Jesus Christ, are pleasing to God, are in conformity with God's wishes, and will be rewarded by God. (2 Tim. 4:6, 7: "For I am now ready to be offered, and the time of my departure is at hand. I have fought a good fight, I have finished my course, I have kept the faith.")

A variety of beliefs exist about good works: **1.** God rewards good works with eternal life: "The day of wrath and revelation of the righteous judgment of God; who will render to every man according to his deeds" (Rom. 2:5, 6). (Also refer to 1 Pet. 1:17; 2 Pet. 1:4.) **2.** Good works must be done by humans in order to justify themselves before God and to glorify him: "Let your light so shine before men, that they may see your good works, and glorify your Father which is in heaven" (Matt. 5:16). (Also refer to Matt. 23:3ff.; 2 Cor. 9:8; Col. 1:10; 2 Thess. 2:17.) **3.** Faith alone is not enough; good works are also required: "Even so faith, if it hath not works, is dead, being alone" (James 2:17). **4.** Humans cannot do good works unless graced by God—unless they are in a state of GRACE. "For by grace are ye saved through faith; and that not of yourselves: it is the gift of God. Not of works, lest any man should boast" (Eph. 2:8, 9). One of the implications that has been seen in Christianity in this belief about good works is that humans are saved by God *for* the production of good works and are not saved *by performing* good works. The Reformation, for the most part, accepted the notion that good works never merit God's reward or God's grace. God bestows reward not out of a debt for good works but from his free grace and mercy.

The Reformers, such as Martin Luther (1483–1546) and John Calvin (1509–1564), rejected the notion of good works primarily because they believed it undermined the intentions and motives of those doing good works. The motive to do good for the Christian would then become the achievement of MERIT in order to attain eternal life. The Protestant tradition stressed that the motivation for good works was: the love and gratitude to God for giving us the gift of salvation and grace; the desire to please God; the total obedience to God's plan of salvation through Jesus Christ. The Roman Catholic tradition stressed the notion that some good works were more meritorious than others. For example, the religious works of a saint, martyr, monk, or priest are of higher value than those of say a carnival operator or an owner of a bowling alley.

works of mercy, the seven corporal. See CORPOREAL ACTS, THE SEVEN.

wounds of Christ, the five. The wounds Christ suffered during his CRUCIFIXION, on his two hands, two feet, and his side (or breast). See also PASSION, INSTRUMENTS OF THE.

Wrath of God. According to Christian tradition, humans as sinners sense God's wrath (anger, rage, indignation, ire) in the attempt by God to extinguish SIN. God is a righteous being, expressing righteous wrath and is an enemy of sin, self-centeredness, and greed. Christ's spirit frees a person to make a new self, a new spirit, a new human. Christ frees humans from the consequences of God's wrath, effecting a reconciliation and FORGIVENESS that in turn frees humans from being slaves of sin, releases humans from slavery and its tyranny. See also FREEDOM FROM BONDAGE.

Y

Yahweh. Sometimes spelled *Yahwe* or *Jahveh.* The transliteration of the Hebrew word for the incommunicable divine name (God) that has been translated as "Jehovah" in the Bible and considered by the Jews too sacred to be uttered.

About the Author

Peter A. Angeles received his B.A., M.A., and Ph.D. degrees from Columbia University. He has taught philosophy (logic, history of philosophy, ethics, philosophy of mind, epistemology, metaphysics), philosophy of religion, and comparative world religions at the University of Western Ontario, Albert Schweitzer College in Switzerland, and the University of California at Santa Barbara. Currently, he is professor and chairperson of philosophy at Santa Barbara City College, Santa Barbara, California. He is the author of *A Dictionary of Philosophy; The Problem of God; An Introduction to Sentential Logic; The Possible Dream: Toward Understanding the Black Experience;* and *Critiques of God* (Ed.); as well as articles in journals.